FOR OPENERS

For Openers

Conversations with 24 Canadian Writers

Alan Twigg

HARBOUR PUBLISHING
1981

ISBN 0-920080-07-3

TYPESETTING AND LAYOUT BY PULP PRESS
PRINTED AND BOUND IN CANADA

HARBOUR PUBLISHING
Box 119
Madiera Park, B.C.
V0N 2H0

Acknowledgements

Portions of this book have previously appeared in *Quill & Quire, Vancouver Province, Georgia Straight, Vancouver Free Press* and *NeWest ReView;* or have been aired on the CBC-FM program *Audience.*

A travel grant from Canada Council Explorations Program was essential.

Thanks for support from Jane Rule, Warren Tallman, David Robinson, Bob Mercer and George Melnyk. Thanks for photographs from Dianne DeMille, David Boswell, Eleanor Wachtel, Paula Jardine, Rick Green, Graeme Gibson, Rose-Marie Tremblay, Steve Hiller and Dennis Cooley. And thanks to the participating authors for their cooperation, and for their books.

This book is dedicated to Dale Banno. For all those conversations when we were young.

Contents

For Openers

Literature, as Alice Munro says in her interview, is most valuable to us as an "opener" to life.

Canadian literature is of particular importance to Canadians, as Margaret Laurence says in her interview, because it helps us "to see through our own eyes".

This book has been designed to serve as an informal "opener" to contemporary Canadian literature in English.

The last decade of literary activity in Canada has been a fruitful one. Anyone wishing to know more about Canadian writers and their work is cordially invited to eavesdrop on a two-year talking tour of assorted Canadian living rooms and kitchens, hotel rooms and beer parlours, and Rudy Wiebe's mosquito-ridden bluff overlooking Strawberry Creek, to hear varying first-hand accounts of what Canadian literature has been up to during its coming of age.

No claim is made that you will meet the twenty-four "best" writers in Canada. You will meet a cross-section of writers of all ages, from the disciplines of poetry, drama and the novel, whose opinions, I hope, will offer as much recreation as refinement. Your curiosity is your ticket.

Because the interviews are intended to be only as uniform as their personal subjects, I hope the resultant diversity of tone and content allows you an ideal opportunity to shop and compare authors. If you enjoy a particular interview, chances are you will enjoy that author's work. Take a chance.

Conversations feature candid observations on the psychology of Canadian society and the process of writing by those who arguably know both these topics best. This book is not a definitive introduction to contemporary English Canadian literature. Rather it is an attempt to lead a few thousand Canadians—and anyone else who might be interested—towards a greater appreciation of the pleasures afforded by many of our country's first-rate authors (in the discursive spirit of Robertson Davies' *A Voice From The Attic* twenty years ago and Silver Donald Cameron's *Conversations With Canadian Novelists* ten years ago).

Verbatim transcripts have been extensively edited to make interviews clearly cohere. All quotes are nonetheless genuine and revisions by authors have been kept to a minimum. Profanities have been deleted to safeguard the impressionable youth of Canada. The interviewer readily admits to offering private opinions to encourage the interviewees to do the same. These are inter-views. Three writers got tipsy. Two cried. And I liked them all.

A rare attack of good taste and discretion now precludes a long lecture as to the precarious future of Canadian publishing if present marketplace conditions, briefly outlined by Margaret Atwood in her interview, are allowed to increasingly limit the public receptivity and economic viability of Canadian literature.

Here then is the book I wish I had been given when I was in high school and university in the 60's or "discovering" Canadian literature in the 70's.

It is for and about openers.

A.T.

One of a Kind

AL PURDY

The application of labels to categorize the work of artists is a questionable practice understandably discouraged by artists. To Al Purdy, it's anathema. He therefore gains the singular honour of being labelled this book's token author without a thematic pairing or interview title which extends beyond his individuality.

Al Purdy is one of Canada's premier poets, an enigmatic man who combines his highly developed sensitivity to natural word rhythms with an engaging frankness of tone to produce poems of lasting beauty, sardonic humour and reflective depth.

The Cariboo Horses (1965), Poems for All the Annettes—Selected Poems Prior to 1965 (1968), A Handful of Earth (1977) and a comprehensive collection Being Alive, 1958-78 (1978) are amongst the best known of his twenty-five books of poetry. He is the editor of four other books and a Governor General's Award winner.

Purdy's public persona is that of a non-university-educated cynic with rolled-up sleeves, homemade grape wine and a difficult-to-live-with wife. The Hallelujah-I'm-a-Bum buoyancy of his poetry readings contributes to his irascible raconteur appeal. Underneath the demeanor of an obstinate, self-confessed born loser lurks, according to Purdy, an obstinate, self-confessed born loser.

Al Purdy was born in rural Ontario in 1918. Presently he lives with his wife in Ameliasburg, Ontario.

photo: David Boswell

T: What was your family upbringing like?
PURDY: We were lower middle class, I guess you'd call it. My father was a farmer who died of cancer when I was two. My mother moved to town and devoted her life to going to church and bringing me up. I suppose I reacted against religion. But I remember when I rode the freight trains west for the first time when I was sixteen or seventeen, I got lost in the woods and couldn't get out. So I prayed. I wasn't going to take any chances, no chances at all.

T: If a person reacts that way when he's very young, they say he'll react that way again when he's old.

PURDY: Christ, I'll never make it! I haven't prayed since that time. I doubt if I ever will again. I'm not religious in any formal sense, not in any God sense.

T: Do you think riding the freights appealed to you because it put you in touch with your survival juices?

PURDY: Well, let me give you the story about the first trip I took. I was hitch-hiking north of Sault Ste. Marie when suddenly the Trans-Canada Highway didn't go any further. So I had to catch a train. I waited till after midnight. I got onto a flatcar that had had coal on it. It was raining and so I huddled there, all self-equipped with two tubes of shaving cream and an extra pair of shoes and a waterproof jacket.
    We went all night into a town called Hawk Junction. I was desperate from the rain. I got out my big hunting knife and tried to get into one of the boxcars. I ripped the seal off one of the cars and tried to open the door but I couldn't do it. So I went back and huddled miserably on the flatcar. I didn't know I was at a divisional point.
    A cop came along and said, "You can get two years for this." He locked me up in a caboose with bars on the windows. There was a padlock on the outside of the door which opened inward. Then he came along a couple of hours later and took me home to have lunch with his family. They gave me a *Ladies Home Journal* to read.
    I began to get alarmed. What will my mother think? Two years in jail. The window of the caboose was broken where other people had tried to get out and couldn't do it. But I noticed, as I said, that the door opened inward. There was a padlock and a hasp on the outside. I put my feet up on the upper part of the sill and got my fingers in the hasp. I pulled the screws out of the padlock on the outside.
    I started to walk back to Sault Ste. Marie, which was a hundred and

sixty-five miles. Then I got panicky. They'll follow me. I'm a desperate criminal. I broke a seal. So I thought I'd walk a little way in the woods so they won't see me. But I got in too far. I couldn't get out. I was there for two bloody days. It rained. That was the last time I prayed, as I said.

T: What were your ambitions as a kid?

PURDY: To stay alive. To get along with other kids. Growing up in a small town, the only son of a very religious woman, I was always alone. Until I got into the Air Force at the age of twenty or so, I didn't get along with anybody.

I became a great reader. I read all the crappy things that kids read. I remember there was a series of paperback books way back then called the Frank Merriwell series. This guy Frank Merriwell went to Yale University and he won at everything he did—naturally he was an American—and anyway, he went through many vicissitudes. When I was about thirteen, a neighbour moved away and gave me two hundred copies of Frank Merriwell. I pretended I was ill and went to bed. My mother fed me ice cream and I read all two hundred copies of Frank Merriwell. I stayed in bed for two months. Then I went back to school and passed into the next form.

T: Were you good in school?

PURDY: Not really. I even failed one year so I could play football. I was playing football then. I rather enjoyed it. One year I got ninety per cent or something and the next year I got forty. Don't ask me why. I started writing when I was about thirteen. I thought it was great when in fact it was crap. But you need that ego to write. Always.

T: You sound like you were probably pretty harem-scarem in those days.

PURDY: No, I wasn't harem-scarem at all. I was pretty conventional. Also I was always very discontented. A miserable little kid. I started, out of sheer desperation, to ride the freight trains. There's a quality of desperation about riding the freights. In my own mind, I was sort of a desperate kid. At a certain age you're always uncertain how other people will take you. I was desperately unhappy trying to adjust to the world. Finally I didn't give a damn.

T: Was the RCAF the next step in your life, after the freight trains?

PURDY: I was doing odd jobs around Trenton. What you did was you picked apples or you worked for Bata shoes. You quit one and then the other. I got into the Air Force for a job. I was there six years. I took a course and became a corporal, then an acting sergeant. Then I was demoted from acting sergeant to corporal and all the way down.

T: You got demoted "to the point where I finally saluted civilians". Why?

PURDY: By this time I was uh...going out with girls. I'd been too scared to go out with them up to the age I got into the Air Force. Once, when I was corporal of the guard, I drove the patrol car over to Belleville to see this girl after midnight. I got caught at it. I was acting sergeant at Picton where I had a big crew of Americans waiting to get into training. What I did was appoint a whole bunch of acting non-coms so that I would have plenty of freedom. I went out on the town again.

Actually I was enjoying myself for the first time in my life. I hated the town of Trenton and I was finally out of it.

T: You've described your first book of poetry, *The Enchanted Echo*, as crap. Did you pay for its publication?

PURDY: Sure. Clarke and Stuart in Vancouver printed it for me. It cost me two hundred dollars to do about five hundred copies. About one hundred and fifty of them got out so I guess about half of those have been destroyed. I went back there ten years ago and they'd thrown them all out. Or they'd burned them. I'd been afraid to go back because I didn't think I could pay storage charges.

T: Around this time you got married. Your wife plays a pretty integral part in your poetry, yet we never get a clear picture of what kind of person she is...

PURDY: Oh, yeah, she's good material. She fixes small television sets and bends iron bars. I picked her up in the streets of Belleville, way back when. Her name's Eurithe because I think her parents were scared by the Odyssey or Iliad or something. It's a Greek name. I don't know why they picked such an oddball name because they're pretty straight people.

T: After you got out of the Air Force, you started a taxi business. Was there much bootlegging involved?

PURDY: Oh, sure. Lots of it. But all the cars kept crashing because we hired such lousy drivers. I used to have a fantasy for writing a novel. I was going to put in this one scene, then tell the novel to my grandfather, who I Liked. After all the cars had crashed and there was only one left, I go out of town with several cases of beer and I drive up the northern highway—Highway 62 I think it is. Of course I'm pursued by a dozen bailiffs and I outrun them all. The car is mortgaged to the hilt. I throw the empties along the road, thus ruining the ecology. I come to a high embankment of rock which overlooks a great lake. I've drunk the last beer. I turn the lights on and point the car into the lake and it sinks. I've outrun all of them. So I walk back to the highway and hitch-hike to Toronto. It's silly, but it's one of the fantasies you have.

T: Have you ever tried writing a novel?

PURDY: Yes, I got 16,000 words once but it was terrible. I used to write plays, too. Ryerson Press accepted a book and the first play I wrote was produced so my wife and I moved to Montreal so I could reap the rewards for my genius. She went to work to support me, as any well-behaved wife should. It turned out I had to write a dozen plays before I could get one accepted by the hard-boiled CBC producers. She decided if I could get away with not working, she could too. She quit her job, though I advised her against it.

That's when we built the house which would be in ah...oh hell, '57 or something like that.

T: Were those the good ol' days or the bad ol' days?

PURDY: Oh, the bad old days. We were so broke! We spent all our money buying a pile of used lumber and putting a down payment on this lot. It was very bad for a while. You know how insecure your ego is when you have no money and you're jobless. There's nothing more terrible than walking the streets looking for a job. I'd been so sick of working for somebody else. Things were so bad we ate rabbits that neighbours had run over and gave to us because they knew we were broke.

I was picking up unemployment insurance for quite a while. When I built the house, I was still getting it in Montreal. I didn't dare move the unemployment insurance to Belleville because they'd give me a job. I used to drive to Montreal every two weeks to pick up the unemployment insurance. I'd drive like hell. Finally I had to get a job.

So I decided to hitch-hike to Montreal. It was twenty below zero. I always pick a day like that. I got seventy miles and I couldn't make it any further. I had no gloves and I was freezing to death. Finally I got so disgusted I hitch-hiked back again. Things like that always happen. Born loser.

T: Isn't is possible to perpetuate that "born loser" image yourself?

PURDY: Oh, sure. It's your own attitude. Now I don't figure I'm going to lose hardly anything. But I used to always have that in the back of my mind, that I was going to lose or be defeated.

T: Is a talent for writing something you're born with?

PURDY: I had no talent whatsoever. If you look back at that first book, it's crap. It's a craft and I changed myself. Mind you, there are qualities of the mind which you have to have. I don't know what they are.

Still, you look at some precocious little bastard like W.H. Auden — who was one of the closest to genius in this century — and you wonder. My God, there's some beautiful lines, beautiful poems. When George Bowering writes this book about poets and the people he's met and he calls Auden "that faggot", that's nasty, plain nasty. I don't care if he's a faggot or what he is, he's a great poet.

T: You mention Bowering. He once wrote that you're our "most Canadian poet".

PURDY: That's b.s. If you're born in Canada, you're obviously one hundred per cent Canadian. So what.

T: How did you come to meet Irving Layton and Milton Acorn?

PURDY: I'd been corresponding with Layton because I'd found a couple of his books and liked them. After I got out of working at a mattress factory, I decided to go to Europe. I went to Layton's place in Montreal and slept on his floor before we caught our boat. I met Dudek through him. I can remember being at this drunken party in Montreal and lying on the floor with Layton, arm-wrestling. Dudek was hovering above us, supercilious and long-nosed, saying, "And these are sensitive poets!"

Milton Acorn had come from Prince Edward Island to sell his carpenter tools. He'd visited Layton. I was writing plays and Layton told Acorn to come around and see me and I'd tell him something about writing plays. I couldn't tell him anything. I couldn't even write them myself.

T: What made you head off to the Cariboo when you got your first Canada Council Fellowship in 1960?

PURDY: I was looking for an excuse to do anything. I only got a thousand bucks so I decided to write a verse play. I'd been stationed at Woodcock during the war, which is about a hundred fifty miles from Prince Rupert. Totem poles, Indians and the whole works. We were building an air strip.

T: So did you intuitively think the Cariboo would stimulate you? Likewise for your trip to Baffin Island?

PURDY: Yeah, you do. I thought I was so damn lucky to be able to go up there to Baffin Island. I'm the only writer on the whole damned island! The feeling that nobody'd ever written about it before!

T: Now you've published twenty-five books, fourteen in the 70's alone. Do you consider yourself prolific?

PURDY: I'm not prolific like Layton. I'll publish a small book and there'll maybe be three or four poems which I think are worth including in this one [*Being Alive*]. It's a frightening thing to look backward and see that the earlier books have more poems in this collection than the later books.

T: How closely did you work with Dennis Lee in editing *Being Alive?*

PURDY: He's a friend of mine. There are about fifteen poems which have been changed a bit because he'd look at a poem and say, ''I don't quite understand this'' or ''I think this could be a little bit better.'' Picking the poems was a mutual thing. The idea was to be able to read through the sections and be able to go on to a new section easily. The divisions are not so clear cut as in *Selected Poems.*

It's by far the best book I've ever brought out. It amounts to a ''collected'' but it feels like a gravestone at the end of a road. There's a feeling of where the hell do I go from here? I certainly write less as I grow older. I'm writing very good poems at infrequent intervals. Like ''Lament'' and ''A Handful of Earth.''

T: Do you ever force yourself to write?

PURDY: Occasionally. I think a prose writer forces it out like tooth-paste, but I prefer not to. Sometimes you've got a thought and you want to explore it. I dunno. The title poem of *The Cariboo Horses* was written in about half an hour. Another poem, "Postscript," took seven years.

T: Ten years ago you said people who develop a special way of writing, like B.P. Nichol or the Tish-Black Mountain people, were going down a dead end. Yet they're still travelling after a decade.

PURDY: It's still a dead end. They don't have any variety. The Black Mountain people talk in a certain manner in which they make under-emphasis a virtue. It's dull writing. It's far duller than conversation. I can't understand how people can write it except kids can write it and think, I too can be a poet. They can ignore a thousand years of writing poems, not read what's come before. There's so much to read, so much to enjoy. That's the reason to read poetry, to enjoy it.

T: Margaret Atwood has described your work as "hard-boiled and romantic" at the same time. That's the standard Canlit line on your work. As you get older, do you find yourself moving closer to one side of that dichotomy than the other?

PURDY: I'm probably getting more pessimistic.

T: You don't hold with the theory that nature is hostile and that Canadians are "survivors".

PURDY: I don't understand how anybody could think so. Nature is completely indifferent.

T: Do you have any thoughts on the general characteristics of Canadian literature?

PURDY: The most prominent characteristic of Canadian literature is that it's the only literature about which the interviewer would ask what the characteristics are.

T: I think your best poems are those that cover the eerie meeting place between past and present, such as "Method for Calling Up Ghosts", "Remains of an Indian Village", "Roblin's Mills 1 and 2", "Lament for the Dorsets". Do you believe you have a soul?

PURDY: Well, Voltaire had some thoughts on that. He tried weighing himself before and after death. I don't think he came up with anything. I don't think I do have a soul. But there are areas in our nature that we don't know about. It's possible that we may find something that we haven't found before and we may use that word that's already invented and call it a soul. We use that word because it's the only word we have. You can feel this, of course, what you earlier referred to as transmigration of souls. I thought it was a fascinating concept to imagine everybody living to leave lines behind on the street where they've been in "Method for Calling Up Ghosts." What it means is you're walking across the paths of the dead at all times. Every time you cross the St. Lawrence River you're crossing Champlain's path.

T: You think a lot about death?

PURDY: Quite a bit.

T: Dorothy Livesay complained to me recently that —

PURDY: Oh, she's complaining about everything.

T: She said that writers such as yourself, Milton Acorn and the worker poets have disappointed her expectations because you're not motivated by politics as much as poetics.

PURDY: That's too bad. I'd like to be as nasty as her, but it's hard. To me it's a virtue to disappoint Dorothy. The particular grievance I have against Dorothy Livesay is that she reviewed a book and ended it by saying he's "not self-indulgent and roistering like Purdy." Of course I'm self-indulgent. If I feel like roistering, I'll roister. Why drag me into that review? It's meanness, smallness...of a dull writer. Which you can quote. I had been in Winnipeg when she was there and I didn't pay very much attention to her. I think she resented it.

T: You were born in 1918. Has feminism affected your life at all?

PURDY: Every time I read my poem, "Homemade Beer", it affects me. The audience thinks, "male Chauvinist". It's a bawdy, exaggerated poem. Then I can read "The Horseman of Agawa" and it's exactly the opposite. People think you want to be one thing. You're not one thing. You're everything. Of course women have been second-class citizens for years. To gain a position of near equality, which they certainly haven't done yet, they've got to exaggerate. I exaggerate, too. Those remarks about my wife were facetious, of course, but I'm trying to imply with exaggerations that she's a tremendously capable woman.

T: In "The Sculptors" you enjoy imperfections of the broken Eskimo carvings and in "Depression in Namu, B.C." you write, "beauty bores me without the slight ache of ugliness". There seems to be a streak in you that feels affinity with imperfection, that wants things to be blemished.

PURDY: Don't you ever want to splash muddy water into a sunset? A sunset is so marvellous, how are you going to paint it? How are you going to talk about it? So there is a quality of wishing to muddy up perfection, I agree.

T: You end many of your poems with a dash, as if the poem is not really completed.

PURDY: Yeah, a lot of poems are in process as if things happen after you stop looking at it. A poem is a continual revision, even if you've written it down without changing a single word. I like the thought of revision. When I copy a poem, I often change it. When I've written a poem in longhand, as I always do, I'll type it then I'll scribble it all up with changes.

T: What is there in you that needs to commemorate your existence through poetry?

PURDY: You have to go back when you started to write. I think most young poets begin to write through sheer ego. Look at me, no hands, mom. There's always going to be the element of ego, because we can't escape our egos. We don't necessarily want to. But there has to be a time when we can sit down and write and try to say a thing and the ego isn't so important. When you are just trying to tell the truth, you're not trying to write immortal lines that will go reverberating down the centuries. You're saying what you feel and think and what is important to you.

T: Have the 70's made you at all optimistic about our future?

PURDY: I'm pessimistic about everything the older I get. We're going to wade through garbage. We're going to split up. The Americans are going to take everything, even though they don't need to, of course, because they have it already. The world is going to explode and we'll all be dead. Life is awful.

What Is

ALICE MUNRO

Writers of fiction have been collectively psychoanalysed as injustice-collectors. One writer who does not fit comfortably into that definition (and who helped cancel The Injustice-Collectors *from the list of many possible titles for this book) is Alice Munro.*

Alice Munro's "super-realism" takes the form of a sophisticated and sympathetic awareness of emotional conflicts unencumbered by any penchant for didacticism. As twice winner of the Governor General's Award and a frequent contributor to New Yorker *magazine, Munro has firmly established her reputation as one of Canada's premier writers with her impeccable style and exacting honesty.*

Her four books are Dance of the Happy Shades *(1968),* Lives of Girls and Women *(1971),* Something I've Been Meaning to Tell You *(1974) and* Who Do You Think You Are? *(1979). All have been critically well-received and feature heroines who seek to gain some measure of control over their lives through understanding.*

After two years at the University of Western Ontario, Alice Munro married and moved to Vancouver and Victoria where she became a mother of three daughters and was eventually divorced. In 1972, she remarried and returned to live in Ontario.

Alice Munro was born in Wingham, Ontario in 1931.

photo: Graeme Gibson

T: Your writing is like the perfect literary equivalent to a documentary movie.

MUNRO: That is the way I see it. That's the way I want it to be.

T: So it's especially alarming when *Lives of Girls and Women* gets removed from a reading list of an Ontario high school. Essentially all they're objecting to is the truth.

MUNRO: This has been happening in Huron County, where I live. They wanted *The Diviners, Of Mice and Men* and *Catcher in the Rye* taken off, too. They succeeded in getting *The Diviners* taken off. It doesn't particularly bother me about my book because my book is going to be around in the bookstores. But the impulse behind what they are doing bothers me a great deal. There is such a total lack of appreciation of what literature is about! They feel literature is there to teach some great moral lesson. They always see literature as an influence, not as an opener of life. The lessons they want taught are those of fundamentalist Christianity and if literature doesn't do this, it's a harmful influence.

They talk about protecting their children from these books. The whole concept of protecting eighteen-year-old children from sexuality is pretty scary and pretty sad. Nobody's being forced to read these books anyway. The news stories never mention that these books are only options. So they're not just protecting their own children. What they're doing is removing the books from other people's children.

T: Removing your books seems especially absurd because there's so little preaching for any particular morality or politics.

MUNRO: None at all. I couldn't write that way if I tried. I back off my party line, even those with which I have a great deal of sympathy, once it gets hardened and insisted upon. I say to myself that's not true all the time. That's why I couldn't write a straight women's lib book to expose injustices. Everything's so much more complicated than that.

T: Which brings us to why you write. Atwood's theory on Del Jordan in *Girls and Women* is that she writes as an act of redemption. How much do you think your own writing is a compensation for loss of the past?

MUNRO: Redemption is a pretty strong word. My writing has become a way of dealing with life, hanging onto it by recreation. That's important. But it's also a way of getting on top of experience. We all have life rushing in on us. A writer pretends, by writing about it, to have control. Of course a writer actually has no more control than anybody else.

T: Do you think you've chosen the short story form because that requires the most discipline and you come from a very restrictive background?

MUNRO: That's interesting. Nobody has suggested that before. I've never known why I've chosen the short story form. I guess in a short story you impose discipline rather soon. Things don't get away from you. Perhaps I'm afraid of other forms where things just flow out. I have a friend who writes novels. She never touches what she's written on the day she's written it. She would consider it fake to go back and rework the material. It has to be how the work flows out of her. Something about that makes me very uneasy. I could never do it.

T: You're suspicious of spontaneity?

MUNRO: I suppose so. I'm not afraid spontaneity would betray me because I've done some fairly self-exposing things. But I'm afraid it would be repetitious and boring if I wrote that way. It's as if I must take great care over everything. Instead of splashing the colours out and trusting they will all come together, I have to know the design.

T: Do your ideas ever evolve into something too big for a short story?

MUNRO: Yes.

T: I thought the title story of *Something I've Been Meaning to Tell You* was a good example of that. It didn't work because you were dealing with the lifetimes of four different characters.

MUNRO: You know I really wanted to write a novel of that story. Then it just sort of boiled down like maple syrup. All I had left was that story. For me it would have been daring to stretch that material out into a full novel. I wouldn't be sure of it. I wouldn't be sure it had the strength. So I don't take that chance.

T: Do you write your stories primarily for magazines now, or for eventual inclusion in a book?

MUNRO: Writing for magazines is a very sideline thing. It's what enables me to survive financially, but it isn't important to me artistically. Right now I'm working on some stories and I might not be able to sell any of them. This has happened to very established

writers. Markets are always changing. They say to beginning writers
— study the market. That's no use at all. The only thing you can do is
write what you want.

T: You once said that the emotional realism of your work is solidly
autobiographical. Is that how your stories get started? when
something triggers you back to an emotional experience?

MUNRO: Yes. Some incident that might have happened to me or to
somebody else. It doesn't matter which. As long as it's getting *at*
some kind of emotional core that I want to investigate.

T: Do you ever worry that goldmine of your past will dry up?

MUNRO: I never know. I never know. I thought I had used it all up
before I started this book. Now I'm writing out of a different period.
I'm very interested in my young adulthood.

T: Has there been a lot of correlation between your writing and
raising your daughters?

MUNRO: Tremendously. When I was writing *Lives of Girls and
Women*, some of the things in there came from things my daughters
did when they were ten or eleven. It's a really crazy age. They used to
go to the park and hang down from their knees and scare people, pre-
tending to be monkeys. I saw this wild, ferocious thing in them which
gets dampened for most girls with puberty. Now my two older girls
are twenty-five and twenty-one and they're making me remember new
things. Though they live lives so different from any life possible to me,
there's still similarities.

T: Do you feel a great weight has been lifted now your kids are older?

MUNRO: Yes. I'm definitely freer. But not to be looking after
somebody is a strange feeling. All my life I've been doing it. Now I
feel enormous guilt that I'm not responsible for anybody.

T: Maybe guilt is the Great Canadian Theme. Marian Engel writes
Canada is "a country that cannot be modern without guilt." And
Margaret Laurence says she comes from "people who feel guilty at the
drop of a hat, for whom virtue only arises from work." Since intellectual work is not regarded by many people as real work, did you face
any guilt about wanting to write?

MUNRO: Oh, yes. But it wasn't guilt so much as embarrassment. I
was doing something I couldn't explain or justify. Then after a while I

got used to being in that position. That's maybe the reason I don't want to go on living at home [Huron County]. I notice when I move out and go to Toronto, I feel like an ordinary person.

T: Do you know where you got your ambition to write?

MUNRO: It was the only thing I ever wanted to do. I just kept on trying. I guess what happens when you're young has a great deal to do with it. Isolation, feelings of power that don't get out in a normal way, and maybe coping with unusual situations... most writers seem to have backgrounds like that.

T: When the kids play I Spy in your stores, they have a hard time finding colours. Was your upbringing really that bleak?

MUNRO: Fairly. I was a small child in the Depression. What happens at the school in the book you're referring to is true. Nothing is invented.

T: So you really did take a temperance pledge in the seventh grade?

MUNRO: Yes, I did.

T: Sounds pretty bleak to me!

MUNRO: [laughter] I thought my life was interesting. There was always a great sense of adventure, mainly because there were so many fights. Life was fairly dangerous. I lived in an area like West Hanratty in the book [*Who Do You Think You Are?*]. We lived outside the whole social structure because we didn't live in the town and we didn't live in the country. We lived in this kind of little ghetto where all the bootleggers and prostitutes and hangers-on lived. Those were the people I knew. It was a community of outcasts. I had that feeling about myself.

When I was about twelve, my mother got Parkinson's Disease. It's an incurable, slowly deteriorating illness which probably gave me a great sense of fatality. Of things not going well. But I wouldn't say I was unhappy. I didn't belong to any nice middle class so I got to know more types of kids. It didn't seem bleak to me at the time. It seemed full of interest.

T: As Del Jordan says, "For what I wanted was every last thing, every layer of speech and thought, stroke of light on bark or walls,. every smell, pothole, pain-cracked illusion..."

MUNRO: That's the getting-everything-down compulsion.

T: Yet your work never reads like it's therapy writing.

MUNRO: No. I don't write just out of problems. [laughing] I wrote even before I had problems!

T: I understand you've married again. And that it's quite successful.

MUNRO: It's a very happy relationship. I haven't really dealt much with happy relationships. Writers don't. They tell you about their tragedies. Happiness is a very hard thing to write about. You deal with it more often as a bubble that's about to burst.

T: You have a quote about Rose in the new book, "She thought how love removes the world." With your writing you're trying to get in touch with the world as much as possible, so does this mean that love and writing are adversaries?

MUNRO: Wordsworth said, "Poetry is emotion recollected in tranquillity." You can follow from this that a constant state of emotion would be hostile to the writing state.

T: If you're a writer, that could have some pretty heavy implications.

MUNRO: Very heavy. If you're a writer, probably there's something in you that makes you value your self, your own objectivity, so much that you can't stand to be under the sway of another person. But then some people might say that writing is an escape, too. I think we all make choices about whether we want to spend our lives in emotional states.

T: That's interesting. My wife's comment on *Who Do You Think You Are* was that your character, Rose, is never allowed to get anything. She's always unfulfilled. Maybe she's just wary of emotion.

MUNRO: She gets something. She gets herself. She doesn't get the obvious things, the things she thinks she wants. Like in "Mischief" [a story about middle-aged infidelity] Rose really doesn't want that love affair. What she does get is a way out of her marriage. She gets a knowledge of herself.

T: But only after a male decides the outcome of the relationship.

MUNRO: I see that as true in relations between men and women. Men seem to have more initiative to decide whether things happen or don't happen. In this specific area women have had a lack of power, although it's slowly changing.

T: When you write, "Outrageous writers may bounce from one blessing to another nowadays, bewildered, as permissively raised children are said to be, by excess of approval," I get the feeling you could just as easily substitute the word male for outrageous.

MUNRO: I think it's still possible for men in public to be outrageous in ways that it's not possible for women to be. It still seems to be true that no matter what a man does, there are women who will be in love with him. It's not true the other way round. I think achievement and ability are positively attractive qualities in men that will overcome all kinds of behaviour and looks, but I don't think the same is true for women.

A falling-down-drunk poet may have great power because he has talent. But I don't think men are attracted to women for these reasons. If they are attracted to talent, it has to be combined with the tradition-ally attractive female qualities. If a woman comes on shouting and drinking and carrying on, she won't be forgiven.

T: Whenever I ask writers about growing older, they not only answer the question, they *respond* to the question. I suspect you're enjoying getting older, too.

MUNRO: Yes. Yes. I think it's great. You just stop worrying about a lot of things you used to worry about. You get things in perspective. Since I've turned forty I've been happier than ever before. I feel so much freer.

What Can Be

JANE RULE

In an era of perpetually uncertain consciousness-shifting, Jane Rule continues to encourage change by creating characters who struggle to step beyond the limitations of social convention to achieve self-determination and self-acceptance, two prized prerequisites for love born of strength, not weakness.

Desert of the Heart *(1964) remains her best known work. It is a compassionate and unsentimental account of two women who meet and fall in love in Reno, Nevada.*

This Is Not for You *(1970) is an out-of-print novel which takes the form of a letter in which one woman attempts to justify her non-involvement with the woman she loves.*

Against the Seaon *(1971) and* The Young in One Another's Arms *(1977) focus upon the difficulties encountered by people of all ages who try to evolve a sense of community from essentially voluntary relationships.*

Theme for Diverse Instruments *(1974) is a book of short stories and* Lesbian Images *(1975) is a psychological study of twelve female writers. A new novel,* Contact with the World, *is forthcoming in 1980.*

Born in Plainfield, New Jersey in 1931, Jane Rule came to Canada in the late 1950's to teach at the University of British Columbia. She now resides on Galiano Island, B.C.

photo: Steven Hiller

T: You've written, "Knowing what should be isn't hard. Accepting what can be seems to be the problem." Do you think that serves as a fair description of what you're writing about?

RULE: Certainly on one level that's probably right.

T: Do you consider yourself an American writer or a Canadian writer?

RULE: Well, simply a writer in English is always best. Some of my work is set in England because I lived there for a while. Then I went back to the States and found it very alien. When I came to Vancouver and found a beautiful place to be, I simply elected the city. I came on a beautiful August day, twenty-some years ago, so that it was still a little charming city. I didn't even think of it as Canada. I mean I knew it was Canada, but I was that kind of American. It was north of Seattle and it was a place called Vancouver. Now I've spent just about half my life in Canada—all my adult life—so, since I didn't really have roots in any specific place in the States, my commitment to a nation is really much clearer as a Canadian.

T: Have you resented being pigeon-holed as a "lesbian" novelist?

RULE: I reacted to it at first, but I don't much any more. If there was a usefulness in resenting it, then I would. But I also know that it's politically important to other people. I'm a responsible person so it seems to me I have to put up with it.

T: Do you put much faith in politics to solve social problems?

RULE: Well, it seems to me politics is housekeeping. I don't look to politics as a place to change anything. We get the politics we deserve. Politics really are to clean up the house. You have to do it every week. I don't find it interesting, just as I don't find sweeping the floor every week interesting. I do it. I vote.

I prefer to work wherever there's a possibility of changing things. I work with lesbians, I work with gay men, I work with the women's movement. I really believe through the counter-movements in society change can be made. We're living witnesses of it. The last ten years have shocked even the most optimistic of us.

T: Are you consciously evangelical for your own politics when you write?

Rule: No, I don't suppose so. In fact, the thing that is peculiar for me about reaction to my books is that I've had an awful lot of reviewers take me to task for not being political, for having no other great interest than writing some kind of gentle soap opera. *Desert of the Heart* got a very bad review in Quebec because I got all the social analysis correctly, I understood everything that was wrong, then I bloody well accepted it instead of blowing the place up! [laughter]

Of course I do get reviewers who say that I'm a revolutionary, that I really ought to be called to confess my revolutionary zeal which is hidden under a slick surface. But I don't feel politics lurk in my books or dominate them.

T: Actually it's often not politics people find threatening. It's ideas. People read "only the good can be guilty" in *Desert of the Heart* and it shakes them.

Rule: Sure. That's why I expected to get absolutely fried with that book. But what I didn't expect was to hear from all the readers who were in anguish. I was shocked by the number of people who were needy for that book.

T: Coming from a different generation, I'd almost say I don't understand what the fuss could be about.

Rule: Absolutely. I think it would be very hard for anyone to imagine what it was like in the fifties. I think about the only valid criticism I got when *Desert of the Heart* was released was that there's no hostility surrounding Evelyn and Ann. The landlady is consoling. There isn't any climate of hostility. But I chose that consciously. So many people in those days were trying to get sympathy for homosexuals by showing how mean everyone was to them. I didn't want to get into propaganda. I wanted them to say what they really would say and feel what they really would feel. I consciously didn't want to drag in a lot of social pressure to overshadow that.

T: I think many readers would agree today with Virginia Woolf's description of *The Well of Loneliness* as a "meritorious, dull book". Do you think *Desert of the Heart* will ever replace it as "the" lesbian novel?

Rule: I don't suppose so, alas. Radcliffe Hall wrote *The Well of Loneliness* as a piece of propaganda and therefore included all kinds of theory and minor characters. It's also a tragic story and I think that as long as people are willing to be broad-minded, *The Well of Loneliness* is an ideal book. Because the people suffer and get punished. *Desert of the Heart* has already taken the place of *The Well of Loneliness* for lesbians, but for the range of society, no. Because Evelyn and Ann apparently get it together. It's not tragic.

T: After having written *Lesbian Images,* where do you stand on the question of rationalizing the origins of lesbianism?

RULE: I think there is only one origin: that you love another woman. The person you love is the motivation.

As physical creatures, we react to sexual stimulus. So it's probably true that we are capable of responding sexually to either sex. Of course the predisposition for reproduction is heterosexual so the majority of people move in that direction. But there are lots of people who are so frightened of sexual feelings that they don't feel anything for either sex.

T: Would you agree with Havelock Ellis that sexual inversion tends to occur in individuals who are above average in intellect and character?

RULE: No. That was one of those defensive statements that you'll find coming out of any minority that feels threatened. You know, that Shakespeare was bisexual. And Plato. To get your act together and claim everybody under the sun is good, strong, brave and true.

T: Where do you suppose you got your strength for living a life of non-conformity? from your family?

RULE: Partly, yes. But partly also by not finding it easy to conform. A lot of people find strength because they have to have it, not because they go around courting it.

For instance, I didn't grow up in one place. Therefore I never experienced a lot of intimate social pressure. It didn't really matter to me much what people thought because I knew I'd be gone in a year. I could really base my choices on what I wanted to do. My parents were also very supportive and taught us all to be non-conformists, even though they're confirmists themselves. They conform because they can.

T: Which brings us to Jane Rule on morality. "Morality is a test of our conformity rather than our integrity."

RULE: Yes, I do think morality is simply part of the quality of life, sometimes a very bad part and sometimes a very good part.

T: One of your characters says, "What you lose is what you survive with." Does that statement come out of your life?

RULE: No, it comes from observing more than experiencing. Some of the people I know who have carried the heaviest burdens are people who figured how to let those things work for them. So I wanted to create a character who had that kind of guts. As long as you're alive, what you lose becomes part of your understanding.

T: With that what-you-lose-is-what-you-get angle, was *The Young in One Another's Arms* meant as a definitive novel of the sixties?

RULE: No. The experiences that come from me for that book go back to the end of the Second World War. In that respect, it's really too bad when something like draft-dodging gets to be associated only with the sixties. I'm always startled when a reviewer says, "Oh well, this is about the sixties, no point, dead issue." I think fiction isn't about those issues. Those issues are part of the climate of fiction. The notion that a book should be "new" is new since television.

I remember I sent a short-short to *Redbook*. A short-short is only about a thousand words long. I wrote it at the time of the Cuban Crisis and sent it off. They accepted the story two months later but they said they needed me to invent a different world crisis because the Cuban Crisis was dated. Crazy, just crazy.

T: But *The Young in One Another's Arms* is essentially about people trying to set up an economic and emotional commune. So it is a reflection of the sixties.

RULE: Sure. But the word is politically loaded for me. At that time I was listening to an awful lot of young people out at UBC who were so earnest about living in a commune you knew it wouldn't last. Everybody had to have exactly the same amount of space. I remember saying to one girl, "What happens if I'm a writer and my friend Tak Tanabe is a painter? I could work in a closet and he couldn't." She said, "Oh well, those are only hobbies." And every Tuesday night you have a criticism period. That whole era is what "commune" got stamped with.

T: Were you personally affected by all that sixties idealism floating around?

RULE: No. But it certainly affected the young people I knew at the time. I was very busy being a teacher and trying to find time to write. We always had draft dodgers with us, or people who couldn't cope with the university, but I was too involved with the commitment I had made to writing. Consequently I've never been one to think of solutions for my own life coming from things I do with other people.

T: Yet you're writing these books where you're almost prescribing communalism, or at least the notion that a communal way of life is a very real and worthwhile alternative.

RULE: Well, I know it is. It can be done. But art is a job that has to be done alone. My next book is about artists and what it is like to be committed to that kind of job. [*Contract With the World*] The kinds of good friends I have are people who are perfectly willing to have me say I'll see them in six months, and live right next door. A number of people do that with me, too. But you don't do that and live in a commune.

T: How do you feel about the anti-academic sentiment of the sixties and seventies?

RULE: I am "anti" a lot that's going on, at the big universities particularly. But I'm an academician. I really care about the academy. When I feel critical, it isn't that I'm being anti-intellectual. I'm saying this is one of the important places and you better clean up your act. I feel very strongly that they haven't been emphasizing teaching and that's death to learning.

[Whimsically] I'm a schoolmarm. I pick up a book of Margaret Laurence's and I say what's she doing with point of view here? She'll never get away with this in a million years. Five pages later I've forgotten the question of course, and I write her and say, Margaret, if you got by me with this one, it works. Because I usually don't forget. If you're going to write you have to read that way.

T: Is it important for you to keep in touch with other writers?

RULE: Not as a thing in itself. But it's very important for me to keep in touch with people who happen to be my friends and are writers. Certainly in Canada we're very fortunate in that the government helps us keep in touch. We all go to Ottawa once a year on the government. I need to see Marie-Claire Blais once a year. And Peggy Atwood. And Margaret Laurence.

T: With the setting of *Desert of the Heart,* you gave equal time to how
relationships work and how society works. But as your books become
more technical, it appears social analysis is becoming less emphasized.

T: That's probably true. Essentially what I've been trying to teach
myself over these last few novels is how to deal with a group of people.
Technically that is more difficult than doing the structural things, as in
Desert. Desert is the most structured of anything that I've ever done.
From natural to social to individual. The characters were provided
with certain intellectual chores that they had to get through in that
book, never mind make love to each other and all those other things.

The Vancouver setting for *The Young* was nowhere near as
important. And in *Against the Season,* the setting was even less
important again. I was mostly interested in people living in a no-place,
a place that was dying. Also in that book I wanted to try to write that
conventional kind of English novel. It has an omniscient narrator
which I hadn't done before. That's conventional. But it wasn't
conventional for me. It was far out to sit there and let the quips come
and have them be my own.

T: That's something I really enjoy about your books—the humour.
Your characters' talk is very modern, like people I know. They're
always using humour to break social ground, as a reaching out.

RULE: Well, I have a feeling that the kind of dialogue I write is very
West Coast. I get an awful lot of flak from eastern editors saying this
is absolutely unbelievable dialogue. Their claim is that the only people
who are witty are people who use lots of references to books and other
intellectual paraphernalia. There's a kind of snobbery in the east, and
also a slowness. People are not kindly offhand. There's not the kind of
teasing that has nothing to do with anybody needing to be defensive.
A sort of joking attentiveness that goes on in a more relaxed world.

T: I think another strength of your writing is the repeated appreciation for the aged. What accounts for all the elderly characters in your
books?

RULE: I spend a lot of time with people a good deal older than I am. I
always have. I grew up with grandparents and was very close to them.
On this island, most of the population is over sixty-five. Elisabeth
Hopkins down the road is, I suppose, our closest friend. [Eighty-six-
year-old painter and recent author of *The Painted Cougar,* a children's
book.] So older people are very much a part of the world I live in.

T: Living on an island is another recurring motif. Do you get special comfort or stimulation from being here on Galiano?

RULE: No, I suppose I think of this mostly as "away". One of my characters in my new book says, "If there was a town called Away I would drive to it." Galiano is for me a bit of a fortress. I was beginning to be bugged in town, I couldn't lead my own life. Coming over here, I can spend my time as I want to. When I go to an event here, it's as the treasurer of the Galiano Club. I take the quarters. Nobody pays much attention.

T: One last highly pertinent question. Do you really drink Coca-Cola for breakfast?

RULE: Yes, I do. Except they don't sell Coca-Cola on the island. I had to switch to Pepsi. The guy who owns the store over here had a fight with the Coca-Cola people and he won't buy it. [laughing] I said, "Vic, I am nearly fifty years old. This is a lifetime addiction. You didn't tell me when I moved onto this island that you were going to have a fight with the Coca-Cola company."

T: So Jane Rule took the Pepsi challenge.

RULE: I did. And I can't tell the difference.

World of Wonders

ROBERTSON DAVIES

Dr. Robertson Davies is not unlike a wizard. Although his formal manner and versatile intellect suggest a somewhat pompous and conservative personality well suited to serve as Senator of the Stratford Shakespearean Festival and Master of Massey College at the University of Toronto, in fact Davies' international reputation as a novelist, playwright, critic, humourist and scholar owes as much to his emotional vulnerability and inquisitive nature as it does to his formidable air of confidence and credibility within the halls of academe.

Fifth Business (1970), The Manticore (1972) and World of Wonders (1975) comprise his Deptford Trilogy, one the most impressive storytelling feats in Canadian literature. These particular novels combine Davies' fascinations with Jungian psychology, the nature of evil and the charms of magic.

Born in Thamesville, Ontario in 1913, Davies was educated at Queens and Oxford, with the Old Vic Drama School, as a journalist with Saturday Night and as editor and publisher of the Peterborough Examiner before he turned to a full-time literary career.

He is the author of twenty-five books. The Manticore received the Governor General's Award.

Robertson Davies lives with his wife in Toronto.

photo: Alan Twigg

T: Why have humourists fallen from fashion in Canada?

DAVIES: Oh, I think it's because of the extremely sore skin of our times. Humour very often consists of shrewd perceptions about people. It's usually funny at someone's expense. Nowadays if you're funny at anybody's expense they run to the U.N. and say, "I must have an ombudsman to protect me." You hardly dare have a shrewd perception about anybody. The only people you can abuse are WASPs. They're fair game. But most of the people who want to mock them aren't very good mockers because they don't understand what a WASP is.

T: But humour always makes a comeback.

DAVIES: Of course. It has to find an outlet because it's a basic element of civilized life. But there are always people who mistrust it and dislike it. You find whole periods of history where humour is completely choked off. For instance, if you look at the period from about 1640 to 1660 in British history, you won't find much humorous writing in it. The people down on humour then were the same people who are down on humour now. The Puritans, the people who are terribly touchy about any kind of criticism or evaluation that isn't made exactly on their terms.

T: Are we experiencing a New Puritanism in a liberal age?

DAVIES: Oh, yes. It's a very puritanical age. It's not puritanical about some of the usual targets of puritanism like sex, but it's extremely puritanical about human rights. And children. All sorts of things like that.

T: Do you put a value judgement on it?

DAVIES: I think it needs exploding. But it's going to take a very good man to explode it. He's going to have all the blacks, all the Jews, and all the minorities down his neck, chasing him with knives.

T: Do you have any desire to become that man?

DAVIES: I have to see if the opportunity presents itself. Any group that becomes too serious about itself, and this means most minorities, needs reminding of the ordinary humanity that encompasses us all.

T: In your essay on Stephen Leacock you say humour is the result of

tension in the mind. Are there particular tensions in Canadian society
that form the basis of a distinctly national humour?

DAVIES: I think we do have something which more or less approaches
a national humour, and it's something that Stephen Leacock evolved
with great brilliance. The characteristic of it is a kind of patterned
innocence which covers a very great bitterness. Never is it so sharply
shown as in Leacock's *Sunshine Sketches.* You analyse what he says
about the little town and it's a snake-pit. But he says it with such
charm! The charm is convincing because it probably seemed charming
when it happened.

T: What about the tension of Canada feeling itself a dutiful daughter
of the British Empire in jealous competition with the undutiful
daughter, the United States?

DAVIES: That was the case. It's not the case any longer. Canada is no
longer a dutiful daughter. It hasn't been since at least 1945. You see
the whole British world-wide connection began to crack up about the
time of World War One. By World War Two it was already
becoming tenuous. When Britain served notice on Australia that
whatever happened in the Pacific they shouldn't expect any help from
Britain, that was the end of a great sentimental link with the Mother
Country.

Now Britain's cultural influence is very much on the wane in
Canada. But it's always been a one-way thing. It's been our feeling
towards them, not their feeling towards us. They couldn't care less
about us.

T: In your play, *Hunting Stuart,* Henry becomes Bonnie Prince Charlie
and in your Deptford trilogy Boy Staunton is killed essentially by his
desire to be like the Prince of Wales. As a young person, were your
role models essentially British?

DAVIES: My relationship to Great Britain was not as strong as that of a
lot of Canadians because my family was not English. Part of it was
Dutch and American.

T: Would you agree the Canadian public thinks of you primarily as a
man of intellect and education; whereas you think of yourself primarily
as a man of feeling and intuition?

DAVIES: Yes.

T: Doesn't this variance limit people's appreciation of your work?

DAVIES: I think that it does. This business about me being so elaborately educated isn't true. I am very spottily educated. This is both because of the kind of schooling I encountered and because I was not capable of assimilating a fully rounded education as it existed at the time. Now I tend not to think my way through problems but to feel my way through them. I judge them on intuition and values. That's a feeling person rather than a thinking person.

T: Is this why you turned away from a career in psychiatry?

DAVIES: Oh, yes, I think so. The extreme tightrope-walking involved in psychiatry would have been too hard for me. As a psychiatrist, you've got to keep your cool all the time. That's very, very hard work.

T: Also psychiatry is a banishment of wonder. It's basically putting explanations on sensations.

DAVIES: [amused] Yes. And when you become a professional explainer, you're in great trouble.

T: This would explain why you've developed a fascination with insanity. It emphasizes the frailty of reason.

DAVIES: Yes. Attempts to explain what is happening in the mind of the insane person are often very wide of the mark.

T: Didn't Freud once say that neurosis is a form of creation?

DAVIES: Well, yes. But other people have said physical illness is also a form of creation. You can say those things and they sound very fine. But when you start to analyse them, sometimes they're not up to much.

T: I suspect you've also been curious about the possible benefits of mind-altering drugs.

DAVIES: I've thought a good deal about it and I've seen instances of people who have tried it. The thing is, their minds are altered but not enlarged. Attempts to gain some sort of instant enlightenment are apparently rooted in the idea that the drug is going to extend the mind. It doesn't really. It may clarify it or make it possible to observe something which is not ordinarily accessible, but people don't have wonderful visions under the influence of drugs which are beyond their power of imagination. And it can be frightfully destructive.

The road to enlightenment is hard, hard, hard. You can't do it with pills or needles.

T: Perhaps the popularity of drugs over the past few decades has something to do with advertising. The promise of instant gratification.

DAVIES: Precisely. Happiness can be yours!

T: Magnus in *World of Wonders* says he grew up in a world where there was much concern about goodness but little love. Is that a fair description of your environment?

DAVIES: No, my family was more highly temperamental than that statement would suggest.

T: What about your society?

DAVIES: Oh, my society was very cagey about using the word "love." But there was a great concern about goodness or what would win approval.

T: And with this concern for goodness, there was a lack of giving the Devil his due?

DAVIES: Yes. A lack of recognition of what the Devil might be.

T: *World of Wonders* can be read entirely as an exploration of the nature of evil. Do you think our writers have been leery of that in the past?

DAVIES: I think they have. Though now they're getting to it. Margaret Atwood's latest book [*Life Before Man*] is interesting in that regard. And Marian Engel's *Bear* was an attempt to come to terms with the primal aspects of life. On the surface level, that novel was absurd. Any attempt like that to form a relationship with a bear would probably be impossible—and if possible, highly dangerous. But as a dream, as an allegory of the relationship to the size and spirit of the country, it's something very different and very powerful.

T: Did you become dissatisfied with mainstream Christianity because most Christianity is concerned with Good, whereas Art is concerned with Good and Evil?

DAVIES: Yes. I think that is perfectly true. Also anything that becomes a mass movement is reduced by the mass. I am essentially a cradle Protestant. I feel that your devotion to God has to be personal and individual. To do it with a great gang who are really trying to get away from thinking about God but want to do a lot of good for the Boat People may be very fine but it's not a religion. It's an escape from a dire confrontation with whatever is beyond.

T: A great many people would violently disagree with you there.

DAVIES: Yes, I think they would.

T: About the Boat People analogy, I mean.

DAVIES: Yes. It's all very fine. But it's so easy. You get out and cheer for the Boat People; you're so obviously doing good and you can congratulate yourself; you can mix with a lot of people who think as you do. But just facing your relationship to what is ultimate in life, quietly, is much harder. It's not so self-honouring.

T: Ah, but what happens if you have faced yourself and then decide to say, to hell with the Boat People.

DAVIES: Fine. But again you may not. You might just as conceivably say, to Hell with the Boat People.

T: You're probably most out of step with the times when it comes to your opinions on education. I look at Canada and I see a country that has made great progress in terms of developing a fairly high median level of education. Whereas I think you look at Canada and see how our middle-class society has discouraged excellence.

DAVIES: My opinion is very much conditioned by the fact that I teach in a university. I'm perpetually meeting young people who are products of our Canadian system of education. Sometimes I am shocked and alarmed on their behalf by the things they have not been introduced to and which I think they need if they're going to do the kind of study and work that they want.

I feel that in the yearning to make education acceptable and possible to everyone, certain tough things have been omitted. We have gone for breadth of education rather than depth. You can't really have both because there's only a limited amount of time you can spend going to school.

In the old days, when education was somewhat narrower, I think that it was in certain respects more effective. To come down to an example, I think that the modern training in history is not nearly as effective as it used to be. You get people trying to study something like literature who haven't really any notion of the historical background of what they're reading. This is shortchanging them. People like myself have to give them a quick course in history before they can get to literature.

But all systems of education are riddled with faults. The plain fact is that we are not enjoying the fruits of a splendidly organized and completed educational set-up. We are still in the midst of a great educational experiment which began about a century ago. It was decided everybody ought to be made literate up to a certain standard. We're still trying to find the most effective way of doing it. So no wonder we've got problems. We're in the middle of something, not at the end of it.

T: "We have educated ourselves into a world from which wonder, and the fear and dread and splendour and freedom of wonder, have been banished."

DAVIES: Yes. I was recently visited by a young man who was obviously a very good high school student. He wanted to talk to me about the Deptford trilogy. He came in and he sat in that chair where you are sitting now. He looked me right in the eye and he said, "What do you think is the chief structural flaw in your trilogy?"

I laughed heartily. We began to discuss this thing and it turned out he had been taught by his teacher to find flaws, to see through things rather than enjoy them and find what they had to say to him. I thought—that boy is a very good boy who has been given a very raw deal by the educational system. He's not been taught to blossom and enlarge. He's been taught to zero in on something he can understand because it's negative. It's very hard to understand positive things. It's pretty easy to understand negative things.

T: You also hold the unfashionable view that art is aristocratic, not democratic.

DAVIES: What I mean when I say art is aristocratic is that it is selective. It's not a mass thing. There never is a mass art that lasts very long or explains very much. But I don't mean aristocratic in the sense that it's produced by high-born people for high-born people. I just mean it's produced by special people for people who can understand.

T: Do you feel you were born with an artist's temperament?

DAVIES: Yes.

T: Can we assume then that artists are born and not made?

DAVIES: I think that's true. All kinds of people come to see me and want advice on how they can become writers. But if you're a writer, you know it. You can improve what you are and become a better writer. But if you come to me and ask how can I become a writer, there is no answer.

Yet many people have this curious notion about writing. They know perfectly well they can't be a painter but everybody thinks somehow they may be a writer.

T: That's because everybody can write on a certain practical level of efficiency.

DAVIES: Yes. And a lot of technical writing or writing on factual matters may be very good indeed. But when you get over the bridge to what is imaginative and intuitive, then either you can do it or you can't. Nobody can teach you.

T: How far along were you in your writing career before you came to the conclusion that the function of literature is equivalent to the function of dream?

DAVIES: I don't think I ever came to any such conclusion.

T: It's in one of your essays.

DAVIES: Well, all art has some association with dream because it arises from the unconscious. Novels, poetry and plays and so forth are not exceptions to the general rule. So virtually everything that is written seriously, and isn't simply manufactured out of whole cloth, has some relationship to dream.

T: Does it follow that Canada is not going to have a great theatre until we recognize our collective dreams?

DAVIES: No, I don't think that is so. The collective dreams of a tribe don't mean the collective dreams of a political unit. One of the great collective dreams of our tribe is *King Lear.* That's one of the great collective dreams of western culture. We can't slough it off and say it's not Canadian, it's not ours. We'd be left with very little.

T: You once said Chekhov and Ibsen are our two great Canadian playwrights. Is that because they both explored self-satisfied small-mindedness?

DAVIES: Yes. And also because they explored a northern consciousness with an intensity that has not been equalled in Canada.

T: Are you pleased so far with the growth of Canadian theatre?

DAVIES: Yes. Though I think that it's shortly going to get sick of what it's doing and try more ambitious things. At the moment it's involved in a theatre of discontent. Of protest and underdoggery. It will have to get rid of that because it's not a sufficiently big theme to engage a whole theatre community for a long time.

T: I would agree that the underdog theme is prevalent. But what do you see replacing it?

DAVIES: Upperdog. Because the underdogs run the country. This is one of the things artists have always to bear in mind. It is interesting to explore the consciousness and lives of the dispossessed. But if you're going to talk about a whole nation, you've got to also talk about the people who make it work. That's not the underdog.

T: Who amongst the new playwrights do you see as particularly interesting?

DAVIES: I think [Michel] Tremblay. I wouldn't want to express an opinion beyond that.

T: It appears you're content to have moved out of the playwriting sphere.

DAVIES: Pretty much. Because I have been more or less successful in achieving an audience as a novelist. Although my plays did very well in their time, they're now old-fashioned. I'm not particularly interested in trying to establish a reputation writing in the new line. I've had my shot, as it were.

T: What do you make of that tag, "The Bernard Shaw of Canada"?

DAVIES: I think it's absolutely absurd. Nobody who had any notion of what Bernard Shaw was or what I am would ever use it. Canadians can be so shallow in their judgments! Any man with a beard is the same as any other man with a beard.

T: One similarity is that you've both emphasized that revolution is rarely a path towards freedom.

DAVIES: [laughing] It's usually the path towards another form of tyranny!

T: And you've both examined the pretensions of the middle class and decided roguery functions as readily within the law as outside it.

DAVIES: But you see, my outlook on life tends to be romantic. That certainly was not applicable to Shaw.

T: As the emphasis of your career has shifted from humour to drama, then from drama to novels, have these changes corresponded with changes within yourself?

DAVIES: Well, those changes of emphasis are not so great as they might appear on the surface. I think novels contain a great deal of humour and drama. Inevitably themes are broader in later work. So it's more a question of development than total change.

T: But the talents of a playwright and the talents of a novelist are quite separate.

DAVIES: Yes.

T: Wasn't it difficult making that switch?

DAVIES: No, I don't think it was. It seemed to be more or less inevitable. At the time I was writing plays in Canada, the opportunities for getting them produced were not very great. Productions were often unsatisfactory, for reasons that were really nobody's fault. It wasn't a time when we had a theatre that could work very well with a new script. The temptation was therefore to write a novel where you can control the whole atmosphere.

T: Do you wish you had applied more time to writing novels at a younger age?

DAVIES: No.

T: Would you agree with Liesl in *World of Wonders* that man isn't a good animal, but a noble animal?

DAVIES: Yes, yes, I agree with that one hundred per cent.

T: Even if it isn't true, it's a noble thought.

DAVIES: Of course. Better a noble lie than a miserable truth.

T: You once described Canada in Jungian terms, saying we had a "shadow" which was our habit of emotional repression. Does having such a strong shadow help Canadian artists or hinder them?

DAVIES: I think it has helped them. It gives a nation one appearance externally and something very different inside. That has evidenced itself time and time again in our history. And in our literature. For instance, in the work of writers like Margaret Laurence and Hugh MacLennan. It's there with the people who have written seriously about Canadian life.

T: You said back in 1972 that Canada expects nothing of its writers. Do you think that has changed?

DAVIES: Not really. Nobody pays any particular attention to the opinions of a writer about Canadian affairs. It is really quite extraordinary. We haven't got any writers who are really looked up to and whose word is awaited about public affairs.

T: Why is that?

DAVIES: Because their opinions are not immediately applicable. When you're asked an opinion about politics in Canada, it's "Do you think Joe Clark is going to make it in the next hundred days?" You're not asked, "Are we doing what we should to create a coherent nation?". The questions are always these Johnny-on-the-spot things.

T: And yet in the process of doing this book, it seems to me that our writers possibly know this country better than politicians.

DAVIES: That is quite possible. A writer hasn't an awful lot to gain except his own enlightenment when making his acquaintance with the country and its people. A politician is always looking for some kind of advantage, some kind of angle. So their perception is likely to be shallow. The perception of the writer is not. Nobody cares what he thinks so he's able to look more intently.

Also the politician is always on the spot. There's always somebody pushing a microphone in his face and wanting to know what he thinks. He probably doesn't think anything but he has to say something.

T: Writers are essentially tuned into the psychology of a nation.

DAVIES: Yes, but it's very hard to persuade a country like Canada that it has any psychology. Or that a psychological observation may be a weighty one.

There are things which people in the main regard as trivialities which I think are extraordinarily interesting and important. For instance, when Mr. Clark formed the government, he immediately began redecorating the Prime Minister's residence in Ottawa. How did he do it? He had all the red removed from the decor. It was replaced with blue because that's a Tory colour. Now what kind of a man thinks of decorating his house in terms of the colour of his political party? It tells us a great deal about him.

The Prime Minister's house is the place where our most important visitors to Canada, not the Tory party, are entertained. To decorate it in political colours is to narrow the office of Prime Minister and the head of state absurdly. But just try to get people to consider that as important and you'll have your work cut out for you.

T: I think this comes near the root of why your work is refreshing. You give the reader a sense that self-analysis can be pleasurable as well as painful. Do you yourself ever recall experiencing any memorable moments of personal insight?

DAVIES: Nothing like a flash of lightning. It's more a matter of a thing that happens in the course of a few weeks.

T: So it's a comparison of before and after.

DAVIES: Yes. You can't say on such-and-such an afternoon I came to a conclusion about something. At least I don't.

T: Do you think psychology is on its way to becoming our new religion?

DAVIES: Psychology and religion have always been very closely linked. Nowadays people are extremely cautious about committing themselves to any sort of religious statement so they tend to put psychological tags on what might formerly have been considered religious insights. But I don't think that it matters very much. Basically it's the insights that are important, not the tags that go with them.

T: Can you articulate the connection for yourself between a sense of wonder and religious feeling?

DAVIES: A sense of wonder is in itself a religious feeling. But in so many people the sense of wonder gets lost. It gets scarred over. It's as though a tortoise shell has grown over it. People reach a stage where they're never surprised, never delighted. They're never suddenly aware of glorious freedom or splendour in their lives. However hard a life may be, I think for virtually all people this is possible.

This is very unhappy, very unfortunate. The attitude is often self-induced. It is fear. People are afraid to be happy. Puritanical parents used to say, "If you laugh before breakfast, you'll cry before night." This sort of thing has been driven into us so much that we're almost terrified to rejoice. Or to think we're lucky.

How lucky people are! Look out of that window. An absolutely superb autumn day. Both of us are sitting here, neither of us are experiencing any pain. We're not hungry. We're aware. This is happiness. So many people tend to think that happiness must be a kind of glory which is absolutely unrepeatable. But it's an endlessly renewing thing.

Boondog Universe

PETER TROWER

Peter Trower is a kindred spirit to Robertson Davies from an alternate discipline, a distant locale, a different class, an opposite style and decidedly dissimilar work experiences who also strives to chart and perpetuate the limitless realms of wonder.

He was born at St. Leonard's-On-Sea, England in 1930. He emigrated to British Columbia at age ten following the death of his test-pilot father in a plane crash. His mother married a West Coast pulpmill superintendent who drowned soon after. Trower quit school to work in logging camps. For the next twenty-two years, when he wasn't haunted by the violent hazards of his trade, he haunted Vancouver beer parlours, skidroad hotels and scruffy rooming houses.

Moving Through the Mystery (1969), Between the Sky and the Splinters 1974) and The Alders and Others (1976) express his deep feelings of admiration and resentment at the magisterial power of nature when compared to the frailty of human existence. Ragged Horizons (1978) is a compilation of his previous books.

Insecure. Isolated. Extremist. Stereotyped. Lyrical. Working class. There are numerous reasons why Peter Trower is one of Canada's most gifted overlooked writing talents.

Peter Trower now writes for a living in Gibsons, B.C.

photo: Dianne Demille

T: When did somebody start taking notice of your poetry?

TROWER: I met Al Purdy in 1972. We cut up in the Marble Arch Hotel one time. We were drunk and playing pool. Purdy can't play pool worth a damn. And I don't even try any more. So the balls were flying off the table. It had nothing to do with literature. We were just drunk in a bar.

T: You more or less had to drop out of school to go and work. Do you think your life would have been different if there had been more money around and you could have gone to a university?

TROWER: Yeah, like if World War Two hadn't happened I might have gone to Oxford or something. All my family have followed tremendously traditional paths. But the way things went down I ended up in this weird maverick situation.

T: Do you think you could have been an academic?

TROWER: No, I think I would have blown it sooner or later. I would have been an angry young man or something. I would have been involved in some haywire trip. I couldn't have stuck that stuffy nonsense. I enjoy maverick situations. It's like all the best writers in the world have been mavericks. Like Purdy. Or even Earle Birney, falling out of a bloody tree at seventy-two years old...

T: Have there been special people for you in the way of influences?

TROWER: I used to read a lot and never paid much attention to style. I read Ray Bradbury. Early Bradbury fantasy stories were full of poetic imagery. Bradbury's a lousy poet but he writes good prose. It's peculiar. His book of poetry is absolutely rotten. But he was grinding stuff out for cheap pulp magazines using poetic imagery. So I began to become aware of science fiction. I had wall-to-wall science fiction stories. I read every science fiction magazine there was and I never read anything else. Then one day I woke up and the real world was still there.

T: It seems to me that some of that sci-fi has rubbed off into your poetry in that you have this mystical sense of the powers of the forest. It's not quite science fiction but you're very aware that there's another world there.

TROWER: Yeh, it's what the Indians already know.

T: Exactly. Like at the close of "The Animals" you say "As the day dwindled / the season took aim on us / and the animals knew." Then again there's another bit in "Booby Trap" where you're falling a tree and it just misses killing you. You say, "around us the woods hiss disappointment."

TROWER: I've heard some strange stuff happening with guys falling trees. There's a story I haven't written about yet. I came to this camp and a guy had been killed just a couple of weeks before. He got pinned between the butt of a tree and the stump. He was a very tidy guy. As he was dying, because he was already cut in half, he took out all his ID and put it all out on the edge of the tree that killed him. When they finally found this guy all bust open, there was no blood on any of his ID.

T: Do you usually write from an incident like that or does it comes from a phrase that sparks you?

TROWER: I write totally from real life. I don't build words from words. Like there's a poem in *Ragged Horizons* about a little girl dying of cancer. That comes right out of a heavy duty real experience. It was unbelievably heavy. For years I couldn't even write about it. But I thought, dammit, I better write about it...The first poem I ever wrote that was any good was "Grease for the Wheels of Winter." I was just trying to describe leaving the camps. It was a heavy thing because they'd been my life. It was always where I ran away to when nothing went right. The danger incidence was starting to close in on me. It was like I better quit this before I get killed.

T: Do you ever take your poems and songs to the camps and read to working class guys?

TROWER: I haven't done it yet. I've often wondered about that. The young dudes might like it but some of those old guys might think I was some kind of smartass. I made this film a couple of years ago [*Between the Sky and the Splinters*] when we went into a logging camp called Jackson Bay. I had to act in this film. All my life I've been waking in bunkhouses, putting on cork boots. This time, I woke in the morning and instead of being a logger I was an actor. It was weird. The guys in the camp started looking at me like I was some phoney-baloney. I'd come back to play the part of myself when I was young in a logging camp where they were doing it for real. I went through some funny head changes.

T: You mentioned earlier that you're going to move uptown now. What do you mean by that?

TROWER: I mean, man, I'm going to maybe quit being broke. But I ain't going to change my way of living. I don't like staying in fancy hotels with a bunch of smartass TV people. I'll stay around here, or the Marble Arch or the Cecil.

T: Where did the title *Ragged Horizons* come from?

TROWER: It's just a title. I thought certain mountains I've seen look like they've ripped through the sky. And also I thought of being raggedy-assed in the street. It's a double trip. But if I think about all that it means I can't explain it. I dunno, many times I thought I would never make it. Like that suicide poem about the Marble Arch is a true poem. There ain't nothing in that book that's b.s. There's no place in that book where I can't drag out some old dude from the past to verify it. That's what scares them back east. Mostly back there it's games playing.

T: In "Kisses in the Whiskey" you wish you "could be that ignorant again / embark on some old sophomoric fling / far too callow to understand / that life is other than a Friday thing." Does that bother you, that you feel like you've gone beyond your youth?

TROWER: Not really. I can look back at myself walking down the street when I was nineteen and I was stupid. Very naive. But I ain't even finished growing up yet. Anybody who thinks they have is really dead. Everybody's just a kid growing old.

T: What was it like when you were young in Vancouver?

TROWER: It was heavy. Maybe it's just as bad now but it's not organized. There were actual kid gangs. You could get in trouble just by walking into the Marble Arch Hotel at 1:30. In those days it was more structured. There was a book called *The Amboy Dukes* and everybody was copying that. Big rumbles with gangs from the next district. It was heavy even though it was all bogus.

T: Were you a real part of that scene?

TROWER: I was always an observer, sort of neutral. In those days I couldn't talk to anyone. It was a redneck era. I used to go to bars, man, and sit down at a table but all people could talk about was hockey games and work. Boring stuff, I'd get so bored, man, I'd just o.d. on beer and slide under the table.

T: How do you feel about doing promotion for *Ragged Horizons*?

TROWER: I want the book to sell. I put everything I got behind it. Possibly if I really bust ass in another ten years, I might be able to do a better book. I can still write from the gut. I hope I don't get soft and start writing from the mind. I went through that once but it all came out crap. I have to use experience. I've read a hundred books of poetry by people who purport to know what's going on in the universe. It's just a bunch of fakery. I'm just fed up with academic trips by people who think they know what's going on. Nobody knows what's going on.

T: Are you ambitious for yourself?

TROWER: If you said I had a fierce drive for success, it would be true. I've wanted to make it but I kept getting kicked in the face.

T: Does a poem happen for you in an hour or in a couple of days?

TROWER: It can take twenty years. That poem ''Atlantic Crossing'' took twenty years. I couldn't get it across because a lot of what I write about is melodramatic in the material itself.

T: So that's one of the key things about your poetry then—

TROWER: Right. the hardest thing is to get the balance between melodrama and reality. If you go over the edge with melodrama, as I frequently have, you end up with Robert Service.

T: And that's why this book is a success?

TROWER: Because my editor kept the melodrama out. Someone once told me I was a cross between Dylan Thomas, Robert Service and William Burroughs. I dunno.

T: Which of your poems do you think will outlive the other ones?

TROWER: ''Grease for the Wheels of Winter.'' Maybe ''The Last Spar-Tree.'' I guess they'll stand because nobody else has said those things.

T: The one that struck me was ''The Animals.''

TROWER: That's the one Purdy liked. Purdy and I were sitting in the Arch and he said, Jesus. Like I blew his mind or something. A lot of poets write to be heavy or intellectual. I write directly for communication. I'm trying to communicate to the world. I've read so much that's pure b.s. People who purport to know more than other people are liars and fakers. Look what happened to Ezra Pound. He died in his own intellectual garbage. T.S. Eliot died of dry-rot. The answers aren't in going to university for a million years and getting endless doctorates and never facing the world. Going to UBC I feel like I'm entering another country. You go into the faculty lounge and it's a weird place, man. These people work on a different wavelength than me. I don't understand their trip. They've never been out and scuffled. They've never had the crap kicked out of them. They don't know anything about the real world... And you can quote me on that. I got the boondog universe.

Garbage and Flowers

LEONARD COHEN

Leonard Cohen is the most internationally recognized writer Canada has ever produced. He is a poet, novelist, songwriter, singer, cult figure to a generation—an exquisitely gifted combination of con artist and mystic on the outside, a beautiful loser on the inside.

He has published two novels, The Favorite Game *(1963) passes ambivalent judgement on the emotional self-centredness of a sexually prolific artist and suggests the roles of artist and lover are mutually exclusive.* Beautiful Losers *(1966) is a monumentally audacious and hopelessly religious transcendence of reason and morality.*

His record albums are Songs of Leonard Cohen *(1967),* Songs from a Room *(1969),* Songs of Love and Hate *(1971),* Live Songs *(1972),* New Skin for the Old Ceremony *(1973),* The Best of Leonard Cohen *(1975) and* Death of a Lady's Man *(1977).*

His poetry books are Let Us Compare Mythologies *(1956),* The Spice-Box of Earth *(1961),* Flowers for Hitler *(1964),* Parasites of Heaven *(1966),* Selected Poems *(1968) and* The Energy of Slaves *(1972).*

Death of a Lady's Man *(1978), which celebrates and bemoans the failure of his marriage in poetic prose, is a highly personalized abdication of his role as Canada's number one (and perhaps only) exotic personality.*

Leonard Cohen was born in Montreal in 1934.

photo: David Boswell

T: How important to you is experiencing failure to creating art?

COHEN: It's a good question but it's kind of beyond me. I write from the centre. That kind of question invites you to move out to the edge and look in. I've never been good at those questions. Like I read this review by Sam Ajzenstat [in *Books in Canada*] and he talked about my work as being, uh...

T: A soliloquy on failure.

COHEN: Yeh. I don't know if that's an accurate description of this new book or not. If it is, I didn't set out to do that. Writing from the inside you're just writing about the experience. After a while, some people can step back and look at it, but I can't.

T: But *Death of a Lady's Man* is definitely a book about the failure of Leonard Cohen, the husband. After ten years of marriage it's saying you need to return to being Leonard Cohen the—

COHEN: The nothing.

T: [laughter] I was going to say the artist. Do you think your marriage came apart because you like to write well and you were having difficulty writing while married?

COHEN: It may have something to do with the antipathy between the life of an artist and the life of a married man. But I don't completely buy that. I don't think my marriage came apart because I was a writer. It's too easy to lay the blame at the feet of your activity. It's not just artists' marriages that are coming apart right now, marriage itself is under the wheel in some way.

T: Are you generalizing as a male when you describe yourself as "the appendix" of your wife?

COHEN: I wouldn't want to speak generally about things. There's a certain point when you feel like you're just some useless organ attached to a very vital organism. I certainly felt that. Especially when great beauty is involved and you stand back and look. It seems that women can do without us. If we can believe a lot of their propaganda, they hardly need us. I don't think it will last. But it's certainly in the air right now.

T: You once said you looked forward to the day when we would have a matriarchal society.

COHEN: I think I spoke too soon. We got one very swiftly.

T: And you're not satisfied?

COHEN: I've got no complaints. You find your life and your society and your civilization as you find them. There are some people who try to change things that can't be changed. I don't think I'm one of them. This is our predicament. I feel at home living out my predicament.

T: What's your present marital status?

COHEN: Search me. I'm trying to figure it out. I have children but I was never married officially. And there's a mother of the children. And so I guess it's a marriage with everything else but the document. Or it was. It seems dim now. You know there's that poem by Emily Dickinson, "The heart is slow to learn / what the swift mind beholds at every turn." This woman has told me that she doesn't want anything to do with me ever again, but I keep feeling it's not over.

T: What does she think of the book?

COHEN: She helped me arrange the first draft of it. . . and she liked it a lot at the time. I don't think she's read the second draft yet.

T: I ask because in many ways it's a very intimate book, written to her alone. You use the names of several women, repeated several times, but you're careful never to make her name public in the book.

COHEN: Those other names are not the actual designations of people either.

T: And there's that passage, "This marriage is locked. It is difficult to enter. It is a marriage that operates like one, healing itself the moment it is condemned. In every house there is a marriage that cannot be explained. In our day it appears fragile and easily violated, but it is still the profoundest of initiations, and one into which no stranger can intrude."

COHEN: I think maybe the only way you can enter this book is through your own marriage. That's why I think I'm in the way of the work. If I could get out of the way, through death or through time, this book will be seen a lot more clearly. If you just fell upon this book some day in a second hand bookstore I think it would reveal itself a lot more swiftly. I'm in the way of the thing with my songs. And there's the idea that the guy's out there always screwing around.

T: It's certainly one of the reasons reviewers dump on you. People don't like the idea of some guy who knows a lot of beautiful and famous women, lives on a Greek island and has thousands of women wanting to spend just an hour with him...

COHEN: The guy you're describing, I don't like him already.

T: Critics especially react when you describe yourself as a failure. That idea that losing is more spiritually rewarding than winning has always been central to your work. Is that why you rejected your Governor General's Award?

COHEN: I don't know. I just didn't feel right about it. I remember I drove to Ottawa the night the awards were given because I'd heard there was going to be a party that Jack McClelland was giving. The fiction winner that year was Mordecai Richler. He was very angry. He approached me and said, "C'mere. I want to talk to you." We went into the bathroom. He said, "Why did you reject the Governor General's Award?" I said I didn't know.

T: Maybe he felt you'd made him into a second-class winner?

COHEN: I don't know. Something like that. I didn't look at it that way. A few ideas came into my head at the time but I really couldn't think of anything to say. I don't have any position on it.

T: In Stephen Scobie's book on you, there's an A.J.M. Smith quote from 1928 that says Canadian literature will not improve "until we have been thoroughly shocked by the appearance in our midst of a work of art that is both successful and obscene." If that's true, then obviously *Beautiful Losers* makes you deserving of a Governor General's Award.

COHEN: It's successful now and certainly it's obscene in some places. In some ways maybe this new book might open things up for writers to follow their own imaginations, too. It's hard to say. *Beautiful Losers* only sold one thousand copies when it came out. Then the landscape opens up as more people have a certain kind of experience. Not that it's so important that this book becomes clearer. I understand it's only a very small thing in this world.

T: You once said there's nobody in this country who can appreciate your work.

COHEN: I don't know if that's true. Critics have to make a living. If instance, I just read an analysis of *Beautiful Losers* in a book called *Savage Fields* by Dennis Lee which is pretty good. It's certainly better than anything I could do. His approach is so comprehensive and brilliant. Once every couple of years I get that brilliant. [almost laughing] I'm pretty well writing out of the trench. Trying to get my nose and eyes over the edge of the trench to see who's shooting at me. But he's up there on a watertower looking over the whole landscape.

T: Speaking of critics, what do you think of the theory that your work has arisen out of the fifties? Scobie writes, "Cut off from social contacts and responsibilities, the self turning in on itself becomes perverse and morbid, seeking death."

COHEN: I don't know if that's true. Critics have to make a living. If an argument is put forward forcefully enough, I'll go along with it. In fact, I'm even starting to buy critics' versions of my work.

T: Do you buy the version that you're a Black Romantic in the tradition of Baudelaire, Genet and Rimbaud?

COHEN: I don't reject these things. If somebody says something to you, it's more like an opportunity to evaluate where they're coming from. Black Romantic. I don't even know what that means. It sounds okay. Black, I guess, is solemn, lightless, heavy, desperate.

T: Black romanticism is the negation of self. Like that line at the very end of your album, "I guess you go for nothing, if you really want to go that far."

COHEN: I don't know. I think maybe some writers move in an atmosphere of bewilderment and astonishment. They sit down at a table two hours a day and try to locate themselves. Or justify themselves.

T: That bewilderment could be the result of growing up in a comfortable Westmount family where you're sheltered from too many knocks.

COHEN: Could be. That would certainly be the Marxist interpretation. But that's like saying if my grandmother had wheels, she'd be a wheelbarrow. I was born into a certain kind of predicament. It was just my life. I don't feel I should have been a member of the working class.

T: Do you vote?

COHEN: Yeah. I registered for the referendum in Quebec.

T: So you care whether Quebec secedes?

COHEN: I care about the situation very much. I'm in it. I've seen alarm, anxiety, jubilation. It can't fail but touch you. I like what this movement has done to a lot of my friends who are French-speaking. It's turned them on.

T: What do you hope is going to happen there?

COHEN: Well, I say this in a humorous way, but there's actually something serious to it...I've been suggesting Montreal separate from Quebec and Canada. Montreal is a special kind of city-state. We shouldn't tie our destinies to either Quebec or Canada. It's not like either of them. The Free State of Montreal.

T: I get the impression that the Parti Quebecois is like some big union where your rank-and-file member is not anywhere near as zealous as the figureheads. Is that spirit of self-determination really prevalent in the lower and middle classes, too?

COHEN: It probably doesn't break down so much on class as it does on age. The older people are more reluctant to redefine themselves. The very rich, of course, are not so interested in the proposition.

T: How would you vote on a referendum?

COHEN: Which way I would vote is hard to say. I'd have to see how Rene puts it. But the first thing you have to understand is that Quebec is not going to float down to the coast of Florida. It's going to still be there. We have to participate in the adventures of this land mass. Secondly, they probably won't change the money. If they said turn in your dollars for pesos or something, there would be real resistance. The thing that really worries me about the nationalist movement in Quebec is that given the nature of the Parti Quebecois, which is not thoroughly democratic, where's it going to lead to? Right now it's okay. You got Rene Levesque and he's a really responsible and attractive man. But who's coming after?

T: Previously you've always avoided aligning yourself with political groups. Could you tell me why you went to Israel "to fight the Arab bullet"?

COHEN: There were a number of things happening with that. One, I wanted to get away from my family.

T: There are other ways of getting away from your family than going off to war.

COHEN: Well, there is a line in the Bible, "You shall not stand idly by your brother's blood." I do feel some communion, some sense of brotherhood with Jews. I do have some old fashioned emotions about those things. I feel a sense of solidarity with their struggle. I also feel it with the Egyptian struggle. That's the trouble. You can embrace both sides of the question.

I didn't feel that good being on Egyptian sand. We shouldn't really be there but I knew we had to be there. The time I really felt bad about it was when an Israeli soldier came up to me and gave me some Egyptian money. He'd got it off a corpse or a prisoner. It was a souvenir. He put it in my hand and he walked away. I thought it belonged to some guy who was probably going to spend it on a beer that night. I just buried it in the sand.

Neither side is right. We know that right off the top. To press people into military service isn't right. The Israelis have lost the cream of each generation. So have the Egyptians. This is the real human crunch. This is the real human predicament. This universe is only to be tolerated, it's not to be solved. All these things are unclear but amidst this incredible lack of clarity we have to act. That's what the whole tragic vision is about.

T: Do you think maybe that's why you went through *Death of a Lady's Man* a second time and put in all those contradicting editorial comments? To give the book tragic vision? Or was it your reaction to critics, like an attempt to explain yourself for the first time?

COHEN: First of all it's a literary device. It does participate in that feeling I have that there aren't any critics around. I may as well be my own. But also I really did want to confront the book. I really did want to take those pages one at a time and really see how I felt about them. It's like when you read a book by Shelley or whoever and he swoons, he dies, he falls... Was he really swooning and dying and falling? Or did he get up, fasten his belt and go down to the cafeteria for a cup of coffee? That's what I tried to do with the commentary, just bring in another mind or two.

T: A lot of people are going to figure the ambivalence that results is a cop-out.

COHEN: Well, with a lot of work that we call poetry—that intense writing—what really emerges are the harmonics. You put different ideas or approaches together and they strike fire in some way. Something emerges from that juxtaposition that has resonance.

T: So you're just trying to tune in on an energy when you write?

COHEN: I consider a lot of my work to be a kind of *reportage,* trying to make a completely accurate description of the interior predicament.

T: So it isn't always rational.

COHEN: It isn't always rational. It doesn't follow the laws of logic. Or even of rhetoric. You have to juxtapose elements to get something that corresponds to an interior condition. All poetry is based on differences. Wherever there's tension, wherever there's life, wherever there's the positive/negative, female/male, yin/yang. That's what creates the universe.

That's the kind of writing I like to do. Where you're writing on an edge, where you're really trying to get it right. I don't mean so it endures and the next generation looks into it, although it would be nice if it happened. I'm interested in only one thing: if it lives.

T: How long have you been into zen?

COHEN: About eight years. I have a friend who happens to be a zen master. But our association is really one of friendship between men. I'm probably the worst student he's ever come across in terms of discipline. I'm a monster of idleness.

T: What's its appeal for you then?

COHEN: The training of zen is towards self-reform. The ego is affirmed. There has to be an ego because we live in a world of ego. That's ordinary life. You can't exist as a selfless, egoless creature.

T: You've written somewhere that you believe in God...

COHEN: Because I've experienced the absolute.

T: And the absolute is zero?

COHEN: It's a zero that is continually manifesting as one, two, three, four, five, six, seven, eight, nine, ten.

T: A totality?

COHEN: It's the fundamental ground or field which is nothing, the still centre or whatever metaphor you use for it. It's neither dead or alive. It is an indescribable energy. That's zero. It's so empty that myriads and myriads of form rush in to fill it at every second.

T: You've said having sexual intercourse is the greatest peace. Is that zero?

COHEN: The sexual embrace is beyond self. You don't exist as you. Your partner doesn't exist as your partner. That is the place we all come from. Then we come back to life. That zero or emptiness or absolute is when we don't have any questions.

The self we have is just the result of a question. The question is who am I? So we invent a self, a personality. We sustain it, we create rules for it. When you stop asking those questions in those moments of grace, as soon as the question is not asked and the dilemma is dissolved or abandoned, then the true self or absolute self rushes in. That's our real nourishment.

A real religious education makes that experience available to people. The kinds of religious education available today are mostly concerned with a very specific definition of what God is. Just to define God specifically is a great mistake. It's better to have a kind of education that doesn't even mention God, that allows people to experience that absolute or the dissolution of the particular self.

T: In *Beautiful Losers* you write, "disarmed and empty, an instrument of grace." Can you make that condition happen?

COHEN: Those conditions arise spontaneously. Often they're the result of writing. I have in a poem, "How sweet to be that wretch, forgotten by himself in the midst of his own testimony". When an experience is embracing or total you don't know who you are. When you jump into a pool of really cold water, when you hit that water there's no you.

T: How often is your writing a dive into cold water?

COHEN: From time to time. There is no explanation for it. It's free from an explanation. It's like explaining the kiss you give your wife. You can explain it from a sociological point of view, from an erotic point of view, from all kinds of points of view...but it really doesn't have anything to do with that moment of the embrace. You can speak about it, but it's just a kind of gossip.

When you're writing out of the total embrace of the experience of the emotion of the moment, what comes out of there is really authentic. People ask what does that song, "Suzanne," really mean? The people who lay back and are ravished by the song know exactly what it means.

T: In high school I used to listen to that song all the time. I didn't fathom it at all but you're saying I understood it simply because I enjoyed it instinctively.

COHEN: Yes. If the thing is authentic you tune into it immediately. You embrace it immediately. It includes you. That's what I mean to say. The song also includes you because it's really authentic. Afterwards you can say why it included you, but that's not so important.

T: I think that's why people knock the new book. People have difficulty feeling it includes them.

COHEN: It doesn't include them yet. Hopefully it will include them. It's not written anywhere that my book has to be good, or a success, or that it even works. But I think it works. I think it's alive.

T: You're not an orthodox Jew. How do you raise your kids?

COHEN: I haven't given them any formal training. The only thing is I have a continuous bedtime story. I tell them about the adventures of Jonah, a seven-year-old boy who starts off with the whale and has a whole bunch of adventures. I try to tell my son he's a Jew, that he's a member of this tribe which has a history. There aren't that many interesting traditions going. Most of the other ones are in pretty bad shape.

T: So Jewishness is an anchor.

COHEN: Yeah. You've got to know who you are, especially in Quebec. Quebec's like it was in the fifties now. There was no such thing as a Quebecois. There was a French Canadian, an English Canadian or a Jew. That's what it's back to.

T: How old are Adam and Lorca?

COHEN: Four and six. I try to spend a lot of time with them. Being a writer and doing a lot of your work at home is good that way. I drive them to school every morning and pick them up every afternoon. I put them to bed and hang out with them. I'd just as soon hang out with them as anybody.

T: I'm coming around to that, too. Friends don't interest me that much now I've got a kid.

COHEN: A child is the real mystery, the real joy. This is what we're here to do. I feel people who don't have children—and obviously these are personal decisions—lose so much by not resurrecting with a child. A child is an opportunity for resurrection.

T: Yet you've said, "Having children is the only activity that connects you to mankind and makes a serious assault on the ego." Did that assault on your ego make you dissatisfied with family life?

COHEN: I'm not dissatisfied with it. I love it. It's where I like to be, with my children and a woman. To see the world through the eyes of growing children, well...there's nothing like it.

T: You sound like you enjoy getting older.

COHEN: Yeah, I do. Very much. But it's also like Paul Simon says, "Still crazy after all these years". Layton tells me it just gets worse. Your hunger, lust and appetite inflame as you grow older. There really is no stabilization. You don't sort of cool out.

T: Are you getting any wiser?

COHEN: I don't know. I don't think I'm getting wiser or any more cautious. Certainly not more cautious.

T: There's that line, "I punished her by telling her some of us still take acid". [laughter]

COHEN: Actually I haven't used acid for a number of years. It's too powerful. I wouldn't know what I'd do on a trip now.

T: Do you ever have to force yourself to write as you get older?

COHEN: I don't look at it that way. It's just like picking up my guitar every day. I need a guitar. It's not like I'm a singer and I've got to practice singing. It's like you want to lift your voice in song. You just want to greet your experience with the kind of expression you're used to. There's this singer in New York named Alberta Hunter. She's eighty-three. She sang opposite Paul Robeson in 1929 in *Showboat*. Then she retired and became a nurse and wrote songs for Bessie Smith. Anyway she's back on the boards now. I was listening to her and it was very moving. In fact I wept every set she did. She made me want to write. Just to answer her. Just to answer her.

T: You were wondering whether Shelley wrote the literal truth or not. I was wondering about your line, "I wept for the injustice of the world"...

COHEN: That's a literal description.

T: Does that happen often?

COHEN: It used to happen a lot. Of course the communist poets like Tom Wayman are going to put me down, "Who cares whether he's weeping for the injustice of the world, what's he doing about it?" I guess I'm not doing anything. I've got letters from people dying of cancer saying my songs helped a lot, but maybe that doesn't count in the Marxist view.

T: One more question and we'll talk about your music—

COHEN: I like your answers better—

T: Yeah, sure. [laughter] Explain "The universe is sustained by the old interior quarrel of the limited versus the unlimited".

COHEN: It's something I've experienced. It means that all the forms that arise are based on yes and no.

T: Do you correlate that with the sexes?

COHEN: It's unwise and somewhat unproductive to try and define what the female element is, what the male element is. The *I Ching* does that as thoroughly as anything, but I think it's unwise to specify. It's the nature of the absolute to manifest in these two forms. Male and female. Of course both the male and female are based on zero. There is a fundamental reality that has no genitals. But to try and dissolve those differences is inappropriate to this world of forms.

T: How close is the connection for you between sexual activity and writing activity?

COHEN: Both celibacy and licentiousness represent excesses. Maybe they are appropriate excesses sometimes but I don't think you're going to get to God or The Great Poem through them. If celibacy is carried on too long you'll just have a poetry of total desire. If promiscuity is carried on too long you'll have a poetry of complete self-disgust. It's the middle path that I guess is the wise one.

T: You and Bob Dylan have both suffered in your careers recently because people are angry that they were naive enough to believe you and he were prophets who knew it all. Do you ever talk to Dylan about that?

COHEN: No, I never have. As a popular singer you're going to have periods when you're in and out of fashionability. But I think Dylan remains the supreme artist of his generation. It really doesn't matter whether some people like his new record and some people don't. To me it's always fascinating and always nourishing. I was glad to see the *Georgia Straight* cover about why everyone is dumping on Dylan. It's true. We've got this beautiful poet in our midst who keeps on producing magnificent work. What else are you going to say? I just say thank you. That's all I'm interested in saying.

T: How did you happen to collaborate with Phil Spector for *Death of a Lady's Man*?

COHEN: Phil is a client of my lawyer and agent. The first time I met him was after a couple of weeks at the Troubadour in Los Angeles. Phil had wanted to go down to the concert. My lawyer had tried to prevent him from going because he usually calls out and puts down the singers that he's watching. But Phil insisted. So he came and kept quiet throughout. That's apparently unusual behaviour for Phil. Then I went over to his house afterwards. I couldn't stand staying there for more than ten or fifteen minutes.

T: Why?

COHEN: First of all, he keeps his place at about forty degrees. The air conditioning's on and you're shivering all the time. And he's very loud. It's behaviour that's interesting to see for four or five minutes. The more people there, the more wild and theatrical he becomes. But it's shyness. When you're with the guy one-to-one, he's a different man.

T: And you chose to associate yourself with a guy like that . . .

COHEN: I was hoping there'd be a lot of the kind of treatment he used in that song, "To Know Him Is To Love Him" where the lyric is very, very clear. Or "Unchained Melody". More like his Debussy stage. But I found him in the full flower of his Wagnerian tempest.

T: Were the songs already written by you?

COHEN: Three of the songs already existed in some modified form as poems. "Mist Leaves No Scar", "I Left A Woman Waiting", and "Fingerprints".

T: They're about the three best songs on the album.

COHEN: Well, as I've often said, if you don't look for me it's a good album. It's very strong. It has a special kind of vitality.

T: But the intimacy of the previous albums isn't there.

COHEN: No, you have to play it loud. Also I never did more than one take. I wanted to go in when he was mixing it and put on different vocals, try different things. But Phil took the tapes under armed guard. He went into hiding. I couldn't even find him.

T: Are you bitter about that?

COHEN: No, I was angry at the time. But in some ways his instincts were right. It's something that is not purely Phil and not purely mine. Probably *Rolling Stone* will do a retrospective in 1985 and find that this was one of the records that lasted.

T: Do you try and write with the melody and lyric coming together at once?

COHEN: Different ways. Usually that's what happens. That's certainly the way "Suzanne" was written and "Hey, That's No Way To Say Goodbye" and "Famous Blue Raincoat".

T: Do you ever get tired of playing those same songs?

COHEN: No. From time to time you get tired of them on the road, but when you're in the midst of things and you're playing with good musicians it changes every night. And there's people there. I take that pretty seriously.

T: You haven't done a concert in Vancouver in a long time. I think people have lost track of you.

COHEN: Yeah, they have. Maybe it's just as well.

T: You've always had this fear that power is destructive. Since fame is a form of power, do you ever look at what happened to other "stars" like Hendrix and Janis Joplin and Hank Williams and think twice about what you're doing?

COHEN: Yeah, it's definitely a two-edged razor blade. I think about those people from time to time. Phil Ochs. Tim Buckley. Guys that I knew well. Plus a lot of ones that were not so famous who are no longer around. But I think it's stabilizing in some ways now.

T: As a matter of fact, Errol Flynn finally died of an overdose in this very hotel...

COHEN: Yeah? It gets risky, I know. But I'm too old to commit suicide. It would be unbecoming.

Mystic Eyes

BILL BISSETT

bill bissett is the embodiment of William Blake's adage, "The soul of sweet delight can never be defiled".

The subject of considerable controversy in Parliament and media (over whether his chanting oratory, unconventional spelling and frequent use of four-letter words is worthy of Canada Council subsidization), bissett attempts to communalize his energy as a performer, transcending the standard performer/ audience dichotomy by enunciating his vulnerable yet indomitable spirituality with boyish enthusiasm and audacity born of pain.

Prior to 1980, he has written 43 books. Sailor is likely his most mature and representative collection that is accessible on a literal level.

bill bissett also founded blewointment press which has published dozens of small literary titles over the past decade.

bill bissett was born in Halifax in 1939. He lives somewhere in Vancouver but does not disclose his address even to publishers or friends. He can be contacted only via a post office box.

photo: Rose-Marie Tremblay

T: I've come to collect your life story. So let's start at the beginning.

BISSETT: I was born in Halifax. I started working when I was thirteen and fourteen in record stores. I used to do commercials for one store where I had two characters. I was like a hip young kid and I would push the rock n' roll and then I had this other voice where I would push classical music and stuff. So it was really bizarre and stuff. And I worked in a gas station. Crap like that.

T: Was your family middle-class?

BISSETT: If there hadn't been so much sickness in the family it would have been like upper-middle-class. But there were hospital debts continually. My mother was sick for years. Then I was sick for three years when I was ten, eleven and twelve. Two years in the hospital, then another year to get better.

T: What did you have?

BISSETT: I had peritonitis. That's when you have an appendicitis operation and something goes wrong. The doctor leaves a hand in, or a glove. I dunno. The poison spreads through your blood and you can't crap. I couldn't go to the bathroom for two years. They put tubes in you so you get these scars.

Now it's so far out because I've been meditating for almost eight months. I worry less, have a more relaxed body system, smoke a little less tobacco, drink a little less coffee. I'm starting to get healthier without going on a head trip. It's just sorta happening. So anyway, hair is starting to grow on my belly. It's covering the scars and it's so far out. Like in Halifax when I'd go swimming they used to yell at me all the time. They wouldn't play with me sometimes because I had too many scars. [laughing] So I'm getting more confident on beaches!

T: Thanks to some hair on your belly.

BISSETT: Yeah. It took a long time for me to get better. They didn't think I would live. After the twelfth operation it was okay. I missed two grades and just carried on. I couldn't do sports or nothing. I finished high school and went to Dalhousie University for two years.

T: What did you take?

BISSETT: English and philosophy. I was supposed to be a lawyer cuz my father was one. He was a very idealistic lawyer who would take cases from people who couldn't afford to pay. A lot of that. He was never sick so he was always grumbling about doctor bills. That's where everything went. So no one wanted me to be an artist. I think my mother mightn't have minded but she had gone into spirit by then.

T: Were you the eldest son by any chance?

BISSETT: Two daughters and me. Then I wanted to leave Halifax. I used to run away all the time. When I was legal age, I split. I ran away to a circus once. The cops used to always get me back. So I came out west and starved here. Then I got a job with the library downtown and went to UBC. I did two years but I could never finish.

T: When would this be?

BISSETT: Around '64. I'm not sure. Anyway, I remember I was in this other course with a guy named Dr. Daniels. It was a Milton course because they thought I had promise as an English student person. But I didn't have that much promise because there was this seating plan and stuff and I would never sit in my right seat. I couldn't deal with this seating plan at all. There was a lot of other crap I couldn't deal with either. I wanted to write and paint.

[laughing] I remember I had to get this dumb language credit. I was writing this exam for German or something. I didn't like studying that stuff. I'd already bummed out of two other language courses. It was cool but it was weird. So I just put my pen down and walked out of the campus. It was my own little interior drama. I never came back.

T: Did you have many art friends in those days?

BISSETT: No. I hardly knew anybody. I worked at the library and I read. I started meeting other writers and stuff downtown eventually, but I never melted with the university scene.

T: Did you have any books out by then?

BISSETT: No, the first issue of blewointment started in '64, I think. I went directly into that when I left school. In '65, maybe there were three issues. It was a group thing. By '67 we were doing about five books a year. In the '70's it's been averaging seven books a year.

T: Where did the impetus to start blewointment press come from?

BISSETT: We started it in the '60's cuz no one else would print us. Visual writing was just too weird for other magazines. I guess that's the way most presses start. You get a bunch of people who are organically together and no one else will print them. It just grows and grows.

T: When you started blewointment, was it the starving artist routine? eating potatoes and Kraft dinners?

BISSETT: Yeah. Living on welfare and stuff like that. In '66, a movie was made about me called *In Search of Innocence*. It took about six months with the director, Morris Embra. It was a beautiful movie.

T: Then you got busted?

BISSETT: Yeah, me and this folk singer from Seattle got busted. We were like the second bust in Vancouver. It was really a hot thing. A big deal and crap like that. The social workers were trying to take our child away. The police were coming all the time and I was getting beaten up. It was really getting bizarre. Crap was flying in every direction. The cops would come to bust the place and they'd tear my paintings apart. They would scream, "Why do you paint like this? This is insane!"

One day two social workers came to the door and they bought $800 worth of paintings and told us to get out of town. Or we couldn't keep our daughter. Before that they took our daughter away from us a couple of times. Because she didn't have pants on or something. We got hassled because we were artists.

T: Did you get dragged down by all that?

BISSETT: Well, we understood it all and fortunately we had a really great lawyer, Sid Simons. And Warren Tallman [UBC poetry professor] was a character witness. But like if our daughter walked down to the neighbourhood pool and took her pants off, which all the other kids did, the police would bring our daughter home. We'd get picked on. I suppose the movie we made didn't really help, even though it was a really peaceful movie about writing and painting. But there weren't any hippies yet. They didn't have a word to identify us. They didn't know what we were.

T: Post-beatnik, pre-hippie.

BISSETT: Yeah, they didn't know what destruction we might do. [laughing] All we were doing was painting and writing and living and smoking a little dope. Stuff like that.

T: Who's we? The mother?

BISSETT: Yeah, Martina. We've all gone different places but it's still together.

T: Where do they live now?

BISSETT: Different places.

T: Then you got busted again later in the '60's, is that right?

BISSETT: For possession. It was another big hoopla with a two-year trial. But it was like old times for me. Then things got raging in the '70's when blewointment got a bit more Canada Council support. In 1978, we got a $2,000 increase so we're printing nine books on $6,800.

T: Compared to other publishing houses, that's not much.

BISSETT: It's the fourth lowest block grant in the country. Me and Allen [Rosen] are running seven thousand dollars in debt all the time. You keep hanging in there and conditions eventually improve. The dope thing isn't so heavy any more. No one is frightened by paintings any more. And concrete poetry doesn't scare people so much now.

T: So you more or less survived that era intact.

BISSETT: Yeah. Warren [Tallman] put his house up for me on the second trial for bail. Just incredible really.

T: Do you ever look back on those years in the hospital and speculate how being aware of life and death at such an early age might have affected you? Most kids growing up these days aren't tuned into that.

BISSETT: Unless you're in Chile or Vietnam. Yeah, that was pretty bizarre all right. Everything was backwards. I used to get presents before each operation. It was tempting to have an operation, just to get a present. I used to think a lot about dying. And movie stars. That's when I got into movies. It's in my book, *Stardust.* I used to have movie stars all over my wall. They were my friends. They talked to me. They were closer to me than anything.

T: Do you ever get tired of people asking why you don't capitalize your name?

BISSETT: It's just because there's nothing to emphasize with it.

T: Yeah, I know but—

BISSETT: It's fun when people ask because then I get to talk about spelling and stuff like that.

T: So let's talk about spelling and stuff like that. You're someone who seems to believe there's a power-mongering segment of society "up there" somewhere so if you spell in a way that's foreign to those people, it keeps the poetry safe. Maybe it's a protective thing. The only people who will read them are people who want to read them.

BISSETT: Yeah, I never thought of that. Wow, far out.

T: They open a book and feel instant irritation. So maybe there's also a political side of you that wants to provoke a reaction, too.

BISSETT: Far out.

T: Also if you spell phonetically like you do, it gives you an affinity with people who aren't literate. Like children.

BISSETT: Like a lot of people don't spell right. Like maybe two-thirds of the world or something. That's really neat. Those are three super reasons right there, aren't they? Of course the other reason is simply to get words closer to the way they really sound.

T: Have you ever been actively involved in politics the way you're involved in your art?

BISSETT: Not for a while. I used to do a lot of stuff with the Viet Nam war trip. And Ban the Bomb marches. And art auctions to raise money, that sort of stuff.

T: Do you see the pendulum in society swinging back to the right these days?

BISSETT: Yeah, there's a conservative backlash. But that conservative backlash is funny because the revolution never got off the ground. [laughing] We're having a backlash without even having had a revolution. It's very Canadian!

T: Do you think the reaction to your poetry in Parliament is political grandstanding? Or do you think these politicians are genuinely shocked?

BISSETT: I don't know. I find it real puzzling, like a tempest in a teapot. I can't figure out what their motive is. Maybe they think they can mobilize a vote. These five Conservative MP's have written this letter and xeroxed copies of my poems for all their constituents, which may be a copyright infringement. They're trying to get their constituents to write letters to the Council and try and take the autonomy of the Council away. But without the Council, it would be really rough. I'm a taxpayer too, but I don't tell an engineer how to build a bridge. That's going back to Plato and *The Republic,* right? The only trouble with the Canada Council is that it needs more money.

T: You've said that if you were really writing pornography, you wouldn't need grants.

BISSETT: Yeah. So shame on me for writing what I feel. Why do they get upset about writing? We're not going to be a puritan culture. We're going to have erotic literature as well as any other kind of literature. We're going to have a culture that includes a whole range of experience.

T: Would you agree Canada has a tendency to be liberal about artists just so long as we can ignore them?

BISSETT: Unless you're saying something they can use for their benefit, it's a freak-out. That's the trouble with politicians. I think political activity can be tremendous if it can be communal in some way. Like the world is a commune. Politics should be for getting things together. Like providing guaranteed minimum incomes or fixing things so that senior citizens aren't eating cat food. Or cleaning the water. There are legitimate things that our politicians should be concerned about. Like the defense budget or the food in Super-Valu. Or what the Bank of Nova Scotia and Noranda Mines are doing in Chile, for example. We stood by while Allende got eliminated.

T: Is there any difference for you between where your paintings come from and where poetry comes from?

BISSETT: I think they come from the same place. I approach them both the same way, feeling what can come through me rather than directing it. Sometimes when you look at a linear or more traditional poem, it might look like it's been worked. But it's still receiving. Like it's an "always learning" thing. I might direct with notation and polishing in different drafts, making it closer to how it really is, but it's still trying to listen and hear and see how it is. To let the poem or the painting become what it is. Like one time I was painting and the brush started dancing. It was really exciting because the figures came alive.

T: Are you aware of a common theme in your painting? Because I notice a lot of your figures are illuminated with a glow, like a sun radiating from out of the figure's inside.

BISSETT: I'm sort of aware. Like when I came out of surgery after my brain thing I started seeing people with auras.

T: Tell me about that accident. What happened?

BISSETT: I was at this party after this concrete poetry show I'd been in. There was a folding door made to look like a wall, so it would blend in. The door was supposed to have a latch, because if you went through it was twenty feet to the concrete. I was leaning against this door and I fell through. Or at least that's what they tell me cuz I don't remember. [laughing] Those cells have gone.

It took two years to get better so we took it to court. The insurance company was bucking it. The thing that came up in court was whether the cat had gone down for its milk or not. They unlatched the door to let the cat down for its milk. So there was this testimony as to what time I had fallen through. If I'd fallen through after the cat had already come upstairs, that would prove I couldn't have fallen through. Even though I did. On that basis, the judge threw us out of court. [laughing] I don't remember any bowl of milk! I never even saw the damn cat!

So they took me to the hospital and took the glass out of my hand. But my brain was bleeding. People from the party had left me there for a while because it was a party, you know. Then they got it together to take me to the hospital. They left me in emergency. Then this shrink came in. He started yelling at me. He thought I was catatonic. I couldn't move so he was taking me to Riverview for shock treatment.

I couldn't walk. My hearing would go and then it would come back

again. I couldn't say words. I couldn't move. It was really weird. This
shrink was bundling me up into a stretcher. I was going off into an
ambulance to Riverview. But my brain was bleeding so that would
have killed me and stuff.

   Then this neurologist who was an intern came in. She was fantastic.
She said, "Stop! That's an inter-cerebral bleed." He said it wasn't, it
was catatonia. "He's a screwed-up artist and we're going to shock
him and rehabilitate him."

   So they made a deal. They'd take me to the operating room and go
into my brain. If it was an inter-cerebral bleed, then I'd go to a
neurology ward. If it wasn't, he would get me. She won.

T: How long were you unable to communicate?

BISSETT: About a week. I was paralyzed on my right side for about
three weeks. They sponged up the blood in my brain. I was a staff
patient. I didn't have a private doctor. They took me back to a ward
and they'd use me as a demonstration for classes. They'd bring in these
students and say this is a person who has not got long to live. You see
I had aphasia, which means the echoes were not meeting in my head. It
means you can't function. Then also I had edema, which is something
connected with memory loss. Plus a swelling of the brain or
something. And I was paralyzed so I was like a write-off.

T: Could you talk yet?

BISSETT: No. But I got inspired by this neurologist. She was there all
the time. There was this light coming from her head. I knew she was
on my side. She said my chances were very little but if we really push
we could make a good try of it. She said she was the only person there
who thought I might live. She wanted me to believe that, too, if
nothing else than a joke before dying.

   I remember Gerry Gilbert came over one day and they were having
this group poetry reading which I was supposed to be part of at the
Art Gallery. He wanted to tape me. He said it would be great. My last
poetry reading. [laughing] Some other people there at the time got a
little uptight. They thought it was a little morbid. I couldn't really
handle a reading anyway.

   Warren Tallman was so far out. He brought me tapes of Allen
Ginsberg, Ezra Pound, Robert Duncan. No one could stay very long
but nurses would come in and play the tapes for me. It was to remind

me that I was a poet. It was so far out. Everything would just go. I couldn't remember who anyone was half the time.

But there was something lucky about it all. The accident happened just after I got out of Oakalla. I'd paid my five hundred dollar fine and done my time. But the federal justice department was uptight. They figured I hadn't been punished properly after the two-year trial, a $500 fine, and a little bit of time in Powell River, and some in Burnaby, and some in the city bucket here, and a few weeks in Oakalla. They were appealing. They had to appeal within thirty days of my coming out. They came to the hospital with the papers. The head nurse told them I'd be dead within a week. So that was that.

BISSETT: Have you ever tried to get in touch with that neurologist?

BISSETT: Yeah. I'm going to try and find her again. She was so incredible. She was maybe twenty-five. To all those sixty- to seventy-year-old doctors, she was a toy to them. And I was a dead person. They didn't believe her at all because they'd seen so much. But she just kept believing.

Then I got epileptic and started having seizures.

T: And that really convinced them.

BISSETT: I was a complete write-off! A combination of aphasia, edema, paralysis and epilepsy is about it! But she was fresh. She kept working on me. She started bringing me balls to squeeze even though I couldn't move my hand. She would leave the ball in my hand anyway. She said you'll get the idea, you'll make the connection. She was sticking pins in me everywhere. Normally you have one echo test every two days. I had ten tests every day. She came in with these blackboards and taught me the alphabet all over again. She said, if you live your right side is never going to work, but we don't care. She said there's a lot of people worse off than that.

She got me into occupational therapy as soon as she could get me there. There you see people who are so bad off, like in *Coming Home*. They have so many parts missing from their bodies, or if they have parts there's no feeling cuz their spine got blown away. So you don't get self-pity at all.

She started programming me with my left side. The first day in occupational therapy, it took seven people to get me there. They held me up in front of this ping-pong table. Two guys were sending the ball towards me and they were in worse shape than me! I mean, they had lots missing!

T: I'm sorry. I shouldn't laugh.

BISSETT: [laughing] Well, it is funny. I couldn't laugh but I made gurgling noises. Anyway, two toes twitched one night. My neurologist had this very crackpot theory but she wanted to share it with me. The epilepsy was supposed to mean you're finished, but she figured it might mean there's something that's ticking. She figured with all the electricity it was getting drier in there and a scab was starting to form. So she was getting really excited.

She had me in a sling. She said you're a painter, you're going to keep painting. Enough of this b.s. It doesn't matter what kind of machine we have to make for you to sit in. We can put batteries in you, we can do lots of things.

After the epilepsy, I became spastic. The other people all hung their heads but she and I were getting real excited. At least it was movement. Playing ping-pong, I'd miss the ball and fall on the table. It was a riot. She said rest was fatal. She took my sleeping pills away. She'd say if all you can sleep is four hours a night, that's all your body needs. If there's nothing to do at night, you've got balls to squeeze. Or you can prick yourself with pins.

T: Are you completely recovered now?

BISSETT: Pretty well. I remember the first time I ate in public. It was really far out. I was living with a whole bunch of people as an out-patient. My whole right side was spastic. We had a wood stove. I started to cook some food and everything fell into the fire. I started crying. Everyone freaked out.

We lived in this old warehouse and no matter what was going on, I'd always coped. Things used to get pretty raging there. We had this big bolt on the door because we used to get raided and stuff. We'd be smoking outrageous things inside and the cops couldn't get in. So we'd always been crazy there but they'd never seen me like this before. So I had to go out by myself to this restaurant where everyone used to hang out. I ordered food. It was bacon and eggs, the first thing I'd eaten all day. They brought it and I picked up my knife and fork. That was it. It was all over the floor.

Little by little I got less and less spastic. I had dyladin for about six months. I had barbells and weights. And I had to type. They would check to see how many hours I spent typing. It was terrible. You'd feel like breaking the typewriter.

But it was neat the first time she made me paint. It was so far out. They got me propped up there in this sling from the ceiling. It was a metal thing on a hook. There was paper kept down with masking tape. They taped a brush around my fingers. They pulled this sling back and then they let it go. They had paint on the brush. I would make a mark. Then she'd say you've done your first painting, you're back in business. You could never beat her. So I was really lucky.

T: After all this, you started seeing auras.

BISSETT: Yeah. Hers was the first. But they still thought I would just die in my sleep one night. I got freaked out and crawled out the window once. They found me spastically walking along Broadway and brought me back. She calmed me down and got me inspired again.

T: So do you think your art has come out of this experience to a great extent?

BISSETT: Yeah, a lot.

T: Maybe when you have to relearn almost everything at a later age, you really pare things down to essentials.

BISSETT: It's like a fresh start. You get reprogrammed with a new bunch of cells. [laughing] It's really far out. More people should have it happen.

Patricius

HUGH MACLENNAN

Hugh MacLennan has loved and understood this country for as long and as deeply as any Canadian author. He is the most significant member of what Margaret Laurence has referred to as the first generation of non-colonial Canadian writers.

According to MacLennan, justice is the basic theme of all great literary art. Oedipal struggles for power usually generate the central psychological conflicts of his novels, Barometer Rising *(1941),* Two Solitudes *(1945),* The Precipice *(1948),* Each Man's Son *(1951),* The Watch That Ends the Night *(1979), and* Return of the Sphinx *(1967).*

The latter novel was hostilely received for arguing social unrest in Quebec during the 1960's had psychological rather than political or socio-economic roots. Having received international exposure and acclaim during the 1940's and 1950's, MacLennan is a prophet largely unheralded in his own land now that his prophecies have come true.

Born in Glace Bay, Nova Scotia in 1907, MacLennan's classicist education included a Rhodes Scholarship and a Princeton Ph.D. in Roman history before turning to writing. He now lives in Montreal, having taught for many years at McGill University.

Hugh MacLennan has been the recipient of the Governor General's Award an unprecedented five times. His most recent novel is Voices in Time *(1980).*

photo: Alan Twigg

T: There's a remark in *Return of the Sphinx*, "If you ever let them see inside your soul, they'll crucify you to save themselves from seeing what's inside their own." That explains why artists have been persecuted throughout history.

MacLennan: That's right. Often painters got the worst of it because we will go insane at a new vision if it destroys an old one. I remember once in Montreal somebody did a damn bad piece of sculpture out of wood on Sherbrooke Street in the early 50's and two guys came along with axes and chopped it to pieces. With two policemen watching, looking on. And even the Group of Seven was denounced in Montreal in 1927 for obscenity. For trees and rocks!

T: How much do you think you expose parts of your soul in your work?

MacLennan: Well, I don't write straight autobiography but you know Flaubert's famous remark, "Madame Bovary, c'est moi." It's just a question of empathy.

Of the stuff I've written, the one that ripped out my guts the most was *Return of the Sphinx*. The epilogue of that I can't read very easily even now. I said more there than anything I've ever been able to say. I didn't realize it until the very end when I found myself writing, "One more step would have set us free but the Sphinx returned." And it has.

T: Yet that novel wasn't well received.

MacLennan: It was well received in the States. But every paper here panned it, I must say that hurt me. I'd never had that much hostility in this country. Now that there's a book of my essays out, I'm getting my first reviews which haven't been hostile in twenty years in this country.

T: I think *The Sphinx* is valuable because it argues that a man's morality is not necessarily determined by his political opinions. That's somewhat of an unfashionable opinion these days.

MacLennan: It certainly was in 1967. What happened was that *Return of the Sphinx* arrived in the bookstores less than a week after DeGaulle's famous speech in Montreal where he said, "Vive e Quebec libre!" To my utter astonishment the book was regarded by Canadian reviewers as an insult to Canada in her centennial year! One of them wrote Edmund Wilson about it and he told me. An insult to Canada in her centennial year! I thought we'd grown up beyond that.

T: I think it was received that way because you were arguing that Canada's problems were essential psychological, not political.

MacLennan: And of course that's nonsense. Politics, for God's sakes, is simply property. It begins in the nursery. That book wasn't about Canadian politics. I had a very universal subject there.

You know what that book turned out to be? It's Sophocles' *Oedipus at Colonus*. I didn't know when I wrote it that one of the most prominent leaders in Quebec—and there were more than one—had to have his son arrested. I met him later when he was out of office. I think that's why he was out of office. He thought I had his son in mind when I wrote it.

T: It was the same with Willi Brandt's son in West Germany.

MacLennan: It happened all over the world. Families were torn asunder. God knows it was not a happy time.

T: You claim in your books that the generational strife is psychological, that it's sexual rivalry.

MacLennan: Of course it was! Of course it was! I've been waiting, assuming and knowing there was going to be a violent patrist reaction to all this insane permissiveness. I never dreamed it would come from the Arabs in Iran. But it has.

T: Did you have difficulties with your students in the sixties?

MacLennan: I never had any trouble with my students. They wanted an anvil to beat on and they got one with me.

T: Have you been branded a reactionary for refusing to view social problems in strict economic terms?

MacLennan: Sure. But not originally. Originally I was branded a revolutionary as obscene and so forth. Then I was branded a nationalist in the 50's when it was more fashionable to be an Angry Young Man. Then in the sixties people tried to reduce everything to politics. Now I'm simply not sexy enough.

T: Certainly the pace of some of your novels is more leisurely compared to many novels today. Is that because you felt obliged to supply a sense of place when you wrote about Canada?

MACLENNAN: Yes, I had to. It was necessary then. I was panned by some highbrow critics for this but people have to know where they are. Drama depends upon the familiar. Otherwise it's just an accident. It's necessary to build the stage. That takes a lot of craftsmanship. They ruined *Two Solitudes* as a movie because they didn't understand that. The French and the English never met socially. That's the idea of *Two Solitudes*. But the scriptwriter directed it and he didn't understand the book. The reviewers absolutely massacred it and I couldn't disagree with them.

T: There's been an obvious progression in your work from understanding where Canada is coming from, with novels like *Two Solitudes*, to worrying about where we're going. Why do you object to being called a nationalist writer?

MACLENNAN: Because nationalism that you have with the Parti Quebecois and nationalism in various European countries is a substitute for religion. I have no use for that.

T: But I think you are a nationalist writer because you've been so intimately concerned with the growth of Canada as a nation.

MACLENNAN: The growth of any nation starts with a family. Then it becomes a tribe. Then it becomes a confederation of tribes. Ultimately maybe a nation. It can't be done overnight. It's a matter of evolution. All I've been asking is for people to know what their potential is.

T: Would you agree that Canada's potential is particularly fascinating because we're coming of age at a time when mankind seems to be coming to a major crossroads?

MACLENNAN: Sure. Western civilization is dying. Civilization, as we know it, is in decline. As it happened with the Romans. That puts Canada in a unique position. An Irishman named Dennis Brogan, at some conference I was at in the early 50's, once said: "Poor Canada. It's the most successful country in the world. What a tragedy it should become successful in the middle of the twentieth century."

T: Few Canadians are going to appreciate that tragedy because few of us appreciate the extent of our success in the first place.

MACLENNAN: That's exactly right.

T: You wrote that if Sisyphus was a saint, he could serve as your patron. As a Canadian struggling to become a writer in the 1940's, what made the uphill struggle so steep?

MacLENNAN: Voltaire said that if he had a son who wanted to write, he'd strangle him out of the goodness of his heart. It was particularly hard in Canada because we had no publishers except Ryerson, which was owned by the Methodist Church. So you could forget about them. Then later, if you signed with a Canadian publisher, you had to give them rights to the whole world. It was terrible. The war just made it worse. *Barometer Rising* was a book society choice in England but they didn't have enough paper for more than 15,000 copies.

T: And the money was poor. I understand that at age 50 you had only $1,000 after 35 years of writing.

MacLENNAN: When I published *Barometer Rising* in New York, it got great reviews and drew a huge response. It sold 20,000 in hardcover and 100,000 in paperback in the first year. But out of that I got less than $700. When *Two Solitudes* sold 68,000 hardback copies in Canada at $3 each, I made $4,500.

T: Do you ever question how much international attention you might have received if you had been writing as a citizen of a more powerful country?

MacLENNAN: It would have been much greater. No question of that. The territorial imperative is mighty in literature. Because language is so powerful.

I remember I was in England with C.P. Snow and we were dining with some reviewers. One of them said, "Look, Charles, don't you think it's about time we started putting down these bloody South African writers?" I took offense and said, "You you think you've got anybody in England as good as Alan Paton?" He said, "My dear chap, you can't be serious. He's a South African." It was all boudoir politics. So I told them Alan Paton could write the pants off any Englishman they had, with the possible exception of Evelyn Waugh.

That's why I didn't wish to be known as a Canadian writer. It's still a diminutive term, even after you've been translated into thirteen languages.

T: We often hear that Canadian writers felt obliged to set their stories in American or British locales. You never did that.

MacLennan: No, I didn't. But certainly anybody connected with movies had to. It still happens. For example, when Margaret Laurence's *A Jest of God* was sold to the movies, they set it in the States. Personally I've had some hilariously funny interviews with Hollywood people about this. They would set *Barometer Rising* somewhere other than Halifax. [imitating an American drawl] "Gotta be American. Boy meets girl in Paris, France. Okay. Boy meets girl in Winnipeg. Who cares?" That's a literal quotation.

T: What about the spectre of censorship back then? Was that ever a problem for you?

MacLennan: I never worried about it with my work. After all, it certainly didn't bother Tolstoy that he couldn't use four-letter words. What did bother me was when they tried to actually ban books. I got involved in two court cases, not for myself, defending books. The worst time was when the Americans tried to ban Nobel Prize winners in the 50's.

T: Does it worry you now that some school boards are removing Margaret Laurence from school libraries?

MacLennan: They did that to all my books.

T: How much response did you get to your work in the 40's compared to the 60's?

MacLennan: More. The Canadian reading public took to books very, very eagerly. A young writer had a much better chance to be read than now. In the first place, you weren't in competition with television. Secondly you had a much better chance of being reviewed. Thirdly, hardbacks were cheaper. In 1959, *The Watch That Ends the Night* was 160,000 words and sold in New York for $5. Now people wait for paperbacks. The big contracts are in paperbacks. That's not been good.

T: How have the older writers like yourself and Morley Callaghan and Hugh Garner felt about seeing some of the garbage being passed off as literature these days.

MacLennan: There's always been garbage. The point is that garbage made money in other countries. It hasn't made money here.

T: *Each Man's Son, Two Solitudes* and *Barometer Rising* were all set

before or during World War One. Was World War One the turning
point for Canada as far as you're concerned?

T: It certainly was. Canada entered the war as a completely colonial
nation, not a power at all. Then Canada found herself.

Canadians were the first to go under gas attack and hold the line.
Then when Canadians broke the Hindenburg Line on the 8th of
August, 1918, Ludendorf called it the black day of the German Army.
"Wherever the Canadians were," he said, "we knew we were in
trouble." And finally Canadians ended the war by capturing Mons.
After that, the feeling of pride in this country was enormous.

But our casualties were appalling. We had one-quarter more killed
in action than the Americans lost. That was 69,000 killed from a
population of seven million. We lost so many of our best men that for
twenty years Canada had no fundamental leadership. Do you know
what the casualties were the first battle of the Somme? On July 1st,
1916, 50,000 died in three hours. The next day they tried it again and
lost 70,000. They kept on insanely charging barbed wire and machine
guns. It was almost like committing suicide. The average life of a
second lieutenant in the British Army those days was two weeks.
That's why Churchill wrote that Anthony Eden was almost the only
person of first-class ability to survive the First World War.

But the worst tragedy of World War One for Canada was that the
Orange Society in Toronto deliberately jammed conscription down the
throats of the French Canadians. This meant, with their huge families,
a farmer might have had six or seven sons drafted. The French served
in the First World War and had magnificent regiments. But they
never forgave us for that. And we're still paying the price for it.

T: So the First World War not only gave Canada a sense of identity,
it also served to split us apart.

MacLennan: Yes, it did. The French Canadians were perfectly
willing to go along with both wars, providing they had a volunteer
system for those who wanted to go to them.

Can anybody say there was any sense to it at all? The only thing
worse than that war was the peace treaty. It guaranteed a second one.

T: *Barometer Rising* was very critical of the way Canada was used by
the Allied Forces during World War One. Did you come under any
fire for those opinions?

MacLennan: No, because three-quarters of the country agreed with it. I was writing a column for the *Toronto Star,* syndicated across the country, when Winston Churchill wrote his version of the Second World War in the 60's. God knows I admired him. But in the first four volumes of 90,000 lines—I very carefully measured them— Canada got only 53 lines for her contribution. Of those, 28 were in some letter to Mackenzie King about Newfoundland. Canada's contribution to that war was enormous! But the English couldn't have cared less. It was a great shame that Canada's two most stupendous efforts were made as part of the British Empire, not for Canada.

T: I loved that comment about Churchill in *The Sphinx,* the one made by the Russian ambassador.

MacLennan: The one where he says you people love to quote old Churchill, especially when he's rude? That's a reference to Churchill's remark about Atlee, of course. You remember? He said, [imitating Churchill] ''Mr. Atlee is a very modest man with much to be modest about.''

T: The explosion you describe in *Barometer Rising* happened when you were ten. Were you living right in Halifax at the time?

MacLennan: Yes. And I had had a sixth sense that something like that was going to happen. Kids are queer like that sometimes. I knew the Germans had these two enormous submarines, the *Braemen* and the *Deutschland.* The whole of Halifax was blacked out at night because it would have been possible for these submarines to have had aircraft with folding wings like they had in the Second World War. They could have simply surfaced off Halifax harbour and bombarded the place. It would have been worthwhile doing.

When the explosion hit, that's what I thought it was. All the windows came in. One step further I'd have had my head knocked off. There was silence. I did verification of temperatures and things like that to write *Barometer Rising* but there was nothing else I didn't know. I remembered everything about it.

T: Do you think that was a great psychological shock to you as a child?

MacLennan: Well, you did see some pretty horrible things. Then rumours were soon flying around that there would be another one. And there damn near was.

I remember a terribly cold day when a man came into the school, shouting at us to evacuate. He said there was going to be another explosion. We were dragged out on sleighs into the hills and told to get under cover. We nearly froze to death for three hours. When I got home my mother didn't know anything about it. But it turns out the guy was right. There was a ship called the *Picton* and it caught fire. The Halifax stevedores were handling these six-inch shells with heavy gloves but the shells were so hot they scalded their hands lowering them into nets in the water. Finally they towed her out. She didn't go up but if she did it would have wrecked the whole south end. Halifax nearly had three of those things.

T: There's often a psychological explosion in your books, with a youngster involved. Do you think there's any correlation?

MACLENNAN: I suppose there's something, but it's hard to know where these things come from.

T: What were your main literary influences?

MACLENNAN: I never read any novels at all, except *Treasure Island* and *Ivanhoe,* but I read all of Homer in the original. And a great deal of Greek literature. When I finally got to Greece, looking up the coast towards Athens, apart from the slight difference in ground cover, I could have been on some marvellous bay in Nova Scotia. What Homer was describing was exactly like the coast of Nova Scotia. It was the same kind of life. People going out to sea in small boats, people going off to war. Homer described what I knew better than any other writer.

T: Did you read Homer at a young age?

MACLENNAN: I suppose I was reading Homer in Greek when I was about sixteen.

T: Do you regret that Latin and Greek are no longer standard subjects?

MACLENNAN: Oh, yes. A Russian diplomat, round the time of Napoleon, said it was a terrible international disaster when Latin ceased to be the language of diplomacy. Because you cannot write a sentence in Latin which is both grammatically correct and ambiguous. That's the curse of English. It's so ambiguous. Just pick up any newspaper. American English is so ambiguous that nobody knows what they're talking about half the time.

T: What do you think of the federal government's bilingualism policies?

MacLennan: I want to defend this thing of bilingualism as an idea. Anybody from Vancouver who is transferred to Quebec can probably get an English school. If they'd only handled it as simply as that for the French, people wouldn't be saying it's been jammed down their throats. The tragedy with the Liberal government was to say that pure bilingualism was going to save the country. Mike [Pearson] did it up to a point and Pierre's done it too much. But it can't work. It's been too badly handled.

T: Was the invocation of the War Measures Act justified?

MacLennan: Again, all I can say was it was a mistake not to have had a better defined Act. But if that was the only thing they had on hand, I was damn glad they did it.

It was all very well to sit somewhere and complain about it. But if you had been chased by two cells for seven miles yourself, you took a different view of it. There were 50,000 phone calls a day threatening people's lives and things were just ready to explode. Hearing the crowds screaming and roaring, anybody who had seen Nazi mobs as I had could tell perfectly well there were agitators there. I knew, which a lot of people didn't, that foreign agents were at work in Quebec. Really serious boys. Because Canada was the biggest prize in the world.

T: Wait a second. When were you in Germany?

MacLennan: The last time I was in Germany as a student was just a few months before Hitler took over. I saw the damn thing coming. I was even arrested in Germany as a British spy in 1932. But that was just because I knew so much about the German navy from the First World War as a kid. Anyway, in 1937 it was all staring you in the face. But the ruling classes in England and France as well as a very powerful Catholic lobby in the United States, were dreading communism. They turned a blind eye to what Hitler was doing.

T: So you didn't turn a blind eye to the FLQ, is that it?

MacLennan: Six months before it happened I prophesied a kidnapping for the fall. Because there were constant bombings, violence and incitements to violence. People were going practically nuts. They'd given up the Catholic Church and didn't know where they were. I knew some of these people. They were just kids that came out of prison. But somebody got hold of them.

Certainly there should have been a better act than the War Measures Act. But some show of force had to be made.

T: Do you see the danger of the Parti Quebecois being that it's possible they may try to nationalize industry and therefore invite military intervention from the States?

[MacLennan requested to go off the record while discussing the extent of CIA involvement in Quebec. He concludes, "God, this country is innocent!"]

T: Would you agree your work has been essentially about the frictions between generations?

MacLennan: I suppose you'd have to say that's true. This crossing over of generations... oh my God, I've seen some tragedies there. It's a bad thing.

T: Was there a strong generational clash between yourself and your father?

MacLennan: Not as bad as the sixties. But I would say there was. He was a stern Victorian yet he was a highly emotional Highlander. So he was a difficult person, yes.

T: What are some of your memories of him?

MacLennan: Well, I remember my mother and sister and I were living in a single room on captain's allowance, which was only a few dollars a day, while he was overseas in the medical service. He was overage and he nearly killed himself with overwork after the Sommes battles. Then he nearly lost an arm from an infection. He came back to be an invalid at home in 1916. What little money he had vanished with the war. We rented a house sight-unseen in Halifax and it blew up as soon as we got in it from gas in the walls. They were both in the hospital. Then my father got back to practicing medicine again and was back in uniform.

He was a helluva good surgeon. He was the only person east of Montreal who could do a labyrinth operation, which is practically a brain operation. He'd gone to Vienna and learned how to do it. He died as a result of his last operation when he was dragged on a sleigh in a winter blizzard into the fields somewhere near Windsor, Nova Scotia to operate on a farm table. He came back and had a stroke the next day.

T: You've used the term "son hungry" in one of your novels. What about the other side of the cycle? Have you had children yourself?

MacLennan: I didn't because my first wife had rheumatic heart disease so it was impossible. But I'm very, very fond of children. For a time I missed having them terribly. That's really why I went back to McGill. To associate with young people. I couldn't do without them.

T: If you don't mind me saying so, I think there's a lot of beauty in your work which comes out of that yearning.

MacLennan: That's nice to hear.

T: I'd even go so far as to say your conception of God is somehow linked to this idea of the perpetuation of the species.

MacLennan: Yes, I think it's a form of energy built into the evolutionary system. But you have to wait and work for it. What I said in *The Watch That Ends the Night* was true as far as it goes. Theology is pretty well hopeless. You should read Dr. Penfield's book *The Mystery of the Mind*. He was the greatest of all brain surgeons and the founder of the Neurological Institute. He developed the science of neurology and was certainly the greatest Canadian of our time. He said to me 20 years ago, "I know I know a good deal about the brain, but I know nothing about the mind." So he called his book *The Mystery of the Mind*.

He had discovered from a Spanish scientist a way in which you could make cross-sections of the brain. Then they isolated and enumerated over 40 million cells. He was finally able to demonstrate that the brain is a computer, a marvellous one, badly computed by the mind. Then he established that the mind belongs to energy. Energy, of course, is indestructible. But it's capable of an infinity of mutations.

Penfield had not been a religious man when he was younger but his own work in science eventually drove him to where the poets and philosophers were centuries before.

We have now learned more about humanity in the last twenty years than has been learned since people knew how to think. And we have our newspapers taking our federal elections seriously! We have student demonstrations! We have people who are complete materialists teaching psychology! They're back in the Stone Age.

T: So what does the future hold?

MacLennan: The Arabs have such fantastic money power they will soon have A-bombs. They can very easily get the plutonium. There's no problem in hiring the technicians. That's all such a terrifying prospect that it makes what's going on in Canada today utterly trivial. I'm not sure the world will survive it. It's very, very dicey.

T: And yourself?

MacLennan: I like to think that 15,000 years ago is only yesterday. And it is. The ice was a mile high on top of Toronto 15,000 years ago. That gives me a certain sense of being more at ease in this universe. With that thought behind me, I'm quite sure I'll be able to finish a new book.

T: Is this the novel you started in 1969?

MacLennan: That's right. I think it would be finished by now if I didn't have so many other things around my neck.

T: I didn't think you were going to write another novel.

MacLennan: [wryly] Neither did I.

Filius

JOHN GRAY

John Gray was born in Nova Scotia forty years after Hugh MacLennan, at Truro in 1947. As such, he is a representative of the third generation of what Margaret Laurence refers to as non-colonial writers.

After his upbringing in the Maritimes, Gray matured as a writer and director while studying theatre at the University of British Columbia. He has subsequently lived and worked all over Canada, forming Vancouver's Tamahnous experimental theatre group and collaborating with Toronto's innovative Theatre Passe Muraille.

Gray's portrait of a Canadian World War One flying ace, Billy Bishop Goes to War, opened on Broadway in 1980 after the original production played to packed houses in every major regional theatre in Canada. The play features only one actor and Gray at the piano, singing original songs.

18 Wheels, his first produced play, is a musical about trucking. Rock n'Roll, a third play based on Gray's experiences in a high school band, is forthcoming.

Though Gray's work promises to reach the lives of more Canadians than any author in this collection, in 1980 he is this book's token unpublished writer.

At present, John Gray lives wherever he is working.

photo: Alan Twigg

T: *Billy Bishop Goes to War* is one of Canada's longest-touring plays. Has its success surprised you?

GRAY: Yeh, it has. Originally our attitude was if the Canadians and Americans like it, that's great. If the Canadians like it and the Americans don't like it, that's okay. If the Canadians don't like it and the Americans don't like it, that's a drag. If the Canadians don't like it and the Americans do like it, we're in deep trouble. We had no idea it would go so far.

T: It looks as if success has come rather easily.

GRAY: I know. I've only written two damn shows. Now I'm starting to worry that I'm going to have to start thinking of myself as a writer. When you do that, there's always a danger you'll start thinking that you have to write, whether you have anything to say or not. I think that's an awful thing.

T: So if a stranger walked up to you and asked your profession —

GRAY: I'd say I work in the theatre.

T: But without having written *18 Wheels* and *Billy Bishop,* you couldn't pay your bills.

GRAY: I know. But admitting you're a writer is kinda like quitting smoking. The worst thing you can do is start proclaiming you're quitting smoking. You'll fail for sure. Hemingway once said don't put your mouth on anything that looks like it might happen, it'll turn to dust every time. In a way, I guess that has something to do with how I write. The worst stuff I do is always written when I have a good idea what it's about. I do much better if I concentrate on the characters and let the play emerge by itself. Then on the third draft I finally start to observe what it's about.

T: It seems *Billy Bishop* is only half about Billy Bishop's life. The other half is about how our generation is linked to Canada's military past. Was that intentional?

GRAY: Yes. Those World Wars explain so much about ourselves, about our attitudes as Canadians. The innocence Canada took into that first war was just appalling. When the figures started coming back — 25,000 men lost at the Somme, for example — people weren't too keen on going, right? That's when conscription started. Then all the French Canadian resentment against English Canada got started.

Then the whole cynicism about government started. All that stuff affects us today.

I think the heaviest years of life are around 19 to 25. Those are really long, big years. They form you. We didn't fight in a war at that age; some of our parents did. They went through an experience that we don't have a clue about. So there's a monstrous gap between generations.

T: What awareness of war did you get growing up in the 50's?

GRAY: I always knew that my father and his best friend had enlisted together. My father got involved in radar and his best friend became a spitfire pilot. This guy's name was John West. When he was shot down during the Battle of Britain, that's when my father vowed he would name his first-born son after his dead friend.

I was always aware of that. I always wondered who this guy was that I was named after. I wondered about this heavy experience my father must have gone through to do that. Now he's an insurance executive. A middle-class person with bourgeois values and fundamentalist religious beliefs.

T: A Canadian.

GRAY: Yeh, right. So what happened to him to make him do this almost poetic gesture?

T: This is why you wrote *Billy Bishop* then. To answer that question.

GRAY: Yeh. And that's why I'm content to perform *Billy Bishop* for a long time. Because it's about me. I don't know if I can tell you exactly how it's about me...but somehow it is. It's my relationship to the events in *Billy Bishop*. You can't really say the play is really telling you that much about Billy Bishop himself. I don't know what he was like. I really don't. And *18 Wheels* doesn't really tell you much about truckers either. So what is *Billy Bishop* about anyway?

T: It's about your perceptions of Billy Bishop's relationship to war.

GRAY: Definitely. It's not really about war at all. It uses war to show that old countries use young countries. Old people use young people to fight their wars. In the process of this, youth is lost. Youth is lost in the sense of a country and also for individuals. Britain lost a whole generation. *Billy Bishop* is about youth and old age.

T: And it refuses to preach about war, right?

GRAY: Right.

T: Many people would regard that as a failing.

GRAY: Yeh, I get a lot of that. A certain number of people go to the show with a checklist of things they want said. When they don't get to check off things they came to hear, they feel the show has failed them. They don't appreciate that not preaching allows us to talk to old people, too. Old people are thrilled to see that people of the next generation can recognize that they weren't stupid idiots for going along and fighting. It was so much more complicated than that. *Billy Bishop* recognizes that their experiences had validity, irrespective of whether the war was good or bad.

To say that the play is encouraging war is incomprehensible to me.

T: If Billy Bishop embodies the experiences of a generation then the audience can come and pass judgment by itself.

GRAY: Right. I wanted to give people some conception of what war is like. We have a particular kind of arrogance that comes from the sixties which makes people say not only are wars bad, but people who fought them are stupid. That's unfair. In the first World War those guys were encouraged to fight by their elders. They were victims. Not only did those guys not know what they were fighting for, they didn't even know where they were! Ever! There was no landscape. It was all blown up. There were no trees or hills, nothing. They were simple someplace in France. It was like the moon. You spend three years there until you get wounded or killed. The alienation must have been phenomenal! Surviving in this little vacuum was probably their only real concern. The larger issues of war on an international scale had nothing to do with them.

T: Do you think that's why your audience at Royal Military College even liked the show? Because you didn't overlay history onto Billy Bishop's shoulders?

GRAY: That's partly it. The other reason is simply that those people aren't stupid. You generally think of army guys as being like football players. It really knocked me out to hear the military commandant give this analysis of our show in terms of Canada's history. My jaw was open. It was very perceptive and interesting stuff. To start thinking all those right-wing guys are stupid is naive and destructive to one's own thinking.

T: In the 60's, our generation was so busy formulating some alternate stance of our own that we didn't even try to appreciate what we were defining ourselves against.

GRAY: Yes, that's why *Billy Bishop* would have been a bomb in the 60's. It would have been a turkey. People would have called it reactionary.

T: How much of your conception of what theatre should be has been formed by associating with Theatre Passe Muraille?

GRAY: Quite a bit. I used to be quite the little elitist. I went to university for seven years. Nothing will hone an elitist like seven years in a university. So I tended to do shows for formalistic reasons. Content really wasn't that important. New theatre forms and staging were just as important to me as what a play said.

Then I saw Passe Muraille do *1837* in Listowel, Ontario. It was very revolutionary, that first Passe Muraille show. All these farmers were yelling and standing up and applauding. And these guys were prosperous right-wing types. It just blew my mind to see how people can relate to content. It made the stuff I was doing seem trivial. Like playing little games. It made me rethink the whole thing.

T: Now there's almost a movement growing out of *1837*. Shows like *Paper Wheat* and *The Farm Show*.

GRAY: Yeh. In those shows, the event of having a particular audience becomes just as important as what's happening on the stage. It's not like there's a little glass cube around the stage and everybody sits there and admires the work of art on display.

T: What specific things did you learn from Passe Muraille?

GRAY: How powerful a monologue can be.

T: Any negative things?

GRAY: Well, I also learned the limitations of having actors play tables and chairs and cows and horses. I've pretty well had it up to here with that stuff. I also reacted against Passe Muraille's tendency to go into a farming community and tell farmers how great they are. I've talked to lots of farmers. They're not dummies. You don't have to flatter them. It's also a bit much when actors go into a community and start telling people what they're like.

T: Yes, it's getting very trendy now for a bunch of middle class kids to graduate from some university theatre program and suddenly become relevant. So they do some didactic piece on nuclear power.

GRAY: And who's going to come? You just consolidate people's prejudices. I don't think theatre is the place for weighty matters like that mainly because you see a play once. You can re-read a novel by Kafka. You can analyse it at your leisure. But theatre's different. Look at Shakespeare, for example. His characters are wonderful and they mouth human issues very articulately and poetically, but Shakespeare doesn't attempt to change the world.

T: You're saying the function of theatre is to reflect life, not comment on it.

GRAY: Yeh, I guess so. Accuracy over opinion. The best reaction you get out of theatre is recognition. Maybe with a novel it's different. But in theatre I know I'm never going to be a person who writes of weighty matters. By that I mean I'm not going to write anything just to give the world my opinions.

T: Did the UBC Theatre Department instill that approach?

GRAY: No, at UBC I mostly just learned how to direct plays. That was very useful experience. Now I can visualize a play happening on a stage. I know how much it's going to cost. You learn not to see a movie in your head when you're writing. Movies are more approximate to what goes on in your head in dreams. Theatre is different. Working as a director at UBC made it relatively easy for me to write things which work on stage. Of course that doesn't necessarily mean that what you write is going to look good on the page either. I had a lot of trouble getting *18 Wheels* produced at first because people would read it and they wouldn't think it would work. It reads terribly. It's all rhymes. But on stage it's fine.

T: Did you always want to be a playwright?

GRAY: Not at all. I was very, very bored in school. I was so bad they kept testing me for deafness. I was right down there with the special class types. As a result I was a loner most of the time. That's why I was always known for being musical. It helped excuse me for being such a lousy student. I got most of my acceptance from people out of music, out of playing. When I finally joined a rock n'roll band it was great.

T: What stuff did you do?

GRAY: We played *Midnight Hour, Land of a Thousand Dances, I Hear You Knocking But You Can't Come In. Splish Splash.* Stuff like that. I had a Hammond organ. It wasn't like playing the organ; it was like driving a car.

T: Unfortunately most of us have a totally commercialized preconception of what a popular song should sound like.

GRAY: And that's a great shame. There's a whole tradition of songwriting where the songs are more complex. Kurt Weill, for example, is my favourite songwriter. And Sondheim is good, too. His songs fit into a show.

T: Your songs definitely aren't written to be covered some day by Frank Sinatra. It seems you're trying hard to fit them into the flow of a play, too.

GRAY: Sure. It's very American to write a scene around a song. I tend to write the other way round. When I get to a point in the script where something needs to be said that a character can't really say, I can say it in a song.

T: One eastern Canadian critic thought your singing detracted from *Billy Bishop.* For me it was very important that your authenticity onstage could act as a foil to Eric Peterson's exuberance. He plays eighteen characters at once so it adds a sense of balance if you play yourself.

GRAY: Yeh, I know. I'm glad you said that. It's the emotions that people go through that are important. If a great singer sung with Eric, he'd have to do things stylistically different than what the scenes require. It would become schizophrenic. God knows I'd never try and become a singer and have people love me for the quality of my voice. But I sing the songs in *Billy Bishop* because I can sing them in the context as well as anybody can. Again you get people coming to the show with a checklist, for Chrissake. When somebody sings a song, they've already decided what it's supposed to sound like. Well, Jesus Christ, how am I supposed to deal with that?

T: Do you have songwriting ambitions that go beyond the theatre?

GRAY: I used to. I had a brief romance with United Artists. I did a few demos and United Artists wanted to make a single out of one. But it was just ludicrous. I mean, there's nothing quite like being rejected by some fifty-year-old bozo with a Beatle hairdo and a medallion on his chest.

T: [laughter] And white shoes!

GRAY: It's very humiliating. It's such a sleazy industry. You get offered a deal that says you sing with us and we get all your songs forever and ever. And if you're really lucky, they'll make a lot of money. It's a very humiliating setup. I just didn't want to be part of it. In Canada it's a branch plant system so you're constantly up against people who can say no but not yes. You're constantly being humiliated just because of the other person's powerlessness. And that person won't admit his powerlessness. There's nothing in it for those labels to promote Canadian artists. Why should they? They've got lots of American artists they can promote up here anyway.

T: Are your songs always so lacking in autobiography?

GRAY: I do write songs for myself sometimes. But I work best in a context. I don't work well unless I have limitations. If I had the world at my feet I just wouldn't write anything. There are certainly other songwriters who seem to thrive on that openness though. People who can just sit down and write a song. Like Paul McCartney.

T: I always get the feeling McCartney is so naturally musical he could sit down at the piano, drunk out of his mind, and write *Yesterday* or something like that without even realizing it.

GRAY: Yeh. And he does so much with so few themes. Face it, with pop music for the radio you've got about five things you can write about. You can write about I love you...I don't love you...

T: You don't love me...We're not getting along...

GRAY: [laughter] Or I love you baby, but sorry I gotta ramble...

T: [laughter] Or this life on the road is sure getting me down!

GRAY: Oh, God, yes! That's a good one. It sure is awful being in a rock band. Oh, the trials of being in a strange city without my baby!

T: I just woke up this morning, called for room service and wrote you this song. At noon.

GRAY: Yeh, I couldn't write another sorry-dear-I-gotta-ramble song. I don't know how they do it.

T: What's your new play going to be about?

GRAY: My rock and roll band.

T: Yet another totally male world.

GRAY: I know. I don't have any women in my shows at all. I don't know why. [almost whispering] I guess I don't really know much about them. I can't get into a woman's head. I only have male visions of women. It's weird.

T: People will invariably compare any new play against the success of *Billy Bishop*.

GRAY: I know. I'm quite reconciled to a turkey. There will be a turkey on the horizon. Then they'll say, well, he wrote two good shows and that was it.

T: People will want nothing less than a follow-up to *Billy Bishop,* using the same format with Eric Peterson.

GRAY: We already thought of that. We'll call the sequel, *Billy Bishop Goes to Seed.* Eric and I will sit on stage and drink for two hours.

T: Or how about *Pierre Trudeau Goes to War Measures*? Eric could run around with a rose in his teeth while you explored that male world of politics.

GRAY: Yeh, it might work. I happen to think maleness and masculinity is a very hot topic these days. Mainly because women have changed their tunes so much in the last twenty years. Men are having to re-evaluate their masculinity now. There is such a thing as masculinity. Just as there is such a thing as femininity. They just aren't the same any more.

T: Have you ever read anything by a guy named Robert Kroetsch?

GRAY: Yeh, I love that guy. I've just started reading his new book, *What the Crow Said.* He's terrific. I once toyed with the idea of a musical based on *The Studhorse Man.*

Male

ROBERT KROETSCH

Robert Kroetsch was born in Heisler, Alberta in 1927. His novels exhibit his conscious resolve to mythologize the past of Western Canada, thereby "unhiding the hidden" causes of maladjusted contemporary behaviour.

But We Are Exiles *(1965) is the story of a jilted lover who flees emotional chaos to work as a boat pilot on the MacKenzie River. On the frozen river, "where man is defined free of the terror of human relationships", the pilot ends up dredging beneath the ice for the body of his rival.*

The Words of My Roaring *(1966) probes Western Canada's self-definition as an economic and cultural poor cousin of Eastern Canada through the story of a young undertaker during the aftermath of the Depression.*

The Studhorse Man *(1969) features Hazard Lepage, a Quixotic anachronism who wanders Alberta in search of a mare worthy of his prize stallion. Determined to keep the tradition of the studhorse alive, Lepage is one of the most memorable characters in Canadian fiction. This comic novel earned Kroetsch a Governor General's Award.*

Gone Indian *(1973) and* Badlands *(1975) are male quests to uncover primitive pasts. Again primarily concerned with virility, the former novel follows the misadventures of a self-styled Indian while the latter studies a raft expedition in search of dinosaur remains.*

What the Crow Said *(1979) is an attempt to take the tall tale as far as it can go. To recount its plot would be akin to Reader's Digest condensing* Finnegan's Wake. *It is a complex intellectual puzzle of meanings that forges larger-than-life characters and occurrences to mythologize life in a small town.*

Kroetsch has also published several books of poetry and non-fiction. He resides wherever teaching posts at various universities happen to take him.

photo: Dennis Cooley

T: Would you agree that your novels are chiefly concerned with probing how sexuality has influenced the sociology of the Canadian west?

KROETSCH: I can only begin to answer that by saying there's a great deal which is repressed in our society. Look at our vicious need for order that makes us all rush out at five o'clock to have a drink. People used to drink on ceremonial occasions. Now we drink automatically at five o'clock because the pressure we've been under all day is intolerable. We live in a very repressive society. It has to be repressive to make people work eight hours a day. Sexuality is too illogical for society so it's repressed. But the impulse towards sexual "disorder" is inherent in almost all of us.

T: Is this why marriage in your fiction is always depicted as a repression of sexuality, not an opportunity for embracing it?

KROETSCH: Yeah, I must admit my novels reflect a terrible skepticism about the state of marriage. Perhaps based on personal experience.

T: On personal experience and Sigmund Freud?

KROETSCH: Yeah, I do admit it. I do acknowledge that. I liked his statement somewhere that work and love are the two things we have in this world. Putting the two together is very difficult because only occasionally are they the same thing.

Often for a writer, work and love can come together. I'm someone who believes very consciously that the writing energy comes out of a confrontation with the Muse and the Muse takes the form of immortal woman. Often one almost hates a dependence on that. But I really depend on that relationship with a woman for that writing energy.

T: A feminist might label your work as male sexual propaganda because in examining the male desire for freedom, you've painted an extremely unflattering picture of the role women played in the settling of Canada. Women carry the dreaded civilization instinct. They thwart the Prometheanism of the male.

KROETSCH: That's too naive a statement. When I look at the male world that I grew up in, I think I mock it now a great deal. I think Western Canadian males are into this macho posture which is grotesque. They're acting in a way which doesn't fit any societal need any more. Have you ever been in a beer parlour in Yellowknife? It's

grotesque. Those men are still hooked on the notion of a quest. They
have to ride out and win the favour of a woman. And the way you ride
out in this society is so grotesque that it's comic.

T: But except for *Badlands,* it seems only your male characters are
"riding out". Don't women have quests, too?

KROETSCH: I don't say women can't. Margaret Laurence with *The
Diviners* has written one of the greatest quest stories of our time. It's
also a quest which happens to take her through a series of males.

T: That allegorized world of women at home in their Yellowknife
kitchens while their men get plastered in the bar is a fair stereotype, I
agree. Do you think that men and women cannot exist in harmony?

KROETSCH: No, I don't think that at all. What I think is that our
roots are very much in small towns and rural communities. Now we
are an urban people. This creates problems we have to solve. We have
come into our glorious urban centres with a way of thinking that dates
back a generation. You come to Edmonton or Winnipeg and you find
the men are still sitting around in huge beer parlours, talking about
women in that naive way men will talk about women. At one time
this division between men and women might have been a very func-
tional distinction. Now it's harmful. The women who want to participate like men are forced into a kind of isolation.

T: So our problem is really how to become an urban people.

KROETSCH: Yes, that's really what is fascinating about Canada right
now. How in hell do we go about inventing these brand new cities?
Calgary, Edmonton and Vancouver are surely the three most interesting cities in Canada. Every one of them is full of people trying to
define a new version of urban. At the core of that new version there's
going to have to be a new definition of the male/female relationship.
I'm not writing about breaking the land any more. I'm writing about
urban people remembering that rural experience. How we remember it
conditions how we act!

Sinclair Ross already wrote about the terrible nature of a 1930's
prairie town in *As For Me and My House.* Why should I try to duplicate
that novel? I'm writing about people living in this rich society where
there's an incredible sense of money, yet people don't know how to
spend the stuff. They were taught to grub and save. Now they've got

all this wealth and freedom and they don't know what to buy or do. So they buy more beer. My friends won't even buy good liquor for me! [amused] That's what I'm writing about!

T: Using a backdrop of rural origins to discuss urban problems.

KROETSCH: Exactly. *What the Crow Said* is not the description of a real community on the Alberta/Saskatchewan border. It's a real community in our imaginations. Where nature and woman can possibly come together. Where an Indian reserve is at one end of town and a Hutterite colony at the other. The book is full of balances and halves which we have to put together. That's what intrigues me now. I'm intrigued by the idea of bringing back together not only male and female, but also the self with that total relationship with the world. Unfortunately the men are still more interested in doing the impossible like building their tower of ice to heaven.

T: A phallic tower of ice.

KROETSCH: Absolutely. And they can't get it high enough to satisfy themselves.

T: Are you at all optimistic about the chances of resolving these warring relationships between men and women?

KROETSCH: That's a serious question. And I don't know. There are days when I feel a little despair and I understand some of the women's lib philosophy that says to hell with men. I don't know if there are mass answers any more. Maybe that's one of the things we have to learn is to do away with the notion of a generalized answer.

That's why fiction is so important. That's why poetry is so important. The inherited system is breaking down. The intrusion into our society of leisure and money has broken down inherited role definitions. We have to work out new relationships. And art can point the way.

T: Let's bury the past and concentrate on the future?

KROETSCH: Yes, I'm against nostalgia. I remember what it was like on the farm. I picked roots and drove a tractor fourteen hours a day. I know how hard these jobs are to do. Mind you, I had a relatively easy life, don't let me fool you. But I did do those jobs. I know that our memory is not of Europe or high culture. Our memory is of work.

Just look at all the good writers on the West Coast who are using logging as a kind of metaphor for getting at an understanding of what they are.

T: I'd be interested to hear your opinion of Leslie Fiedler's "Huck Finn" theory. He has said men came to North America to flee European civilization and form a homosexual bond with a native male.

KROETSCH: I don't think it explains much in Canadian literature. And it's very glib about American literature. What I find much more intriguing is the power of women in Canadian writing. I would say our culture has a much larger percentage of good women writers than American culture. I don't know why. Maybe it's because Old Queen Victoria was back there as a role model.

T: Or else because feminism came to the fore at the same time that Canadian nationalism did.

KROETSCH: That could be part of it. But Nellie McClung and Catherine Parr Traill were back there long before that. Whatever it was, it's certainly healthy. I like the fact that a woman can now say I'm horny tonight. Or today. Or this morning. That's a great breakthrough in our society.

T: They're breaking out of their role definitions but they don't always find new ones to replace them.

KROETSCH: The same as men. In order to go west, a man had to define himself as an orphan, as an outlaw, as a cowboy. With those definitions, how can you marry a woman? How can you enter the house again? You have to lose that self-definition. That's the problem for the male. He must break his self-inflicted definition of maleness.

T: That would explain why so many of your characters are fatherless.

KROETSCH: Exactly.

T: Your novels are so riddled with significance that I can see the very conscious level of creation turning off a great many potential readers. Does that concern you?

KROETSCH: Yeah, it does. Because I think intellectual play is an important part of human pleasure. Why are we, in this culture, so afraid of intellectual pleasure? In a country which has produced such interesting political movements as NDP and Social Credit, why are we afraid to be caught thinking? For instance, right now I just thought of your pun "riddled." When something is riddled it's full of holes or else it's full of meanings. That was a great remark you made. And to me that's fun. That's often what poetry is to me. Intellectual play.

T: So you would never temper down the intellectual input into a novel to make it more accessible?

KROETSCH: No, I wouldn't. I think if I have failed somehow it's not because I'm too intellectual; it's because I haven't given my books enough emotional weight. I realize there's the darker side and sentimental side to life which I could play up more. I'm beginning to acknowledge these things.

T: The disadvantage of being so obsessed with meaning and therefore also imposing form is that it's hard for your readers to gain an impression that your characters are ever responsible for their own actions. There's always an awareness that you manipulate the strings. That's probably why *The Studhorse Man* has been your best received novel, because Hazard Lepage takes over the book from the author.

KROETSCH: Yeah. Since *The Studhorse Man* I've been much more interested in literature as an intellectual activity, as play. I say to my reader, watch me do this, this is impossible. Then I do it. And of course there's a danger in doing that too much.

T: Do you ever ask yourself how a kid from Heisler, Alberta developed the mind it took to write your novels?

KROETSCH: The question has intrigued me because it certainly wasn't a literary background. I grew up on a farm. But there was a great deal of talk in that environment. People were talking about each other and in that sense inventing each other. Uncles were into politics and loved to make speeches; old aunts were repositories of family history. So I grew up hearing a great deal of talk.

T: What sort of reading material were you exposed to?

KROETSCH: Well, the hired men often had very interesting books up in their rooms! I'd find their old pulp magazines and Zane Grey stories. And there were traveling libraries which came to the schools. This great big box of books would arrive and I remember the delight of plundering through the boxes which contained everything from best-sellers to the classics.

But I lived an incredibly free life on a huge farm. You had the run of the place. And you lived in your imagination.

T: What about those biblical overtones in your books. Were you religious?

KROETSCH: Well, I wasn't terribly into the Bible actually. My parents were Catholic but I was an agnostic at a very early age. I don't know why that was. I remember thinking they were putting me on with that stuff.

On the other hand I do like the kind of cosmology that religion offers. The Bible is a total story of the universe. I think that's where some of my interest in what I would call cosmology comes from. Those great yarns.

T: The obvious biblical influence that springs to mind is that litany of hockey players' names in *The Studhorse Man*. It's like a genealogy. Mahovolich begat Beliveau begat Howe etc.

KROETSCH: The catalogue of names is a great old poetic device. The radio announcers we heard were great at inventing hockey games. We only found out later that the hockey game wasn't at all the way Foster Hewitt described it. He was a fiction maker.

T: Was W.O. Mitchell an influence, too?

KROETSCH: I think he was the first Canadian writer to influence me. He gave me the realization that you could write about the Prairies. All the literature I had read was about people somewhere else. Then suddenly I read his *Jake and the Kid* stories and *Who Has Seen the Wind?* The educational system had insisted that all writers were dead. I think I was in grade twelve before a teacher told me there were living writers as well as Shelley and Keats and Byron.

T: Were you old enough for the Depression to affect your upbringing?

KROETSCH: Yeah, I was very much aware of Social Credit coming into power in 1935 when I was eight years old. The radio was the principal device Aberhart had struck on. He was a genius at using it. I remember the men especially listening to the radio, desperately hoping for an answer. And I remember my dad was a Liberal—I don't know if one should confess this nowadays anywhere west of Toronto! But he was sort of the last Liberal in the Battle River country. I remember the really vehement arguments that went on. I suppose I even had a sense of fright as a child to hear men arguing so vehemently.

T: That would account for *The Words of My Roaring.* Were you always aware of this friction between east and west or did that come later?

KROETSCH: Well, I was in a very ambiguous position in that my father had come from Ontario as a homesteader. He had dreamed as a kid of going out west and being a farmer. In a sense he became a fulfilled person. But he had left Ontario when he was seventeen so I grew up hearing about this Edenic world called Ontario. That contradicted my sense of politics because we always heard about these capitalists who were manipulating us from back there. I think I still have that very ambiguous sense of good and evil about the east.

T: You've written that the American and British experiences are concealed within the Canadian experience in the same way that Latin words often conceal Greek roots. Do you think the Prairies are resolving that conflict ahead of the rest of the country?

KROETSCH: I don't know. Certainly the Prairies do have one answer which came out of the Depression. The 30's wiped us all out. Right down to zero. So we started to invent a new concept of self and a new concept of society. Now I'm intrigued to watch that developing in the Prairies.

T: Do you ever look at how many votes Peter Lougheed gets and how many copies of *What the Crow Said* are sold and have doubts about the value of fiction?

KROETSCH: Yeah, it's a little scary sometimes. If you go by numbers, politicians are way ahead of the writers. But the politician as model is getting very tarnished. People aren't so easily fooled any more by a political leader whether it's a Lougheed or a Levesque. There's a terrible skepticism which has come into our culture. And it is really a dangerous kind of skepticism about the politician as hero. Even our hockey players are being undermined as models.

So, in a curious way, writers have reluctantly assumed a task here. Somebody like Ken Mitchell. Or Rudy Wiebe. Rudy Wiebe is a moralist and Ken Mitchell acts out a tremendous obligation to be a person from Saskatchewan. And Margaret Laurence takes on a kind of mother role for the country sometimes. Isn't that interesting? They don't sell many books but they take on all this weight.

T: You share with Rudy Wiebe a feeling that the natural construction of sentences needs to be altered to jar the reader's equilibrium from time to time. Is it possible, since we're so bombarded by the imitative realism of television, that realism in literature might eventually become counter-productive to art?

KROETSCH: Yeah, it has become counter-productive. I find the concept of realism incredibly boring. We can talk for an hour because our culture has sentence patterns and we fill in the slots with words. But I think there's a danger in not learning new models of sentences. Rudy and I fight about the notion of what realism is and we tamper with grammar in different ways, but I think both of us want to dislocate perception.

T: To construct your novels into intellectual mazes, do you have to map everything out beforehand so you don't get lost?

KROETSCH: No, you have to leave room for discovery as you go. One of the pleasures of reading is surprise. To get surprises happening, often you have to be surprising yourself. That's part of what I'm writing about anyway. Metamorphosis. How things get transformed.

T: Do you have to be turned on to write?

KROETSCH: No, I can write every day when I'm really working. Waiting to be turned could just be an excuse not to write. However, you do have to understand when not to write. Because I believe the body writes the book, not just the mind. How your whole body feels is important. When you wake up in the morning refreshed with that incredible burst of energy, just out of a dream state, you're rediscovering the world. You're being reborn. It's not just intellect that writes the book.

T: Would you ever wake up in the morning and say, "My being is not feeling well today. If I sit down and write today, I will not write well"?

KROETSCH: Yes, I would. [laughing] We call that a hangover.

Female

SYLVIA FRASER

Like Kroetsch, Sylvia Fraser has primarily sought to expurgate from society those conditioned attitudes of and about her sex which she sees as negative by means of making the unconscious become conscious.

Pandora *(1972) and* The Candy Factory *(1975) are incisive probes into childhood and adult mores respectively.*

A Casual Affair *(1978) delineates unconscious motivations of two extramarital lovers with the aid of original fairy tales.*

The Emperor's Virgin *(1980) is a historical romance equating social norms in Roman times as a possible allegory to today.*

Although Fraser's latter two books have not received the enthusiastic critical responses merited by the former, she is one of Canada's more exacting spokeswomen on the psychology of contemporary relationships. Extensive experience as a journalist following her graduation from the University of Western Ontario in 1957 has afforded her a wide, well-travelled perspective of sexual politics beyond female chauvinism.

Sylvia Fraser was born and raised in Hamilton. She lives in Toronto.

photo: Alan Twigg

T: Do you ever regard yourself as a "woman novelist"?

FRASER: Well, there was a time when it was considered an insult to be labelled a woman novelist, but now I almost would consider it flattering, because I think women today are miles ahead of men in terms of emotional health and awareness. Essentially, it's the result of the women's movement. Women have done a lot of introspecting and it shows in themselves and in their relationships. By comparison, I think men are nowhere...I'm sorry.

T: Do you think *A Casual Affair* could have been written by a man?

FRASER: That's an unanswerable question. Nobody else would write my books. A book is as individual as a fingerprint.

T: But do you think there is a woman's perspective as opposed to a man's perspective?

FRASER: A culturally determined one, certainly. However, as a novelist, I have no self-consciousness about writing from the point of view of a male character—or someone who is rich, or poor, or young, or old, or of a different race—because one thing I learned as a journalist, from listening and listening and listening to other people, is that the patterns of humanness under these important differences are much more powerful. It isn't necessary to identify with a character to understand them, or to have compassion for them.

T: Why do you think men are less healthy than women?

FRASER: In my generation, which came of age in the fifties, the ideal for North American males was that of the super-achiever. That pattern was broken, to a certain extent, in the 60's and 70's. Now that jobs are scarce, men of the new generation are becoming conservative again, but I don't think that women are quite ready yet to give up the freedom they got a whiff of.

T: I agree that the sociological climate of any country is basically determined by the economic situation. Like in the 60's everybody could afford to hitchhike across Europe reading Herman Hesse novels. But I can't agree that men are necessarily more conservative than women. The males I know are actively fighting against that. Do you think there might be a difference between east and west?

FRASER: Well, Toronto is certainly very achievement oriented. Men that I know who are, say, ten years older than I, which means they are into their fifties, are coming to the end of their achieving lives, and they are finding either that they made it and so what, or that they haven't made it and they're never going to. They go through what is popularly called the male menopause, but the ironic thing is that I know almost no women who have a menopause any more—or let's say that it's never mentioned; it's just a physical thing that's dealt with privately, with a few pills or something. But the number of men I know who are suffering from confusion and depression is staggering. I believe it has to do with having been conned. The best men of my generation were conned into the achievement thing and now they're reaping the limitations of that, whereas the women I know who went for careers—and I am one of them—were not so singleminded about it. They did not trade off their personal lives for success.

So responses to emotional problems are different. When women are blocked on the level of feelings, they go for detail—they make endless lists of things to do, and make complicated little things with their hands. When men are blocked, they go for structure, which is what our government and business bureaucracies are all about.

T: Do you think it's easier to have a liberated marriage these days?

FRASER: Yes, but it's always difficult for two equal people to try to live together. The most encouraging pattern I see emerging has to do with couples recognizing cycles—it's your turn and then it's my turn. A man runs with a career and making money for a while, then maybe he's tired of that and wants to have a sabbatical, or maybe even change jobs. Then the woman has a chance to be aggressive about her career. Humans have both a feminine and a masculine side and it's dangerous to permanently repress either the one or the other. That's the old sexual stereotype, where he was the breadwinner and she the breadbaker. However, as a cautionary note, I should also say that I think it unwise for couples who marry today to expect, as an article of faith, that they will remain married to each other all their lives. That may happen, and it's wonderful when it does, but I no longer think it should be an expectation or a requirement—then it just becomes another piece of baggage.

T: Has your life been affected by feminism?

FRASER: Dramatically, in that it changed the world in which I live, though all my major "feminist" decisions had been made before that word was a popular part of everyday lingo. You see, I came of age in the Doris Day era of Togetherness, when everyone was supposed to want 3.4 children and a two-car garage. Though I did get married, I never wanted children. I didn't want suburbia. I wanted to travel and to have a career, though I didn't know what that career would be. By the time most of our friends had two children and were thinking of taking out a second mortgage the men began to get restless and worried and they became jealous of what they thought to be my footloose, carefree life. They would get drunk at parties and they would come lurching over at me and they would tell me that I was selfish, that I was depriving my husband, even that I was a female castrator. The feminist movement changed all that. The best of those men became more sensitive to what women like myself were about, and the others at least learned to shut up about it. So you see, the feminist movement took the pressure off of me. Ironically, it made it possible for me to be more feminine, less aggressive, because nobody was attacking me any more, and I could relax. So, I've always supported the feminist movement though I'm not politically active. It doesn't suit the life and work of a writer to have too strong a political bias.

T: Do you think extra-marital affairs are, more often than not, to use your own phrase, "venturing into emotional quicksand"? Obviously each individual case is different, but can you generalize?

FRASER: I accept the idea of many kinds of lifestyles, both inside and outside of marriage. It depends what a couple's marriage contract is. People who married out of the 40's and 50's were supposed to be mating for life and promising fidelity. That's not necessarily true now. As for myself, I would like to see the locks come off sex. I would like to see a time when people regard sex as a need, in the same terms that they regard eating. To extend the food metaphor—just imagine that if, when you married, you promised that you would eat only with the person you married for the rest of your life, and that it would be disloyal and immoral to eat with someone else. Therefore, whether your mate is hungry or not, that person must eat with you or you can't eat. Follow that through and think of the tyranny of making somebody eat with you even if he isn't hungry. If he doesn't eat with you, you must go hungry. If he eats with you when he doesn't want to, so you can eat, he may find that sickening. Also, he's committed to eating the same kinds of food you eat. Resentment builds up on both sides. The sexual prohibitions have forced us into extremely unnatural and convoluted positions.

All this has to be unlearned for a healthy society. Understand, I am in no way discarding commitment—that's a different matter. Also, sexual fidelity may be a preference throughout a marriage or for a period of time, but I can't see it as a requirement or an expectation. Mind you, it's very difficult for people to change their lives in midstream. What I am talking about is the future. In the meantime people have to do what they have to do, and of all solutions I think "cheating", and especially the double standard, is the least successful, but I guess that's the only way masses of people today can hold their lives together.

T: That whole thing of possessing one another is pretty deeply ingrained in all of us. It seems to me those changes you talk about are a pretty long way down the line for the majority of people.

FRASER: I'm more hopeful. It was impossible to predict the 60's from the 50's. Analysts usually relate that change to the invention of the pill. Maybe there's another invention just down the road that will free us from our sexual juggernaut. I'm in awe of how fast change does happen these days.

T: Yes, I often think of what it must be like for someone who is eighty years old to be alive today, to come from horse-and-buggy days to this.

FRASER: Well, that's one reason why I write the kind of books I do. The main thrust of all my work is an attempt to make the unconscious conscious—that's the revolution we're all involved in today, I think. Why the self-help business has become a large industry. We're in a period of transition, and people are confused.

T: What is the transition—from where to where?

FRASER: One of the major differences between a human and an ape is the human's ability to absorb information. Just think of how much a child has to absorb before the age of five just to cope on a minimum level—how to walk, talk, eat, use the toilet, manners, etc. So much of this learning is absorbed unconsciously, and this unconscious programming was vital for human survival. All that worked very well as long as adults were bringing up children to lead the same kind of lives that they led. For example, a blacksmith who brings up his son to be a blacksmith—to live in the same town, to marry a girl just like his mom, etc. As long as lives were static from generation to generation, the programming you received from your parents was of prime value.

What's happening now is that we're all out of sync. We're being programming unconsciously by our parents to live lives that no longer exist by the time we are ready to lead them. And since our parents were out of sync too, the problem compounds and will continue to compound as the pace of social change accelerates, unless we learn to de-program ourselves. That's what underlies many of the new therapies—most of them coming out of the States. It's a remarkable revolution, and one absolutely necessary if people wish to make life choices based on real possibilities instead of following blind habit in the name of moral values.

T: If the United States is a remarkable nation because it's at the forefront of "deprogramming" itself, why is it on a per capita basis, there are far more leading female writers in Canada than in the States?

FRASER: Yes, I'm quite interested in that. The energy of the women's movement in the States went into non-fiction and a powerful polemic. The important names in the States are non-fiction writers—Betty Friedan, Kate Millett, and so on. The female fiction-writers are only now just catching up. In Canada, the energy of the women's movement has gone into a flowering of fiction writing.

T: But why?

FRASER: Well, I can only speculate. I suppose it's a difference in national character. The United States is a great pragmatic nation. It's a how-to nation. Americans are always taking surveys, compiling statistics, taking polls. They're always measuring things in the interest of some sort of factual truth. In my opinion, it's a nation that overvalues fact. Fiction tends to be regarded on the one hand as unreal, therefore escapist and trivial, or as being elitist—a snob exercise of the intelligentsia. Now I happen to regard fiction, at its best, as greater truth—which is the European and, to some extent, the Canadian view. So it's a difference in national preference and national psyche.

T: Is that difference reflected in the publishing industry in general then?

FRASER: It has been. What is happening now in Canadian publishing is that we are being hit ten or twenty years late by the paperback revolution. That means mass marketing and therefore a reverence for mass tastes. In the States 90% of the people who sit down to write books are attempting to write commercial books. In Canada, till recently, the overwhelming number of authors were attempting to write seriously. This marks no particular national virtue but simply reflected the fact that there was no mass market available to Canadians, therefore there was no temptation. Now in the States publishing is essentially a branch of the entertainment business. Books written to entertain do not challenge the status quo. They amuse, they reassure, they ingratiate. They provide an escape from life. Serious books focus on life. They probe, they examine. Therefore anyone who reads them runs the risk of being provoked or disturbed, as well as enriched. When a book is judged, by publisher and public, only for its entertainment value, then the serious writer is heavily penalized.

T: Who do you see as your audience?

FRASER: When writing, I don't think about the audience—or let us say that in the past I never have, though the pressure is certainly on now to do so. I mean, I always hope to find an audience, and I don't deliberately set out to alienate people, but in writing I have a very strong idea of what I want to say and I'm willing to do my best to make that as accessible and as popular as I can through the use of craft, but there is a point beyond which I can't divert or dilute what I'm saying and still say the same thing.

My books are full of what I consider hard and challenging truths. Therefore my audience is whomever is willing to take the time and the effort to be a creative reader. To be a creative reader is to participate in the reading of a book with head and heart and all your sensitivities, instead of just letting the words sort of slide through your mind to fill up time, or to collect some facts.

T: To go back to the title of your last book—do you think there is such a thing as a "casual affair"?

FRASER: I think affairs—and I'm talking here about secret affairs—are usually destructive. To begin with, they are usually secret because someone is cheating on someone else, so right there they are surrounded by guilt, lies, hypocrisy. But even within the relationship, there are severe limitations. To a secret affair, you can smuggle in only a part of yourself. Now, it may be that both persons bring the best part of his or herself, in which case the relationship may be idyllic. But how long can that go on; and how often does that happen?

Take the characters in *A Casual Affair.* She's in a state of hysteria most of the time, she's obsessed. Whatever maturity she has, whatever skills as an adult, whatever friends she has are unavailable to her, because she is isolated in the secret relationship. He is a man of considerable professional accomplishment, and a set of traditional values, but these are not what he brings to the relationship. What he brings are his terror of intimacy and his need to play with fire while still being able to control the blaze. Now this can happen in a relationship that is not clandestine, but the real world and ordinary events and the support of friends provides some perspective. In a secret relationship that is not going well the two people are in free fall. Under such circumstances, in our society, it is usually the woman who is most vulnerable because the man, by tradition, is the aggressor and has control of the action. If he has an active professional life and is married, then he will be virtually unreachable for large chunks of time. She is pushed into the position of distorting her life to wait for the call. If she is normally independent this will be doubly demoralizing.

T: So she says to him about his previous mistresses, "I'll bet there was an oversupply of nurses, secretaries and stewardesses. All women in the service professions who couldn't threaten your position."

FRASER: Yes. A man who is emotionally insecure will usually choose someone he can easily control or victimize. The potential for exploitation, one way or another, is naked. It's the pits.

Matrona

DOROTHY LIVESAY

Dorothy Livesay is the senior stateswoman of Canadian poetry. Twice recipient of the Governor General's Award (for Day and Night, *1944 and* Poems for People, *1947), she has always maintained that art need not be propagandist but that an artist must be a "social realist" and ensure that all work is commonly accessible.*

Emancipation of women. Internment of Japanese Canadians during World War II. The Spanish Civil War. Persecution of the poor. Racism perpetrated upon Canadian Indians. These are some of the themes that have prompted her to rattle her literary sabre in the 30's, 40's and 50's, consciously employing poetry to broadcast anti-capitalist, pro-feminist sympathies.

Later, as songs of innocence (early lyricism, radical poetical idealism) have ebbed and songs of experience (intimately private reflections) have begun to flow, Livesay's poetry has expanded beyond its proletarian focus to encompass mature wit, psychological incisiveness and deeply-felt spiritual concerns. The Unquiet Bed *(1967),* Collected Poems: The Two Seasons *(1972) and* Ice Age *(1975) are some of the major books which have subsequently contained much of her best poetry.*

Born in Winnipeg in 1909 and educated in Toronto and Paris, Livesay's often turbulent career spans over half a century and eighteen books. She has lived and worked throughout most parts of Canada, presently dividing her residency between cottages at Winnipeg Beach and Galiano Island.

photo: Eleanor Wachtel

T: Could you explain the significances of the title of your recent book of memoirs, *Right Hand Left Hand, a True Life of the Thirties?*

LIVESAY: I come from a middle class family—WASP, I suppose—and yet I was very interested in the other side of the town, the other side of the fence. Early on I became a social worker and got involved in how people lived, especially during the Depression. I saw how the unemployed lived so often I would have to take a stand on the left, then go home to a very "right" situation. Also there's the Biblical phrase, "the right hand knows not what the left hand doeth."

T: Plus you have a reference in the book to right and left hands when a boss reprimands a female worker. . .

LIVESAY: Yes, I found that little excerpt while going through my papers of the times. It described something I had seen in a factory. A woman was advised to turn the lever with her right hand and pick up all the mess with her left.

T: In the 30's it must have been more difficult for a woman to take an activist role outside the family than it is now. Where do you think you got your strength for your non-conformity?

LIVESAY: Well, there have always been women rebels. But I don't think there have been very many women revolutionaries. For that I would think you have to be a militant since childhood, which I never could be. My father called himself a radical, a man who went "to the root of things." Being a newspaper man involved with sending a news service across the country, he'd never committed himself to the Liberals or the Conservatives. But he was interested in the developments of the CCF. He had an open mind until I went out on the picket lines!

T: Do you think it's more difficult to create social change nowadays because a class structure is not so obvious?

LIVESAY: Yes. What we'd hoped for was that the soldiers would come back from the second World War and be ready to change society. Instead they were very accepting of society. The working class that we used to think of has become very much a middle class, therefore they are afraid of change.

T: It seems to me that liberalism dominates our age but it's unprogressive because it's basically just individualism. How do you feel about social change for the 80's?

LIVESAY: Well, when you get to be seventy, every decade seems to be swinging one way, then the other. *Plus ça change, plus c'est la même chose.* Certainly, though, there's been a great liberalization in the areas of sex. What we did surreptitiously as university students in the 30's, is now all completely in the open.

But as a whole, I would say North America is still very reactionary. In Europe there's a great deal of this splitting up, of wanting to be independent over there, amongst the Bretons, the Basques and what have you. It's happening in England with the Welsh and the Scottish. This is an age not of disintegration but of refraction, of splitting off and becoming culturally and linguistically aware of oneself. In Belgium there are now three different languages. So I don't find it disturbing that this is happening in Canada, too, even though others do. It may be that Quebec can move much faster towards a socialist society than the rest of Canada.

T: When you were a student in Paris you wrote, "I don't see any way out but the death and burial of capitalism." Forty-seven years later, do you still believe that?

LIVESAY: It's taking much longer than we thought, but of course it is happening all over the world. Capitalism has taken on many practical socialist ideas.

T: You've always been a great believer in proletarian literature or writing which is readily accessible to everybody. Do you think Canadian writers are adequately responding to their social obligations?

LIVESAY: No, not at all. We have no writers like Sartre or Simone de Beauvoir who believe that the writer in any country must be committed to seek better things for humanity. If he doesn't speak out then he's committed to reaction.

T: Certainly there must be some writers whom you read nowadays and admire, whom you could recommend to other people?

LIVESAY: I had high hopes for the grass roots poets in Canada like Milton Acorn, Al Purdy and Pat Lane. And Pat Lowther was certainly very much a committed poet before her murder. And Tom Wayman. It would seem to me that these poets and those that follow with them are speaking out, but there isn't anything like the commitment of the writers in the 30's. We were so stirred up by what was happening in Spain. The takeovers by Mussolini and Hitler created an anti-Franco situation in Canada which was very strong.

T: We have lots of capable wordslingers, but very few people are concerned with international matters.

LIVESAY: It's pitiful what some of the young writers are doing. They are completely ignoring what's happening in this world, which is the threat of nuclear war. But it isn't so with the youngest group. I've been in contact with students in Ottawa and Manitoba who are nineteen and twenty and they seem very concerned.

T: In the 30's, when you were writing for *New Frontier,* you were more consciously propagandist in your poems than compared to the work in your most recent collection, *Ice Age.*

LIVESAY: Well, in those days you didn't have any mass media. You didn't have people participating so much in the level of say, folk songs or jazz. Now the scene is changed. Beginning with the 60's, in Canada and perhaps around the world, the poet is now asked to come and speak to musical gatherings or pop weekends. There was never any of this in the 30's. Of course we tried to join in on picket lines and have mass chants that we read, but it was somewhat schematic, or unreal. What's very good today is that poets are now part of popular art. I don't spurn popular art. Many songsters are very good poets.

T: In your poem, "Last Letter," you write: "I am certain now, in love, women are more committed." Do you think that opinion will ever change?

LIVESAY: It's going to be very tough. Young men are having an awful time adjusting to the idea that a woman is a person, completely free to do what she pleases. I have confessions from young men who tell me their problems with their girlfriends. I sympathize with them, but we're absolutely flooded with television and magazines which work against change. The consumer market for women's products is appalling! Girls must have more and more dresses for more and more occasions to attract men. How are you ever going to break that down?

T: It seems there's a freedom now not to conform, but still the majority is conforming.

LIVESAY: Up to a certain age, they do wear blue jeans. But a time comes when most of them change.

T: Speaking of ages, let's talk a little about your latest book of poetry. Is the title *Ice Age* intended to have personal and political implications?

LIVESAY: And human. I had been reading, as we all have, of the possible changes in our world climate. The ice age is moving down again. This is a symbol of what's happening to humanity psychologically and spiritually. And of course personally, as one is approaching seventy, one begins to sense that this will be the end. All I have said will turn to ice.

T: Your style as a poet has not fluctuated a great deal since you began writing in the 30's. How consciously have you been concerned with manipulation of technique?

LIVESAY: I used to be very conscious of punctuation. All my early poetry was very carefully punctuated. But I think my style changed when I came back from Africa in '63. That was the year the Black Mountain thing descended on Vancouver. Earle Birney brought Robert Creeley and Robert Duncan and that whole crowd. I heard them that summer and met Phyllis Webb and all the Tish people. But I got bored with the way they were all talking the same way. Lionel Kearns would use a metronome finger as he read. But I did come around to thinking that capitals at the beginning of a line were unnecessary. So I started arranging my lines as much as I could according to the breath. [George] Bowering helped me quite a bit on that. But I'm conservative. I don't want to make it look far out, like bissett and these people.

T: Many poets nowadays write poetry which is meant to be read aloud. Do you keep that in mind when you write?

LIVESAY: If I'm alone, I'll go over a poem aloud. I'll pace it out. I'll find that a particular stress or syllable doesn't work there at all.

TWIGG: You mentioned at an SFU Heritage seminar on poetry in the 30's that P.K. Page had never given a poetry reading until the 60's. Did you undergo a problem of adjustment becoming a poet as performer?

LIVESAY: Well, I remember the Ford Foundation once invited Canadian poets to come from all over the country to Kingston to discuss the literary scene for a weekend. The government was concerned with setting up the Canada Council. This would be around '56. Between these long sessions with publishers on the state of publishing, we organized little poetry circles. Layton and Dudek were there, people of that sort. I was asked to read. I read a recent poem that hadn't been published called "Lament," about the death of my father, I was absolutely terrified. I believed in the poem before I read it, but while I was reading it didn't believe in it at all. It didn't make much of an impression. Not it's probably the most anthologized of my poems, that and "Bartok." But it was definitely not an easy time to read aloud.

T: Did you get much support from the CBC?

LIVESAY: I don't know when I was first asked to read for the CBC. I had a long standing fight with Bob Weaver who was doing *Anthology*. He insisted that the poetry be read by an actress. I couldn't stand their women actresses. They read it all wrong. I didn't think my voice was that bad. Some of us had a ten year fight with Weaver to allow the poet to read it his own way. They swore an actor could do it better. Part of it was they had to pay the actor, to help them survive. Now it's pretty well the rule that a poet reads his own poems.

T: Most of the power of your poetry comes from your ability to make the personal reflect the universal. Do you ever consciously write poetry as a social function, starting with the universal deliberately?

LIVESAY: My earlier documentaries were full of immediate passion, like *Day and Night*. It just sprang out of my experience. But *Call My People Home* was planned. I had to present what happened to those people. So I did a lot of research beforehand. The same is true of an Indian play I wrote for the CBC called *Momatkom*. This was in the 50's, long before *The Ecstasy of Rita Joe*. I was dealing with these radical conflicts way back. In '45 I was writing a poem about Louis Riel. I had to get a Guggenheim grant for that because there were no Canadian grants. Well, I missed getting the grant and couldn't finish the poem. It's now called "The Prophet of the New World." Now suddenly there's nothing but Louis Riel poems, plays and operas! [laughing]

T: Do you ever look back on things you wrote perhaps forty years ago and want to change them?

LIVESAY: No, I've objected very much to W.H. Auden changing his poems about Spain. I think it's dreadful, sinful. Because that was the feeling at the moment and that's what made the poem. Earle Birney's done the same thing. He's revised and I think it's wicked.

T: Birney was a Trotskyite when you knew him aside from his poetry.

LIVESAY: Yes. We were all against Hitler during the war. That's how I got to know Earle best. He brought Esther home from London and they had a son born about when my children were born. We met often on picnics and literary evenings. But I had known him even in his Trotskyite days. Earle at that time wasn't a poet at all, as far as I knew him. He was a Canadian interested in literature while he was becoming a Trotskyite. Harold Cassidy, who is the father of Michael Cassidy of the Ontario NDP, asked us to come together and talk politics.

Then Earle corresponded with me during the war from Europe. We were always quite close. I dedicated the poem *West Coast* to him. He represented the poem's central figure, the intellectual, who didn't know what to do. So he finally went down to the shipyards to see what that was all about. Then he enlisted. We've had terrible schisms since.

T: Generally do you have a low opinion of Canadian critics?

LIVESAY: They're myopic. They have no vision.

T: Has reading the criticism of your work ever been a learning experience for you?

LIVESAY: I don't think I had any serious critical work done on me in the earlier years. The whole group that centred around Frye ignored me completely. You won't find any of them even looking at my books.

T: Is the Canadian writing scene more fragmented than ever?

LIVESAY: Well, I don't think we ever were fragmented because we were small enough to be a company, a community of writers. We all knew each other. Now it's just become more regional. You have communities in five regions but you don't have a unification for the country. That's significant for the future.

In a remark he made in the introduction of Emily Carr's first book,

Ira Dilworth said she was absolutely rooted in her region, in the history of B.C. and Indian life. But because she was dedicated to that region she's an international genius. It's true of Hardy; it's true of Balzac. The more you really absorb a locale or community, the more international you become.

T: Do you think the Crossing Frontiers conference in Banff [1978] crossed any frontiers between American and Canadian?

LIVESAY: It proved there was a difference. It gave us quite a lift, in fact. We thought, "We are real! We have an identity!" I felt that tremendously.

T: Even though the gathering was organized to throw some light on our similarities?

LIVESAY: Yes, it was a great thing. Canadians identified with the western American experience, but they felt ours was different. The great thing is that Canadians are writing from their roots. A lot of young people are doing this in the West, on the Prairies, and in the Maritimes. The urban experience is common, I suppose, to all North America. So urban writers in Toronto and Montreal don't seem to have much to say that's new or real.

T: Are there poems of yours which you think will stand the test of time?

LIVESAY: Some poems have meaning now and some poems have meaning for always. A poem like "Bartok and the Geraniums" might have meaning for always. It's a male/female poem, but it's also about art and nature. Then there are poems about women's plight. And perhaps a poem which predicts the androgynous future, "On Looking Into Henry Moore." I think he was androgynous. He saw the humanity of man and woman, the complete thing, which I've been striving to express. I also think in the Canadian scene that my documentaries will have importance. *Day and Night* and *Call My People Home* are being put into anthologies quite frequently.

T: Has your writing been affected by your earlier work as a journalist?

LIVESAY: Yes, I think that helps. I hated newspaper work because you have to do such dirty things to people. My year of apprenticeship on *The Winnipeg Tribune* was painful. I had to compromise people to get my story. I hated that. Then I worked for *The Star.* I sent articles

about France and then after the war I did a series on post-war rehabili-
tation in England. I was freer then, but as a younger reporter you
simply had to get a story out of people. I hated that.

T: I don't think there's any particular route one should follow to
become a writer. However, would you recommend a career in
journalism as opposed to the university route?

LIVESAY: Both things that I did, journalism and social work, have
been significant. But I actually would have liked to have been an
anthropologist. There are a number of anthropologists who are also
poets and writers. That sort of area is far better than going into
English. The last thing I'd tell people to do would be to go through as
an English major. I took languages, French and Italian, and that was
far more broadening. But then I'd read all the English literature at
home in my teens. I tell every single promising poet, "Don't go
through and be an English major. It kills your poetry." That's my
great message. [laughing]

T: Yet you were in Vancouver teaching a course on woman writers.
Which are your favorites?

LIVESAY: I've always tremendously admired Virginia Woolf,
Katherine Mansfield and Edith Sitwell. Recently, Doris Lessing,
Rebecca West, Simone de Beauvoir. I don't know American writers
very well at all. I've had to close myself off from that. I'm doing so
much Canadian reading.
    Canadian women writers have been neglected. All the best and first
Canadian women fiction writers have come from the West. The
Canadian novel had its roots in the West, certainly not in Montreal or
Ontario. But when Mordecai Richler came to give a talk in Alberta,
he hadn't read anything by Frederick Philip Grove. He didn't know he
existed. It's that kind of incredible insularity that I've been fighting
against. Emily Carr's style was utterly unusual and she had a brilliant
mind. And the other B.C. writer, Ethel Wilson, also had a totally
individual style. But all people think of back east is Marian Engel or
Margaret Atwood. These weren't the first, and they're not the best.
But I should mention that I have not read as much as I should have of
French Canadian women writers. Gabrielle Roy is absolutely a top
novelist. And Anne Hebert.

T: But it seems like the Canadian theatre scene, as a whole, is coming
along well?

LIVESAY: It's the healthiest. It's not looking at its navel. That's the worst thing about the poets in this country; they're writing from an ivory tower. Even the young ones. All that Tish group is ivory tower in my view.

T: Are there major projects on your mind that you're worried about not getting done?

LIVESAY: Well, I've done a lot of work on the first woman poet in Canada, who was a Confederation poet, Isabella Valancy Crawford. She was an Irish child brought to Canada in 1855 or 1858. She was a remarkably visionary poet. I discovered and edited an entirely new manuscript that had never been seen. There are now about five people writing theses on her.

The other writing I would like to do is some work on popular women writers like Pauline Johnson, Mazo de la Roche and Nellie McClung, who were neglected and spurned by the critics. There needs to be a whole critical book looking at popular writers in Canada. Their work laid the basis for more mature work like Margaret Laurence's. I don't think a mature novel can arise in a country unless there's been a lot of popular writing as a base.

T: Certainly one of the signs of maturity in a country's literature is when all books do not have to aspire to be *War and Peace*.

LIVESAY: Yes! What's wrong with the ballads of Robert Service? It's a genre. It's great fun. A lasting literature has to have a base from which to grow. She who went before Margaret Laurence was Nellie McClung.

T: And Dorothy Livesay. That must be a good feeling, to know you helped lay the foundation for what others are now writing.

LIVESAY: Yes, it is. But I've never felt that the poetry belonged to me. I am the vessel through which it comes. My tentacles are out recording. What's coming through has been for everybody.

Femina

SUSAN MUSGRAVE

Susan Musgrave is not unlike the foreign correspondent on the evening news who reassures us that the rest of the world is indeed in chaos. Subjective poems as precious and desperate as notes in bottles have brought notoriety in Canada and abroad.

Her books of poetry are Songs of the Sea-Witch *(1970)*, Entrance of the Celebrant *(1972)*, Grave-Dirt and Selected Strawberries *(1973)*, Gullband *(1974, children)*, The Impstone *(1976)*, Becky Swan's Book *(1977)*, Selected Strawberries and Other Poems *(1977)*, Kiskatinaw Songs *(1978, with Sean Virgo) and* A Man To Marry, A Man To Bury *(1979)*.

The Charcoal Burners *(1980) is her first novel, a dream-like vision of rituals in a primeval society.*

Born in 1951, Musgrave grew up in Victoria. She has lived in California, Hawaii, Ireland, England and the Queen Charlotte Islands. Presently she lives near Sidney, Vancouver Island.

photo: Alan Twigg

T: What are the types of poems that get the most response from people?

MUSGRAVE: The love poems. I met a woman recently who had carried around one of my love poems for six months.

T: Yet you can still question writing as a profession for yourself.

MUSGRAVE: Well, it's hard for me to get any vicarious enjoyment out of what I've written. Once I've written it, that's it. It's just there to be found for someone else. It doesn't have much to do with me any more. My problem being the creator is that if a poem is really strong, it doesn't need me any more. It's like giving birth constantly, and constantly weaning.

That's not to say I'm only some sort of medium. But I don't feel I can take credit very long for something that I have written. People quote great lines of poetry without even knowing who the poet was. That's sort of how poetry works.

T: Does that mean you would write to create those special lines as much as special poems?

MUSGRAVE: I think so. It's *the* line. Individual lines stick in my head. Every poem usually has a couple of lines in it that are better than the rest.

T: You mean like "Someday we will meet in Warsaw". [laughter]

MUSGRAVE: Yes. It's funny how poetry works. Around New Year's I wrote a poem about looking back at what had happened in the last ten years. Ten years before I had been in hospital on New Year's Eve. "My father rocked in his chair, unable to share his last breath with anyone. That was years ago when we didn't think he would live much longer. He still drives down the highway to see me." When I showed the poem to a friend, what stuck out for her was the line about my father driving down the highway to see me. For me, that is the whole poem. But I can't figure out why. That is what is so great and so tricky about poetry. To get that to happen. You can't really try. It just has to fall into place.

T: When you publish a book, do you wonder what people are going to say about it because you're wondering yourself about it?

MUSGRAVE: Oh, yes. I never really know. I put a book together but I don't have much idea what I'm attempting it to be. One of my problems has always been this approach. If it works, then it's great. If it doesn't work, it's not so great. In my novel, because I didn't set out to do anything, all the way through I had to figure out what was going on. I knew I had this good idea for a novel—but it was like a jigsaw puzzle where I was always the missing piece.

T: But art requires form. My E.M. Forster guide to novel writing says so, so it must be true.

MUSGRAVE: Yes. I'm sure that's right. I can see there's a lot more for me to learn about prose than poetry. These days I'm thinking more and more in terms of prose. Even the poems I'm writing are becoming more narrative. I want to be accessible, at least to myself. I figure if I am accessible to myself, then I will be accessible to other people. I admire writers who are accessible.

T: These days it seems the reader very often has to exert almost as much energy reading a poem as a poet takes to write it. Some of your poems I totally blank out on.

MUSGRAVE: I do that all the time with poetry, too. Sometimes it can just be the way it looks on the page. But I figure, go on, read something else. There are certainly enough good things already written to choose from.

T: Would you agree much of your poetry functions basically on the level of dream?

MUSGRAVE: Yes. A lot of poems come right out of dreams. Lately I've been especially interested in how falling in love, or being in love with someone, is very much like being on a dream level. It attacks the same areas of my head as a poem. It's a kind of vague hit of something, of adrenalin, of psychic energy. I just don't know what it is. But it's all connected. I'm sure that's where the term "dream lover" comes from. It's so much like being in a dream. I know that sounds like a cliche, but in my work I use dreams and being in love the same way. I get the same kind of inspiration from it. It's quite unconscious.

T: The talent of your poetry then is trusting your instincts to such a pure extent that whatever you write cannot be dishonest.

MUSGRAVE: It's all done with mirrors. [laughing] A lot of my early poems, I don't even understand any more. I get quite embarrassed when people come up to me and ask what's this poem all about. I just haven't a clue. In fact, I end up thinking that they're badly written and I obviously missed the point. I trusted the vision, the spirit and the mood and all those things, but I missed what I was really trying to communicate.

T: Maybe you didn't know enough about how to properly shape a poem.

MUSGRAVE: Yes. Eliot, when he was older, said he didn't understand *The Wasteland* any more. He thought it was a case of having had too much to say and not the understanding of how to say it. I think that really applies to me when I was nineteen or twenty. I had an amazing amount in me to write about but I wasn't ever sure really how to do it.

T: Nevertheless, the level of maturity of your first book is really quite exceptional. If you hadn't gone through that exceptional experience of spending time in a psychiatric ward, would that maturity have come so quickly?

MUSGRAVE: I don't know. I feel that I was more mature then than I am now. I had some sort of wisdom but I couldn't cope with it very well. Obviously—because I kept going mad all the time. Which may have meant I was very wise but I wasn't quite sure how to handle that!

T: Do you get hostile reactions from people because of your witch persona?

MUSGRAVE: Oh, I think so. Yes. People try to make it hokey. They try to make it nonsense. More blood and darkness. More preoccupation with morbidity and death. They try to attach words to it that lessen the impact of what I'm trying to talk about. They don't tackle the essential ideas of, I suppose, spirituality. Where could they start?

T: Because we have so little training for that.

MUSGRAVE: Yes. Even people who respond positively cannot articulate why they like my poems. It's like what you were saying yesterday, the pioneer mentality is all hard work, make money and get ourselves set. We don't want anybody undermining that. We don't want anybody saying maybe there's more to it than just that. Maybe you should just sit and look at the mountains for a day. People can't be told that. It upsets what they've come here to do. So people walk out of a bill bissett poetry reading shaking their heads, like we were saying.

T: Yes. There ought to be a book analyzing Canadian literature from a spiritual poverty angle.

MUSGRAVE: *"Canadian Literature: A Christian Interpretation."*

T: Other countries are saturated with a sense of acceptance of spiritual reality so in Canada we need people like Marian Engel writing books like *Bear.* And we need bill bissett.

MUSGRAVE: That could be your next book. [laughter]

T: No thanks. I have a theory that too much theorizing makes you sick.

MUSGRAVE: The theory I'm developing now is that the writer should be slightly afraid of what he's writing about. When the writer is in too much control, that excess will get communicated. For instance, I think Atwood was too much in control in *Life Before Man.* I actually liked the book. It was extremely well written. But people couldn't like the characters because of her control over them. Whereas in *Surfacing,* I felt the author was afraid. Perhaps a really successful book will have both elements. It will have fear and control.

T: You're talking about fishing into the subconscious.

MUSGRAVE: Yes. Writing can be likened to fishing. Except I hate fishing. Things never surface for me. I've never once caught a fish that came to the top. The rod bends double. Something's down there that never comes up. I think how can people go out there and idly catch fish? as if they're not doing some mystical thing? People always think I'm crazy but that's how I feel. You hook the darkness.

T: A novel gives you another world to go into.

MUSGRAVE: Yes. Where my novel fails is that I didn't come to grips with my fear. The fear overcame me in the end. I didn't have enough control. I was so anxious to get it over with because I was so frightened. It could have been a novel of nine hundred pages. But I was too terrified. Next time I'd like to get more balance between control and fear.

T: Maybe if you learn more control in your writing, you'll eventually learn more control over your life. You won't get possessed by people and things.

MUSGRAVE: Yes. When I'm writing, I'm very calm. I'm quite happy when I'm writing. I don't need a quarter as much from the world as when I'm not writing. When I feel those strong attractions happening, I'm not nearly as strong.

T: When you feel that state of being possessed coming on, are you frightened? Or are you expectant? Or do you merely find it intriguing?

MUSGRAVE: A bit of all those things. I get incredibly energetic and ecstatic. That usually is accompanied by a total loss of appetite. And I don't sleep very much. There's some sort of overload going on. It's usually a person I feel I'm possessed by but it's very hard to tell somebody, "I am possessed by something in you that you may or may not recognize or see or know."

T: So that attraction can be highly impersonal.

MUSGRAVE: Yes. Of course a lot of people are confused by that. Not many people are going to be interested in return. I mean, if somebody does that to me, I don't think I'm going to be impressed. [laughing] Matt Cohen, who has known me for a long time, says I don't fall in love with personalities, I fall in love with what is invisible.

T: That fits because your poetry is trying to come in contact with what is unrealized, too.

MUSGRAVE: But also it could just be something I'm projecting. Maybe I'm just projecting onto someone else something that is mine. I attach it to someone else in order to lose it. If I project it hard enough, it can become real. Then when I see that actually that special quality in someone else isn't really there, that I've invented it, it's very disappointing. The magic wears off.

I'm at the stage of wondering what it is I'm doing, what it is I need, why do I keep doing this to people? I was reading something by Jung about poets, he said when poets aren't writing, they regress. They become children. They become criminals. That describes a lot of my behaviour pretty well.

T: Certainly our image of a poet is someone who is outside society in some way. The falling-down-drunk poet is outside society because society expects self-control. Maybe poets are people who are willing to relinquish control more easily.

MUSGRAVE: I don't think it's a case of willingness though.

T: That shows you how *I* look at behaviour.

MUSGRAVE: Yes, I don't believe in words like willingness. I don't believe, to use your analogy, that people set out to get drunk. I believe that drunkenness happens by accident. Suddenly there you are drunk. There are men I know who will say, "Let's go out and get drunk tonight." I don't know how to do that. I don't set out to behave any certain way. Behaviour creeps up and takes over.

T: You get psychologically drunk by accident.

MUSGRAVE: Yes. I don't *like* giving up control. My reaction to finding myself in a position of having given up control is usually an extreme one. That reaction causes huge difficulties in my life, and the lives of people around me. I don't like things to be utterly mysterious to me. Yet at the same time, I suspect there are whole areas of our lives that should remain mysterious. There's a line in *Daniel Martin* where he is talking about his wife and he says that his wife didn't appeal to the unconscious in him enough to make the relationship work.

T: Ooh. That's a heavy one.

MUSGRAVE: Right. You can't live with someone day after day and have that happen. It has to be a mysterious process. "You can't catch the glory on a hook and hold onto it."

T: That has rather depressing implications.

MUSGRAVE: It does. I always want to know, I want to own, I want to keep. Yet there's that line, "Every time a thing is owned, every time a thing is possessed, every time a thing is loved, it vanishes." Knowing that, I still want to do those things. I still want to own and possess and control. That's killing something but it's also a way of getting on top of something and not being dragged down. Not becoming its victim.

T: Is this why you collect talismans? To get power on your side and have control?

MUSGRAVE: I don't know. I've always had huge collections of things. I found a dried-out lizard on Pender Island just the other day. For years I've been collecting these objects, but lately I'm beginning to see that I should trust them more. I'm believing again in power objects.

T: Why do you think people collect things?

MUSGRAVE: To build a little net around themselves. To make external something that is internal. Collected objects reassure people that there is something tangible about life. What's odd about me is that I collect things that are pieces of bodies that once had life, bones and dried-out things. The reassurance there is that it's all ephemeral.

T: If you don't have a body, you can't be hurt. You might simply be seeking the sanctity of spirituality. Have you ever been religious? Or does that word mean anything to you?

MUSGRAVE: I suppose I am religious. Yes, it does. I went through a phase over the winter of being a born-again Christian. I was converted through Bob Dylan. [half seriously] People got incredibly upset. They thought I was a write-off. They thought I was going to start handing them pamphlets. They didn't understand what it means to be born-again. When the light shines on you, it shines on you. It can also stop shining on you.

I used to think of religious people as weak people. I thought it was a weakness to believe in anything. But it doesn't mean you're a fanatic to be religious. For instance, Catholicism makes sense to me. One day maybe I'll become a born-again Catholic for a while. It's a very powerful force. I don't believe there are answers. I don't believe that Christ is the answer. But I believe in all gods. How can I believe in the power of a bone or a lizard skin without believing in Christ?

T: Are you one of those people who wonder if they might not have been better off living in a previous century?

MUSGRAVE: I say that all the time. I say to myself I'd much rather be alive two hundred years ago.

T: Is that just a feeling? Or have you figured out why you feel that way?

MUSGRAVE: I think it would have been easier to cope with problems because you didn't have the choice you have now. My biggest problem has always been choice. Knowing that I have choice. No one is going to say you can't do this or that. I have to make decisions on everything. Whereas in the "olden" days, things weren't socially acceptable so you didn't have to choose whether or not to do them. Nowadays we even get encouragement for getting divorced or leaving a person. You're not condemned to live at the crossroads forever. Even suicides get buried in graveyards now.

T: Why did you drop out of high school?

MUSGRAVE: I was bored. Boredom is the one thing I just can't stand. I would rather have everything be terrifying than boring. I was a straight A student until about grade seven. Then I got bored. I stopped working.

T: At about the age of puberty.

MUSGRAVE: Yes, I think so. Once I became interested in boys, that became a focus. Instead of staying up all night writing papers, I went out with undesirable types.

T: How old were you when you went to live in California?

MUSGRAVE: Sixteen.

T: Did you have any idea that one day you would be able to fill out an income tax form and say you were a poet?

MUSGRAVE: I still don't do that. I cheat. I say I'm a writer. I don't have any problem with "writer" because I could be a journalist. [laughter]

T: But did you have any career ambitions to be a writer?

MUSGRAVE: No.

T: Did you have any ambitions at all?

MUSGRAVE: There are two things I've always wanted to be. A ventriloquist and a tap dancer. I remember Shirley Temple did some great tap dancing in a film I saw once.

T: Ah-hah. Now this interview is finally getting somewhere.

MUSGRAVE: Yes, I want to die in my ruby red tap shoes! Also I remember I once wanted to be a spy.

T: This is all highly significant [imitating computer] Please compute. What is common to all these professions?

MUSGRAVE: They're all disguises, I guess.

T: So being a poet allows you to do all three things at once.

MUSGRAVE: Yes. Projecting the voice, performing, spying. I never thought of that. Here I am, everything I ever wanted to be. I've made it.

Quebec

MICHEL TREMBLAY

Michel Tremblay is Quebec's most gifted and accomplished playwright. His intimate depictions of characters on the periphery of conventional society struggling to gain the dignity of self-acceptance have powerfully mirrored the rise of indigenous cultural chauvinism within Quebec.

Forever Yours, Marie-Lou (1971) ignited painful repressions to obliterate the sanctity of the family cell, suggesting hierarchical imperatives inherent in capitalism have cheated family members of happiness.

Les Belles-Soeurs (1972) features fifteen working-class women who hopelessly try to compensate for their emotional poverty by frantically embracing materialism.

Hosanna (1973) portrays a transvestite who must strip off humiliating insecurities to free himself from the trap of sexual ambivalency.

Bonjour la, Bonjour (1974) is a sympathetic concert of family voices written to declare the playwright's love for his aging father.

Damnee Manon, Sacree Sandra (1977) is a cumulative work presenting two polarized characters from previous plays juxtaposed to dramatize what the playwright perceives as the two essential emotional needs, something to believe and someone to love.

L'Impromptu d'Outremont (1979) marks a conscious departure in subject matter, examining the social functions of art in the Molierean "impromptu" tradition while presenting the tragically unrealized lives of four upper class sisters in a Chekhovian mode.

As well, he has written numerous minor plays, an early book of surrealist prose and a recent novel, La Grosse Femme (1979). Most of his work is available in English.

Michel Tremblay lives in Montreal where he was born in 1943.

photo: Alan Twigg

T: The freedom to love in your work has tremendous political ramifications. Are working class Quebeckers getting more of that freedom under the Parti Quebecois?

TREMBLAY: I really don't know. If the people in Quebec have more liberty to find happiness and love, it may not be because of the Parti Quebecois. It may be because of what happened before. I think it's quite obvious that the artists of Quebec helped to put the Parti Quebecois in power. The generation of people who are less than forty years old gave the people of Quebec back their confidence in themselves so they could elect the Parti Quebecois. So if the people ever find happiness it will be as much because of us as because of any party.

T: For years writers like yourself were arguing that the people of Quebec must become their own government. Now that the P.Q. is in power, are artists having to redefine their roles?

TREMBLAY: Yes, that may be true in certain areas. For instance, before the Parti Quebecois came to power I refused to have my plays produced in English inside Quebec. But when the Parti Quebecois came to power I said yes. So maybe we may now become only artists instead of artists who are trying to replace a government.

But after two years of the Parti Quebecois we are realizing we still have things to say. For instance, I always say that governments of the left have ideas of the right as far as culture is concerned. I know the Parti Quebecois is not from the left at all but they think sometimes they are.

T: Do you see the main problem with the Parti Quebecois that it is basically an intellectual elite divorced from the working class?

TREMBLAY: Yes. It could fall into the elite process. So as artists I think we must be there not to let them do that. An artist must be there to criticize society from day to day. I'm not disappointed with the Parti Quebecois but I have a lot of questions. But at least we have a government we can talk to.

T: Will there always be a strong link between the power of any government in Quebec and the presence of the Catholic Church?

TREMBLAY: Probably. But it's very strange what I feel about the Catholic religion. In a way they helped to keep the French language in Quebec. But they screwed up everything else. I always say the

Catholic religion is horrible but they kept us French. Women and priests kept us French.

T: Do you differentiate between the reactions of Francophone audiences and Anglophone audiences?

TREMBLAY: They're just the same. It's very gratifying to know that the basic things I want to say come across. All that is lost in English is the folklore and the *joual*. I always say I hope Chekhov is better in Russian, but it's not a reason not to produce him in English and French. An author that would be better in translation would be an author with big problems.

T: Maybe your plays translate well because most of your characters communicate best with anger, which is pretty universal.

TREMBLAY: Yes, but not in my novel [*La Grosse Femme*]. That's a big difference for me between novels and plays. Theatre is only people talking. But in the novel I am the narrator. When the characters talk they can be as mad as they are if they're on stage. But in between there is me talking about them and I can show I love them.

T: Is that the main reason you're moving into novels? Because you want to be more compassionate with your characters?

TREMBLAY: Yes. The reason I wrote *La Grosse Femme* was basically to tell the public that I love these characters. I have been much accused the past eleven years of hating them. I love them very much. So I wrote a novel to tell people that I love them. Perhaps that's why it's so successful.

T: It was given a first printing in Quebec of 40,000 copies. Is there a temptation to alter your work as you become more and more aware of its potential audience?

TREMBLAY: No, I don't think so. Since I know years in advance what I want to write, that cannot be changed. I'm very stubborn and cold-headed in that area. Nobody can change what I want. Even before *La Grosse Femme* was published I knew two other novels were coming. Even if the reviews for *La Grosse Femme* had been very bad or even if people had not read it, I would still write those books. Because I need them.

T: Why?

TREMBLAY: Well, what happened was that I realized, after having written *Damnee Manon, Sacree Sandra,* that I didn't have anything else to say. It was very clear. That was the end of something. So when I finished I said, "Oh my God, here I am 33 or 34 years old and I don't have anything else to say." So I went on TV and I said, "Hey, people, wait for me. I want to try something else. Please do wait for me."

T: Was that "end of something" in *Damnee Manon, Sacree Sandra* when the two characters tell the public that they were invented by a small child named Michel?

TREMBLAY: Yes, that's on a public level. I tried to say to people in *Damnee Manon,* please, after eleven years you thought that what I said was the truth but look, I'm just a mere child trying to say things. What I say is not *the* version of *the* reality. It's my own vision. It's art, it's theatre, it's not the real thing. You pay your ticket to see actors earning their living saying lines written by a boy named Michel.

I never wanted anybody to think I was telling the truth. I was telling some kind of truth. When I come to the theatre and I see actors trying to tell me that they are real characters I don't like that. That's why, the way I write plays, you never forget it's a show.

T: But there is truth in your work. There's always the emphasis that people must "take action" against their repression.

TREMBLAY: Sure. When you go home from the theatre you don't just go to sleep and snore. You think about what you saw. Hopefully what you saw will make you do something about what is happening in real society. That's what theatre is about. Theatre is there not only to entertain. We are there to change the world. I'm telling people this is what society looks like now. If you want it that way, that's okay with me. But don't you think you should do something to change something somewhere?

When I sit every morning at my table I don't say hey, this morning I'm going to write a masterpiece. People used to think like that. Now the notion of a masterpiece in Quebec is vanishing. We think, let's be useful.

T: Is that one of the reasons you wrote *Damnee Manon, Sacree Sandra?* because once your notoriety becomes so great people start looking at your work in terms of masterpieces and not in terms of its usefulness?

TREMBLAY: Not as masterpieces but as the truth. I just wanted to help people realize that theatre is only theatre.

When we do a show in Montreal with my director [Andre Brassard] there is always something at the beginning of the play which says it's only a play. For instance, at the beginning of *Bonjour la, Bonour* the last time we did it, the eight actors came on stage and Serge said, "Lights, please." Nobody in the house forgot that. Some people were asking why we did that. But it was for people to say, oh yeah, they're actors. That's very Brechtian and very useful.

T: Yet you purposely don't give any explicit directions in terms of production for your plays.

TREMBLAY: None at all. I decided a few years ago that I would write for intelligent directors. Because I'm not a very visual man. I hear my characters very much. That's why it's so musical. I don't see them at all. That's why I don't like stage directions. I would direct my own plays if I put stage directions. Like I think Eugene O'Neill is one of the greatest geniuses in theatre in the 20th century but I hate reading him. There is more stage directions than actual dialogue.

T: Carmen in *Forever Yours, Marie-Lou* says, "I'd rather be a whore on la rue St. Laurent than an old maid playing with candles." Why don't you ever give your characters a chance to live on middle ground?

TREMBLAY: Because it's theatre. Life can't be grey on stage. It's got to be black or white. There's no middle ground in the theatre because theatre is there to announce, to say things. The basic problems are always all black or all white.

For instance, in the second act of *St. Carmen of the Main* there is a girl who is a western singer and she wants to talk to the people about themselves instead of only yodelling. Her manager wants her to continue yodelling. That scene is very black and white.

T: Some people might argue that black and white isn't real. That a mixture gives balance.

TREMBLAY: If you mix black and white together you get grey. Grey is horrible. Black and white gives life. If you wear something white or black with another colour, the white or black will give life to the rest of you. If you wear grey it will kill everything. [much laughter] I hate grey!

T: That would account for your going from early surrealism in your teens to the point where the political allegory in *La Grosse Femme* is very direct.

TREMBLAY: Yes...I wrote that experimental book [*Stories for Late Night Drinkers*] when I was seventeen years old. I was still believing that anything that was Quebecois was vulgar and ugly. I was raised like every young Quebecois thinking that you couldn't talk about Montreal or Quebec City in a song or book. So when I began writing I never dreamed of talking about myself.

Then one day the flash struck me that I was born to write about my country. I was 23 years old.

T: Tell me about that day.

TREMBLAY: One afternoon I was with Andre Brassard. We used to go to the movies every afternoon because he didn't work and I was working at nights. There were quite a few Quebecois movies at that time and there was something in them that I didn't like. I didn't know why. Then one afternoon, schlack!, we were sitting side by side looking at a film and it struck me. I realized only the characters on that film talked that language. Nobody else in the world talked like that. It was not Quebecois. It was not French. It was some kind of in-between, romanticized Quebecois.

I said to Andre, I think I'm going to try to write a sketch in which two old maids will come back from a funeral parlour. I would just write like people talk. Nobody did that. Three days later I had fifteen characters. Two months later *Les Belles-Soeurs* was written.

T: Does your best work usually come so spontaneously?

TREMBLAY: I'm not spontaneous at all. I'm not the kind of writer who jumps on napkins, writing notes. I keep everything in my head for months, sometimes even years. I have fits with my characters. I make love with them. I yell with them. They yell at me for years. It's the best part. I don't like sitting at my table writing that much. It's my trade and I like it but the process before is much more invigorating. For instance, it took me four years before I wrote a single word of *St. Carmen of the Main*. Then it took me two weeks to write.

T: So the actual writing is almost secondary.

TREMBLAY: Yeah. I could write dialogue forever. Because I'm good at it. I know I'm good at it. I could write for TV and be paid $5,000 to write half an hour. But I don't like TV. It would be very easy to get out of politics and to sit on my big ass and just make money. But I refused $210,000 to write 21 half hours at $10,000 each. I wanted to write my new play and my new novel.

I don't want to make a hero out of myself. It's just a choice of liberty over money.

T: As you personally gain more freedom, isn't there a danger that you may lose touch with your subject matter?

TREMBLAY: Yeah. I did in a way. And since I'm very honest I'm writing now a play about the bourgeoisie in Quebec. Because I lost contact with the working class completely. I know perfectly everything about the 40's, the 50's and the 60's, but I don't know anything about the working class in the 70's. I'm not abandoning them. I'm living other things.

I'm living now in Outrement. I have a big house and somehow people understand that you live somewhere else. I'm being produced in Prague. *Forever Yours, Marie-Lou* just played in Rome. I make a lot of money. It's great. So I would be a son-of-a-bitch if I bought a house in eastern Montreal and disguised myself as a poor man. I have the honesty of saying I'm rich. I bought a big house. I'm very happy in that house. It's just plain honesty.

T: You make a pretty strong correlation in your work between conventional morality and masochism. Or as Leopold says, "There's nothing in the world worse than a steady job." Does a person have to be a masochist in order to work at a nine-to-five job for forty years?

TREMBLAY: Yeh, probably. It's horrible to think that people will do the same gestures all over 2,000 times every day for forty years. And then go and watch TV at night like the women in *Les Belles-Soeurs.*

But then we're four billion people on earth. Somebody has to work, I know that. I was a linotypist myself. In my head Leopold was always a linotypist but I didn't say it in the play. Because I was a linotypist for three-and-a-half years of my life. And they were the worst. I know what it is to have a steady job.

T: Which is probably why you're so strongly against people who live conventional lives. You resent being held back in that position.

TREMBLAY: It's a question of sensibility. No, not sensibility. . .ah. . .

T: Temperament?

TREMBLAY: Yes, temperament. Probably some linotypist just can't understand how somebody can sit at a table and just write.

T: Reading your plays chronologically I thought a tenderness surfaced in *Bonjour la, Bonjour* that was missing in your earlier plays.

TREMBLAY: Yes, *Bonjour* was the first one in which tenderness came. Because of the love between Serge and Nicole and because of the father.

T: I wondered if that play was a result of experiences you might have had handling the social stigma of being gay?

TREMBLAY: Yeah, it was the first time I was talking about myself. That relationship between Serge and his father is exactly like my relationship with my father. He was deaf, too. And I was raised by women. I felt I needed to go to my father and say I love you. But I couldn't do that. North American society kept me from doing that.

T: What was your father's reaction to that play?

TREMBLAY: He was still deaf. [laughter] He came on opening night and he didn't hear anything! My two brothers who were there just cried their guts out.

My father read the play after. He never talked to me about it but somehow I felt the message came across. He was seventy years old, okay, but why couldn't I just do it? I could never do it. I could never, never do it.

It's very strange, North America. There are basic needs which you don't have the right to fulfill.

T: Did you also want to tell your father you were gay?

TREMBLAY: I told him in my plays. He saw *La Duchesse le Langeais* and *Hosanna.* But I couldn't talk with him. That came from him because he raised me. That came from his part of society.

T: Did you grow up with as much sexual guilt as your characters?

TREMBLAY: Like anybody in the 50's and 60's in a way, I lived a double life of ten years maybe. Because I knew I was gay when I was thirteen. I began doing things then. When I found a way to express myself I went all the way. I eventually said it's much simpler to tell people what you are and how you are and how nice it is instead of how monstrous it is.

As I was trying to help people get out of shit in *Les Belles-Soeurs* I was trying to help myself, too. Instead of leading a double life and going out with girls and never sleeping with them and having them suffer, I decided why don't I let people know? It's so simple.

T: I'd be interested to hear your opinion of the movie *Outrageous* which purported to depict the Toronto gay club scene.

TREMBLAY: It was outrageous, funny, and not one bit intelligent.

T: Too much titillating voyeurism for liberals?

TREMBLAY: Well, people say that about me, too. Gay people say that about *Hosanna*. Gay critics, I mean. There was not one single gay reviewer who wrote a good review of *Hosanna*. They all loved *Outrageous* but they say *Hosanna* was a farce. But *Hosanna* was not about homosexuality. *Hosanna* was not at all about the life of a drag queen with his lover.

T: It's about self-acceptance.

TREMBLAY: Yes, it's a psychological strip-tease.

T: Maybe those gay critics weren't judging on the quality of art so much as the extent to which the art can help them be accepted more readily by the rest of society.

TREMBLAY: That's it. Because I love my marginality. I don't want gays to be accepted by society at all. It doesn't interest me. I don't want to be a straight couple with another man. I resign that. But this is what gay people are fighting for. I can understand that if somebody works in a bank and wants to lead a nice simple life with his lover. But not for me. I want to be a marginal. I love being a marginal.

T: So gays are sacrificing gayness for conventionality.

TREMBLAY: And it's very sad. It will kill whatever is alive in being gay. I don't care about going on the street hand in hand with my lover. I would do it anyway.

T: In a book called *Gay Sunshine Interviews* most of the major gay American writers who were interviewed mentioned how they were finally establishing permanent relationships after age forty.

TREMBLAY: That's because they're afraid they're not beautiful any more. That whole macho thing is so horrible. Society is just making soldiers out of gay people now. They are all becoming men with big mustaches. They are being drafted by society. And in a few years they'll be in Vietnam or somewhere killing poor Viet Cong.

T: They're being drafted by society because society realizes there's a great deal of money to be made from gay people.

TREMBLAY: Sure. They buy things. They are rich and they don't have families. They are very useful to the moneymakers.

It's horrible. When you go to a gay bar everybody's dressed the same. The same mustache. The same hair. The same shirt. My God, it's soldiers again. The disco music is very military, too. I freak out. I haven't been in a gay bar for two years because I just feel like unplugging everything. I want to tell them, "Go to the army if that's what you want. You'll be with men and you'll be very happy. And you'll have real guns."

Prairies

KEN MITCHELL

Ken Mitchell is the Renaissance Everyman of Prairie literature. He is best known as one of Western Canada's foremost playwrights. As well, he is an accomplished novelist, short story writer, radio dramatist, humourist, poet, academic and former pig farmer. Mitchell presents the anomaly of the serious man arguably best suited to the comic mode.

Wandering Rafferty *(1972) is a novel recounting the wild travels and tribulations of a destitute protagonist and his ingenuous sidekick as they scour the Prairies on various Quixotic, Candide-like quests.*

Everybody Gets Something Here *(1977) is an agreeable collection of potentially disturbing short stories combining caustic insights and poised humour to successfully limn the author's contempt for those who emotionally exploit others.*

Cruel Tears *(1977) is an adaptation of* Othello *featuring Prairie truckers and original music that has toured throughout Canada with critical and popular success.*

Davin: The Politician *(1979) is a historical portrait of the founder of the* Regina Leader *newspaper who gained immense political power in the 1890's before his downfall and eventual suicide.*

The Con Man *(1979) is a highly realized comic novel, chronicling modern frontier escapades of a reluctant half-breed confidence man victimized by the gullibility and greed of his fellow Canadians.*

Other frequently produced stage plays include This Train, Heroes, The Shipbuilder *and* The Great Cultural Revolution. *As well as numerous other publications, he is the author of* Horizon: An Anthology of Prairie Literature *(1977).*

Ken Mitchell was born in Moose Jaw in 1940. He lives with his wife and family in Regina.

photo: Rick Green

T: The characters in your plays don't seem to be concerned about the so-called search for identity. Do you think people who grow up on the prairies, where there's such strong ethnic presence, are less likely to be navel-gazers?

MITCHELL: Yeh. The ethnic thing is part of it. But, as in Quebec, there's a strong sense of regional involvement. There's where the strength of prairie writing has come from. I believe prairie people know their identity in the same way that Quebecois people know their identity.

Also there isn't a process of abstraction going on here because everybody in the prairies are equally newcomers. Even the native Cree were originally immigrants from the bush country of the east. When everybody's an immigrant there's less development of hierarchical standards of privilege.

The Depression in the prairies was important, too. Everybody survived a large number of adverse factors together. Anyone who was weak — emotionally, physically or culturally — simply didn't survive. Those that couldn't hack it simply went elsewhere.

T: To Vancouver!

[laughter]

MICTHELL: Or back east. That's why prairie people brag about the incredibly difficult conditions. It's a posture that's given them identity.

T: Maybe as a result, you tend to look more outward in your work than inward. It seems writers in the west are less obsessed with tapping their actual experiences and emotions than writers in the east.

MITCHELL: I think that's generally true. Although I would character-ize Canadian writing that way as opposed to American culture. We're less autobiographical, less internalized, less confessional.

Marginally, I do see a difference between east and west but I think it's because the west is more extreme. The further you get from the metropolitan centres — like the centre of the communications industry which is Toronto, where they tend to imitate British and American models much more — the less self-centred it becomes. I believe a natural writer or poet is really somebody who is only a voice for a people or region. Jack Hodgins is a good example. He almost has no identity at all. Obviously he's a very interesting and attractive and clever person. But he's being the voice of Vancouver Island.

T: Jack Hodgins is the perfect example because he's the most physically removed writer from Toronto and he's also the least overtly egocentric.

MITCHELL: I think in the metropolitan, cosmopolitan, cerebral centres people tend to be much too concerned with the rational process and self-analysis. If I give you any difficulty in this interview, it's probably because I have a tendency to resist self-analysis. I think, in part, it's unhealthy for a writer to do that.

T: After editing *Horizon* [an anthology of prairie literature], what other conclusions can you draw about the nature of prairie lit?

MITCHELL: I think that a great deal more literature has come from the prairie than people from Canada have yet to realize. History is slowly realizing that the art which originates from the prairies is stronger, on a per capita basis let's say, than art which originates elsewhere. There's no reason why this physically barren, thinly populated area should turn out any art at all. It goes against most theories of art which say art comes from metropolitan centres.

That's why, if you look back at the Nellie McClungs and Ralph Connors, then to Frederick Philip Grove and Sinclair Ross, and then finally at the contemporary writers such as Margaret Laurence, you'll find they were almost all unrecognized when their work appeared— except in more recent times. Grove died in virtual neglect and was extremely bitter about his relationship with the Canadian public. Other writers were doing quite well from the urban centres. Yet it's history that makes the final judgment on the value of literature. It's the next generation that judges. Mazo de la Roche is probably not going to last and Frederick Philip Grove and Sinclair Ross probably will.

T: Which do you think has had a greater influence on prairie writers, landscape or history?

MITCHELL: You're trying to separate oranges and apples there, I think. Because I believe that landscape deeply affects history and politics.

The thing that makes the prairies unique and a strong source of art is the landscape is one of extreme openness. There are no natural barriers immediately obvious to the eye. That has quite an unconscious influence. It's a very freaky experience for people to come here who are not accustomed to seeing that much sky and openness. Plus the climate is as extreme as the openness of the landscape.

The extremes of temperature and openness make you feel like you are the only thing around. But at the same time you are dwarfed by the enormity of it all. You see the universe around you all the time. You're not allowed to live in a little microcosm. When you can see the stars all the time you are constantly reminded of the insignificance of your being. So there's this kind of tension that develops. Extreme significance and extreme insignificance. You're the only erect thing in the landscape. I believe, in a subconscious way, this brings artists down to very fundamental observations of life. They are close to the roots of existence. Ultimately their work is going to mean more to people than the reproduction of social manners, which is where urban writing tends to be located. People in cities are often too obsessed with the artifacts of pop culture rather than the basic realities of life. Consequently prairie art may not be popular, but it does last.

T: The effect of that openness is certainly reflected in your work. The protagonists in your two novels seem to have an almost obsessive urge to travel. Is that something you felt growing up in the prairies, a need to explore all that openness?

MITCHELL: Yeh, I guess so. I like to travel a lot. But I couldn't say for sure whether people generally like to travel in that part of the world.

After a while you tend to see the whole prairie as a kind of community. You may know the same number of people as someone who lives in a city, but the people you know are spread over a million square miles. My social life tends to exist in an inter-city way, not a neighborhood way. But obviously that's a result of modern technology so it can't be interpreted as a reflection of how people have felt in the prairies historically.

T: In the short stories in *Everybody Gets Something Here* you use humour as an antidote to pain but in the novels [*Wandering Rafferty* and *The Con Man*] it seems travelling takes the place of humour.

MITCHELL: That's a really interesting idea. I'd never thought of that before. But it makes sense. Those are two ways of blunting the painfulness of reality.

T: And it seems there's been a progression in your work from dealing with how individuals "blunt" reality to treating alienation on a much broader scale. Do you think your writing might be becoming more overtly political?

MITCHELL: No. But I do believe that fundamentally I'm quite a political writer. Maybe more than most. I have a political sense of what I'm doing.

However there isn't much parliamentary politics or debate that happens in my work, even in this new play, *The Great Cultural Revolution.* Politics is much larger than the House of Commons. It's only when people realize that politics is a much deeper force than electing somebody and sending them off to Ottawa to engage in legalistic debate that only they can understand, that people will develop a sense of control of the political direction of their own country. Of Canadian unity.

T: How did you come to write the new play about the Chinese Cultural Revolution?

MITCHELL: A friend who directed *Cruel Tears* showed me a play he'd come across called *Hai Jsi's Dismissal.* This is a play of great historical significance because it ignited the Great Proletarian Cultural Revolution in China. He had the idea of presenting it to North American audiences but it was in traditional Peking Opera style. We eventually decided on a fictitious staging of this play in Peking in 1966, at the height of the Cultural Revolution.

One of the things my play is about is the dominant role or influence of culture in political movements. You can see that clearly in China. The Cultural Revolution was very important in deciding whether art was for the people or for the elite. So my play is not so much about China as about the relationship between art — specifically theatre — and politics. It's a question which should engage us here in Canada.

T: Particularly because we had our own form of a government-induced cultural revolution here in Canada to celebrate the country's centenary. Is this play correlative to the cultural scene in Canada?

MITCHELL: Inevitably. There aren't direct references to the Canada Council or the Secretary of State. But we all know that the distinction between art and propaganda is sometimes difficult to define. I think it's a definition that's needed. So much of the art in Canada is clearly heavily influenced by government policies. It's time for artists to take a fairly critical look at their role in society.

T: Did you have that in mind from the outset with this new play?

MITCHELL: No, that evolved in the research. I became fascinated with China and did a lot of study.

T: I understand you've been learning Chinese.

MITCHELL: [He says something in Chinese] My wife and I have both been studying. I have an invitation to go to the University of Nanching and teach English for a year.

T: What are the possibilities of getting a Canadian play about the Chinese Cultural Revolution produced in China?

MITCHELL: That's a very interesting question. I wish I knew more about the process of getting a play produced there. Also I'd like to see a production done here before I go. I wouldn't want to be in China and discover that the play took the wrong political line. I'm not saying I want it to necessarily have the *right* political line either. But inevitably it's going to be contentious. If it's seen as being an attack on Mao, as the original play was, then it might be an uncomfortable sojourn for me.

T: Generally you've been concerned with examining how an individual's sense of his own equality can be eroded by the establishment whereas in *The Great Cultural Revolution* you're dealing with a group of people, the actors, who are oppressed by the majority. When I went to the workshop reading, it struck me you were having some difficulty developing all the characters this time.

MITCHELL: That's just part of the way I work. The first couple of drafts are more concerned with structure, getting the ideas in place in relation to the dramatic development of the script. That reading was encouraging to me because I could see the structure was in place. Now I can concentrate on deeper characterizations. The revisions I've done since then have been concerned more with the characters than with the play's structure.

T: Since you've written over twenty plays, I would expect there would now be a danger of characters repeating themselves. Do you get around that by molding characters on actual people?

MITCHELL: Yeah, there is a danger there. One of the valuable elements of workshops is you can hear what an actor can do with a part. You begin to adapt the character in the play around the capabilities of an actor. It often happens that in writing a play, I'll have a certain actor in mind. That gives the characters flesh and identity.

T: In *The Shipbuilder* [a portrait of an old Finnish immigrant who stubbornly builds an ark in the prairies], wasn't that character based on an actual person?

MITCHELL: The story is based on an historical figure. However I changed the nature of his character a great deal. It's simply based on his eccentricities.

T: Canadian theatre is very healthy and active these days. Do you think that's because so many of our playwrights are dealing with the problems of underdogs and we see ourselves as underdogs beside the U.S.?

MITCHELL: That's a hard question for me to answer. I don't study Canadian theatre as extensively as you. Give me some examples.

T: Fennario, Ryga, Tremblay, French, yourself. . .

MITCHELL: Yeah, that's true. There certainly isn't a tendency in Canadian theatre at the moment to write domestic drawing room comedies.

I think that part of the excitement of Canadian theatre is that it's almost approaching epic theatre. There's a strong sense of Canadian plays being oriented not to the miniature "room" metaphor that I believe most British and American plays concentrate on, but rather on the large scale sweep of history and landscape. That's more consistent with our culture. And I believe, yes, that means there's probably a greater sympathy for the Everyman.

T: We should probably talk a little about your newest play called *Booze*.

MITCHELL: Actually, it's more of a show than a play.

T: Written by a non-drinker.

MITCHELL: Wait a minute. Let me nail this down right now. I've drunk heavily in my life. Like I've been there. I've wallowed in the gutters with the lowest of the low! [amused] I've won drinking contests and all the rest of it. I'm not particularly ashamed of that, although I am ashamed of things that I'd done at the time. But I don't have a moral attitude towards the consumption of alcohol at all. I just try to restrict my own consumption of alcohol to the best champagne that I can find on opening nights of my plays.

T: But every time a Ken Mitchell character is offered a drink, you know he's going to fall flat on his face in the next scene or the next page. It's like when Lucy offers to hold the football for Charlie Brown.

MITCHELL: I didn't realize that. It's not a conscious thing.

T: I think it's consistent throughout your work.

MITCHELL: I'm sure there are exceptions. I'll have to try and find a couple of exceptions! [laughter] However, I think that that's generally true. I use alcohol as a kind of metaphor for social poison. It's an escape from reality which is used quite consistently by exploiters to exploit the exploitable.

Drinking is a habit that has really become quite a destructive pattern of behaviour in our culture. *Booze* is designed to give that awareness to people, to show that alcohol as a drug has a much more pervasive and sinister influence on their lives than is generally believed.

T: If you're writing to communicate an idea, don't you think you might get more mileage by working in an electronic medium like film or television?

MITCHELL: Yeah, that whole relationship between television and a writer needs a lot more examination. I don't think artists can afford to be so contemptuous of the medium as they have been. If you don't accept the challenge and try to use television in some realistic way then the challenge might disappear for good. Technologically speaking, especially with the development of cable systems, television could conceivably be the greatest educational tool ever put in the hands of civilization. For artists to back away from that is an abrogation of responsibility.

You have to allow for the possibility that MacLuhan is right. That after four hundred years, the world of Gutenburg and moveable type is becoming obsolete. That writers who can't learn to tell stories visually are as doomed as the dinosaur. Writing novels takes up a great deal of concentration and energy. I'm not sure it's always worth it because other media might be more productive.

T: Jaanus in *The Shipbuilder* is one of your most successful characters because he falls victim not only to society, but also to himself. The man of steel who doesn't know how to bend. Is that a quality integral to your own make-up?

MITCHELL: Well, I admire it. I've never had to analyse things quite this way, so let me think about it. I think that uh...well, there's something in his defiance or arrogance that I like. He's the man against his circumstances.

T: *The Con Man* is like that, too.

MITCHELL: Yeah, that's a book I've been working on for about eight years now.

T: Do you agree with the character in that book who maintains the whole world is a con?

MITCHELL: He's a cynic.

T: And he's not Ken Mitchell.

MITCHELL: I don't think so.

T: I got the same message from that novel as we get from Brecht's *Three-Penny Opera*. Criminals are merely the people who get caught.

MITCHELL: And that accounts for the cynicism of that character in prison. It also accounts for the cynicism of someone like Richard Nixon.

T: Is that why there's a reference to him at the end of the book?

MITCHELL: Yeah. Politics is a con game and Nixon was as good a practitioner as any. He just got to believe it too much until it destroyed him.

The worlds of advertising and professional sport are other facades for con games. These con games are designed to expropriate money from the pockets of working people and put that money in the pockets of the people who live on their backs.

T: But your con man is different from a con man like Robert Redford in that movie, *The Sting*. Your con man doesn't deliberately con people. He just gets into situations where people want to con themselves.

MITCHELL: Exactly. That's very perceptive.

T: It's as if you're saying Canadians so desperately want to assuage their small town, inferiority-complexed lives that we fall victims to ourselves.

MITCHELL: Yeah. That's the central dramatic point. I'm really pleased somebody is able to refine that because it's not stated. *The Con Man* is an innocent who is really exploited by other people's gullibility. No professional con man could operate in a world where people don't want to get everything for nothing. I've kind of reversed the formula and created a number of worlds where people desperately want something for nothing so badly that they'll create a con man to perform illusions for them. Basically he's a victim of everyone else's greed. He ends up spending his entire life in prison because a con man is needed everywhere!

T: *The Con Man* is innocent and suffers. But all the other characters who understand how the world works have to also suffer because they become jaded and invulnerable. Isn't there any middle ground available?

MITCHELL: Yes, there is. I personally believe there is a large middle ground that most of us occupy. All children occupy it, for example. We have to work harder at expanding that ground to make a better world. That's why I teach. I want to show there is space between the exploiter and the exploited for people to exist and grow.

T: Has it ever occurred to you that writing can be seen as another con game? where you manipulate people's reactions to make readers think a certain way?

MITCHELL: It's not only occurred to me, it's a basic philosophical principle upon which I operate! People love fantasies. They like to be taken away from the brutal reality, if you want to call it, of their everyday life. So writing is the essence of con artistry. Writing a novel like *The Con Man* is a con game where you try to draw people in to perceive a reality they don't normally see. And to make them think that they're getting something for nothing. Or for only $8.95.

Eastern Horizon

MATT COHEN

Matt Cohen is one of two major ascending talents in Canadian literature who is a purposeful contradiction to the write-only-what-you-know adage. He explores his fictions instinctually, often grasping for meanings with the daring of a poet, placing his characters on alien footings to exorcise their unconscious anxieties through extremist behaviour and emotions.

Korsoniloff (1969) is the journal of a philosophy lecturer juggling his non-analytical introspections with conflicting desires for compulsively pure actions.

Johnny Crackle Sings (1971) is a fantasy chronicling the private and public tensions of a rock-and-roll performer who wins short-lived fame.

The Disinherited (1974) is a gothic melodrama successfully evoking the ambivalent loyalties which arise from life on a family farm in Cohen's fictionalized Ontario town of Salem.

The Colours of War (1977) is a futuristic account of one man's desperate homeward journey on a cross-Canada train to escape the politicized fervour of a rapidly collapsing society.

Wooden Hunters (1978) is a destructively blind descent into elemental passions by disparate personalities on a primitive island.

The Sweet Second Summer of Kitty Malone (1979) is the bittersweet but life-affirming romance of a man and a woman rediscovering both passion and innocence in later life, best expressing Cohen's fascination with the dynamics of spiritual fusion from generation to generation and the need to live within a sense of a social continuum.

Matt Cohen was born in Kingston, Ontario in 1942, then raised in Ottawa. Other publications include a collection of short stories, Columbus and the Fat Lady *(1972) and a book of poetry,* Peach Melba *(1975). He lives in Verona, Ontario.*

photo: Alan Twigg

T: Most young writers are advised to write about what they know. You've said you only began to write well when you started writing about what you didn't know.

COHEN: Yes. It started with *Johnny Crackle Sings.* I just made it up. I did the same thing with the best stories in *Columbus and the Fat Lady.* Then *The Disinherited* was like that, too. There was a period of about six months when I was doing the central parts of all those books. My writing totally changed. I had finally written through all the preconceptions I had about what writing was and just started writing about whatever it was that engaged me most deeply.

T: Of those books, I think probably *The Disinherited* was the real breakthrough.

COHEN: Yes. The strange thing was that even though it's an extremely straightforward novel compared to my previous writing, I actually wrote it at exactly the same time that I was writing my most bizarre stories.

I also wrote another novel between *Johnny Crackle Sings* and *The Disinherited*; that was a real disaster. It was my attempt to write a linear novel. M&S probably would have published it if I insisted but I was unsure about it. so they offered me an advance for another novel. I made up a plotline for *The Disinherited,* which I didn't follow, and I was thinking it would be a trashy, commercial novel. But I was living on a farm at the time and I guess that experience was getting through to me. It never occurred to me at the time that it would be a good novel.

T: It's a bit like a Gothic soap opera.

COHEN: Sure. There are a lot of soap opera elements. Struggles within a family are soap opera material. I'd show parts of it to people as I was writing and they'd all say it was terrible.

T: That's interesting about being unable to write a straight, linear novel. On the first page of your very first book there's a mention about how time stretches both ways. Now it seems you're using that lateral sense of time more and more as the stylistic backbone of your novels. Do you intentionally give your stories that elasticity of time?

COHEN: No, I don't. But I'm amazed by what you're saying. It's great to have been so consistent.

T: Don't you agree that you tend to immerse your characters in time just as deeply as plot?

COHEN: It's true that if I feel I have the past and the present—or some idea of the future and the present—co-existing in the same sentence then there's a counterpoint happening which gives the writing an extra energy. I feel at home writing that way, and now I've learned how to create those situations in my novels.

T: Do you conceive of novels in a linear fashion and then jumble the incidents?

COHEN: No, all those replays just happen. Some sort of crossroads is reached which opens up the past. Just as sometimes a sentence might open up for a detail. I never know when it's going to happen.

T: As an example, there's that memorable scene in *The Sweet Second Summer of Kitty Malone* where the boy suddenly recalls being lost in the snow and the wolves kill his dogs. Would that be planned?

COHEN: Not really. When that scene started, I realized there was going to be a flashback. I thought it would be very brief. It was only as I started writing it that the scene developed. It goes on for ten or twelve pages. I probably wrote it in about an hour, which is very exceptional for me. To write that much that fast.

When that happens it feeds one of my theories about my own writing which is that I make it all up unconsciously. Then at the right moment I blurt it out. Then I fix it up. There's a certain amount that seems to form itself beneath my awareness.

T: So you trust your instincts when things come euphorically like that.

COHEN: Usually what I write very fast turns out to be just fine. One of the weirder things is that I have to revise least when I write very fast. When I write quickly, it comes out structurally developed, and always ties in with what has been written before—it's as if I'd prepared it in a dream the previous night.

T: That flashback scene in the snow reminded me of Robert Harlow's *Scann*. Do you purposely try to be experimental with form when you write?

COHEN: No, I don't really care. I just want each book to be right for itself. Styles change so quickly, and people's labelling changes so quickly, that between the time you start a book and finish a book everyone's idea of what's experimental could totally change. I've read *Scann*. And I liked it a lot. But it's a story within a story and I don't think I could pull that off.

T: Aside from that awareness of the dynamics of time, your books strike me as unique because you're so aware of how the dynamics of sex and violence can appear as two sides of the same coin.

COHEN: Yes, I think passion is violent but I don't think all violence is passionate. Passion cuts across what people intend in their lives. It can be inconvenient or it can be totally destructive.

T: That was especially true in *Wooden Hunters*.

COHEN: Yes, in those characters sex and violence were intermingled. They couldn't distinguish between one and the other. To open one was to open the other.

T: A character in that book says sex is like a drug; you get addicted to it. Is that also true of violence?

COHEN: I suppose it could be.

T: It's like if there's something inside us we can't get out, when we finally learn how to get it out, it becomes pleasurable. So it becomes a habit.

COHEN: Right, I couldn't have said it better myself. I think that's exactly true. Once Laurel Hobson becomes more open in that book, she can't stop.

T: Yet passion is also healthy because it reaffirms people are alive.

COHEN: That's one of the problems of destructiveness. There's a scene in *Colours of War* where Theodore is making love to Lise. He hears a noise at the door so he goes out and sees some soldiers have trapped Felipa in a compartment. That's when he gets in a fight with them for the first time. It's only because he's sexually aroused. Otherwise he wouldn't be able to.

So yes, in *The Colours of War* and *Wooden Hunters*, sex and violence come from the same source. I don't know whether that's good or bad, why passion affects different people in such different ways.

T: Because Matt Cohen likes one character and he doesn't like the other.

COHEN: Is this the only difference between good and evil? That you like one person and not the other? Maybe it is the only difference. I don't know. I question the morality of my characters but I don't come up with any answers. I'm still naive enough to think there must be some difference but I can't figure it out.

T: Maybe it's because your characters are all so extremist. Somebody once said life is nine-tenths habit. The people in your novels seem to inhabit that other one-tenth a lot.

COHEN: That's true. Of course one writes books about people in their more or less critical moments.

T: In *Kitty Malone* somebody says, "You might be getting old and droopy but at least you still know how to make a fool of yourself." Are you like that, too?

COHEN: Yes, I guess. But I'm finding it harder and harder to be extremist. It takes quite a toll.

T: You're not the only writer named Cohen to come up against that.

COHEN: Yes, but in some people the impulses stay really strong all their lives.

T: Which is basically what *Kitty Malone* is about.

COHEN: Sure. The whole idea that people should grow up is contentious. I'm not part of the human potential movement. The idea is like health food or something. It is important that I keep seeing my life clearly, but I'm not sure I'm a "better" person than I was ten years ago because of it.

T: What came through strongest in *Kitty Malone* for me was the way you showed how everybody's lives are fused together. That "fusion" thing seems much more essential to your characters than say, a sense of intellectual self-awareness.

COHEN: Yes, it's really a comforting book that way. It's about those solid emotional events that flow under things. It was really an enjoyable experience to write because it seemed I was on such sure ground.

T: I thought the manner in which you described the overlapping of generations in the novel was particularly fine. I suppose you're going to tell me you've never lived with kids now, right?

COHEN: [amused] That's exactly what I'm going to tell you.

T: But that book is such a convincing affirmation of kinship, literal and otherwise. Did you set out to write a positive book then?

COHEN: I didn't set out to do it, but I realized it was going to be positive once I was writing it. I realized it was going to be sort of a romance. I thought that was great. I couldn't imagine how I'd gotten onto such an affirmative footing.

T: Is it amazing to see the different response you get when you write a positive book?

COHEN: Exactly, yes. That's a very odd feature of the whole thing. People like a positive book better, as if it's a better book! Maybe it is a better book! I don't know. But certainly people responded more warmly when I toured with *Kitty Malone* than ever before. Because it's not a political book.

T: The opening scene in *Kitty Malone,* where Pat Frank takes a candle up to the child's room, struck me as perhaps unconsciously illustrating what the book — and most of your other books — seem to be saying. The less far ahead people can see, the more fragile and unhappy they are.

COHEN: That's interesting. I've never consciously thought that. But as you said that, I couldn't help thinking of Violet Kincaid in that book. She is a relatively calm and happy character precisely because she has this highly developed sense of the future.

T: It's probably why the farm atmosphere of Salem in your novels attracts you. In the country you can live with a sense of being in a continuum more than in a city. You can see further ahead of yourself.

COHEN: That's really interesting.

T: It's why Theodore Beame retreats to Salem in *The Colours of War.*

COHEN: Yes, everything is going to crumble around him. That's definitely the place he can cope the best. Because that's where he was brought up. For some people the right thing to do is to leave home and go somewhere else. It's almost inevitable for them. For other people it's almost inevitable to go away and come back. I think I understand those people who come back better than those who go away.

T: This continuum idea is why *Wooden Hunters* is a depressing book. There's no sense of a future till the very end.

COHEN: Yes, *Kitty Malone* is more optimistic that way. But a real difference between the two books is the security of the actual ground on which they stand. In *Kitty Malone,* the actual physical presence of the farm is never in question. They can assume the grandfather's house will remain unthreatened. Whereas in *Wooden Hunters* the island is being logged and massacred.

T: Do you think it's a generational continuum people crave?

COHEN: No, I think it's more the physical presence of the landscape. The crucial experience for a lot of my characters is that they try to get too much from other people. When they try to get less, it's better. They have to relate to other people through the landscape, not at the cost of it.

T: I was going to ask you about your religious background in relation to this continuity business.

COHEN: I'm Jewish but I wasn't brought up very religiously.

T: I thought you taught religion or something.

COHEN: Actually that was in a department of religion, which is very different from a department of theology. I was teaching the sociology of religion. I used to take acid and read the books to get me in the mood for teaching. So it wasn't very conventional.

T: Have you been influenced as a novelist by taking acid?

COHEN: It's undoubtedly true that I have been. I think drugs definitely influence my view of reality. I also changed a lot when I started taking drugs. I wonder if I'm supposed to be saying these things in an interview?

T: If you don't you'll only be censoring something which is probably pretty important. I think it's a pretty fascinating area.

COHEN: Well, I don't know what the value of it has been for me. Like I said before, I don't know what the truth is about my books anyway. But certainly all the ideas for my novels and stories, with the exception of *Kitty Malone,* came during times when I was taking drugs. I'd also say that except for my first novel, most of what I wrote starting with *Johnny Crackle Sings,* up to and including *The Colours of War* and

Nightflights I wrote while taking drugs. I don't know what the significance of that is. Maybe none. I don't know.

T: With me, drugs help you see how there's this gate between your conscious and unconscious. If you take some drugs, the filter can get lowered. What would have come to you unconsciously starts pouring in consciously for a change.

COHEN: Yes, initially I guess drugs helped me become less blocked. But I don't think I had any ideas that I wouldn't have had otherwise. It's just that the hesitation between thinking something and writing it down disappeared.

T: I almost suspect you could write a plausible description of how an elephant feels giving birth.

COHEN: That would be good.

T: But those scenes take me outside the flow of fiction. I have to stop and realize something is being created for me.

COHEN: You're saying there are certain limits within which fiction has to exist. I think exactly the same thing. This is just an instance where my limit is past yours. It's an aesthetic objection on your part.

T: I have another aesthetic objection then. Too many of your phrases pop out at me—like "reminding herself of a neurotic cow" or "suspended like pregnant black marshmallows" or "the brain burning itself out with the sour electric smell of an overheated battery."

COHEN: How do you know brains don't have smells? Maybe people feel that when their brains are burning out.

T: Was there any allegory in *Johnny Crackle Sings* between the life of a rock singer and the life of an aspiring artist?

COHEN: Sure, in a parodying way. The whole idea of the rise and fall of fame applies to everything. What was so much fun about *Johnny Crackle* was that his persona as a rock singer was a total fraud. It was as much comic as tragic that he was rising and falling at all.

T: Are you cynical then about the way some writers rise to the public eye and others don't?

COHEN: I'm never cynical about the way people rise. If writers get good feedback and people read their books, then they probably really deserve it. But I do think there's lots of writers who deserve it equally whose books aren't read.

One of the facts of writing is that it's part of the entertainment business. Some writers may not be happy about that, but that's the way it is. So people come into style and go out of style. They might write a couple of books which are very good and don't do very well; then, with another book which isn't so good, they get what they should have got before.

T: Are you becoming more aware of the entertainment value of literature?

COHEN: No, I've always thought that writing is show business to a certain extent.

T: Show and tell business.

COHEN: [laughing] Yes. I think people should just write the books they're going to write and be aware that it's hard to guess what's going to happen. Even publishers can't manipulate that.

T: Do you ever feel under a pressure because Matt Cohen is being groomed as the new White Hope for McClelland & Stewart?

COHEN: Not really. People have asked that. I know McClelland has sometimes said things in public about me. But I guess I've been writing for so long now that the idea of myself being unformed seems bizarre, in fact I think I could quit writing quite soon.

That's a real eastern habit, though—to make writers into starlets. That was my first perception of the writing scene. I thought how interesting it was that writers get converted into starlets.

T: Which is really out to lunch.

COHEN: It's completely ridiculous.

Western Horizon

JACK HODGINS

Jack Hodgins, like Matt Cohen, is a newly-heralded novelist and short story writer who relies predominantly on imagination and curiosity rather than experience and self-awareness.

Essentially Jack Hodgins is a comic mythologist. By spinning charming folk tales set on his native Vancouver Island, he is extrapolating basic elements (pioneer isolationism) and psychological characteristics (hardy innocence) of the West Coast experience to create larger-than-life fictional histories. His entertaining style accurately reflects rather than factually portrays a sympathetic record of life in a rural paradise fast disappearing with the advent of urban sophistication.

Spit Delaney's Island *(1976) is a collection of short stories featuring picturesque characters who gamely employ familiar prejudices to come to terms with unfamiliar experiences.*

The Invention of the World *(1977) is a contemporary romance that simultaneously documents the mythic exploits of a half man, half bull tyrant who once led an entire Irish village to a life of communal servitude on his* Revelations Colony of Truth.

The Resurrection of Joseph Bourne *(1979) earned a Governor General's Award. In the aftermath of a tidal wave on the fictitious town of Port Annie, an exquisite Jamaican beauty appears on the main street to exhibit such incongruous beauty that the entire town of quaint losers is thrown into an emotional tizzy—from which Hodgins must extract happiness for one and all, including a crotchety recluse named Joseph Bourne.*

Jack Hodgins was born in 1938 in the Comox Valley on Vancouver Island, the son of a logger and grandson of pioneer farmers. He lives with his wife and three children near Lantzville, Vancouver Island.

photo: Alan Twigg

T: Where do you think you got the ambition you need to be a writer?

HODGINS: I don't know because I can't remember not having it. I loved books from the beginning. There weren't that many around the house and certainly very few around the school. The few books I had, I'm sure I read a dozen times before my childhood was over. The library, for most of my schooling, was just one shelf across the back of the classroom. But there was always something magical about books. The feel, the touch and the smell. I wanted to be one of the people who filled up those books, who did whatever the magic thing was.

So right from the beginning it wasn't just the writing, it was the book that was important to me too. I guess in some sense I would feel that you could sit and write all your life and if it never turns into a book then it isn't real or something. When I was ten I remember I wrote a murder mystery that was four pages long. [laughter] I asked my babysitter to type it up, which she did, and then I folded the pages over and sewed them up the back and put a cover on it.

T: Is there anything significant about your family background?

HODGINS: My mother was one of six, my Dad was one of thirteen. So every second person in the community was a relative. If he wasn't a relative, he was a friend. So that kind of an extended family is just part of the way I see the world. It's not something I've deliberately gone out of my way to create, except to some extent in *Joseph Bourne*. I knew everybody in my community. I went to school with the kids of everybody. My best friend through school was somebody who was a best friend even before birth because our mothers were close friends and pregnant at the same time.

T: A lot of people have become writers precisely because they didn't grow up in that kind of social atmosphere.

HODGINS: Well, there was still the loneliness of knowing that what was important to me was something that had no relationship with the lives of the people around me. And if they only knew, they would think I was a real freak. Which I was! That created a problem in that I obviously didn't fit into the adult patterns I saw around me. I think in my childhood I equated this problem to a rural/city question. I felt I probably didn't belong in a rural situation. Maybe all city people were like me. But when I got to university in Vancouver I discovered that wasn't true. You carry your own home around with you. This tuned up my defense mechanisms and then in turn my abilities to know what other people felt like.

T: In one of your novels there's a remark that the city of Nanaimo has gone from a frontier mentality to a Disneyland mentality. Has it ever occurred to you that you may be fortunate as a writer to be able to see your society change so drastically?

HODGINS: Yes. I think someone on the CBC radio once mentioned, in a derogatory fashion, that the B.C. Ferries brought Vancouver Island out of an essential hillbilly culture into the twentieth century. Well, that "hillbilly" culture was my whole life up until my twenties. I've gone from a childhood in a farmhouse without telephone or electricity to being gobbled up by the city of Nanaimo which is bursting at the seams, creating subdivisions all around us.

T: Also there was a story of yours in *Saturday Night* once about a boy whose mother wanted him to become a concert violinist and his father wanted him to be a logger. Do you think it's an advantage for a writer to be a composite of two opposite parents?

HODGINS: Yes, no question about it. If nothing else it gave me a good start at being able to see things from a different point of view. I'm not writing about myself as many do. I write about the people I see out there. If I'm able to do it all, I think it's because I've developed a lifetime habit of being super-sensitive to the way other people feel, almost to knowing what's going on inside them. It may have begun as a child as a defense mechanism, as a timid kid trying to figure out where the dangers were in the world, trying to know what people were thinking before they ever got around to acting.

T: Have you studied people's speech consciously?

HODGINS: Yes. And that's still very conscious with me. I think this is the result of having had to go through a very painful experience of quote, "finding my own voice." In my twenties all my writing was very imitative. I fell in love with the writing of William Faulkner and a few other American writers. Everything I wrote had to sound like them. Then when it did sound like them, it wasn't any good either. Towards the end of my twenties I decided I had to either find my own voice, whatever that was, or else give up writing altogether.

Well, the thing that happened was that I didn't find my own voice at all. But I started listening to the voices of people who live on

Vancouver Island. I think that was much more important than listening to my own voice. I started to notice that no two people talk the same. Not only are voices different, but people have different speech patterns, different favourite expressions and different rhythms of speech. Once I figured it out I thought, that is probably the most powerful device I can use for making my characters seem alive.

Often if I've got a character set up and I know him very well, all I have to do is listen to him talk. I will worry less about the content of his answer to somebody's question than about the rhythm of his speech. Often, I suspect, what we say is controlled more by the patterns we're comfortable with than what we really think.

T: Somewhere in *The Invention of the World* there's a statement that people can never have success if they don't first have a fear of failure.

HODGINS: Is there? [laughing] Well, at least now I have an opportunity to fail. I'm only interested in writing things which have a high failure risk because that's part of the excitement. All through my twenties I wrote, wrote and wrote while doing other ''normal'' things like building a house and starting a family and beginning a career as a teacher. I suppose I wrote about four safe novels to the end. I'd get about halfway through and realize they were going to be clunkers. Puffed up short stories.

T: But you ploughed through them anyway thanks to the good ol' work ethic?

HODGINS: Yeh, my wife would encourage me to finish them. She'd say even if it's no good, the experience of having written it to the end will have taught you something.

T: Profound advice.

HODGINS: Looking back, I think she's right. It would be possible to become a writer who never finishes anything. Or never learned how to end things.

T: Most writers go through a period of finding their own self before they can go on to be writers. Was that a problem for you?

HODGINS: I don't know. I've never consciously looked to understand myself. I think I was at least thirty before a consciousness of myself got to any crisis point.

T: How do you mean?

HODGINS: I reached a point where I had to put up or shut up. Either produce or quit fooling yourself. You see there was a whole pile of people, whose names I now forget, who became overnight sensations when I was about nineteen.

And I sort of took it for granted that if you didn't become a published novelist in your early twenties at the latest, it's like the old fashioned girl who's an old maid if she's not married by twenty-two or something.

T: That's a misconception. The median age for a novelist to publish a first novel is slightly lower in Canada, but in the States it's something like your mid-thirties.

HODGINS: All right, that's a misconception. But remember, I had nobody to advise me. All I had to go by was the people who got the attention. All those overnight sensations! No doubt, all over the world there were people like me gnashing their teeth saying why do I have to wait? Thank goodness I did! I shudder to think what if somebody had published one of my earlier novels. And I suspect that at least one of them is publishable, though not very good at all. If somebody had given me the encouragement of publishing it, I think it would have been very bad. I might have thought, well, I guess I've got it made.

Now I think, if I've learned anything about writing, it's the result of the terrible frustrations of not getting anywhere for so long. I *had* to learn. Because nothing was happening by itself. I had to really work like a dog to make it happen.

T: It sounds like the toughest part of being a writer is surviving the apprenticeship.

HODGINS: During all those years there was that nagging suspicion that this was all a fantasy, all a dream. I had no reason to believe that I would ever have any kind of success whatsoever. I had no reason to believe I'd ever be published at all. I didn't know any other writers as a kid. I didn't know anyone else who wanted to write until I was well into adulthood.I didn't even know anyone else from my own generation who loved reading. So if I wrote, I wrote behind closed doors. I even read behind closed doors. This was just not acceptable behaviour for a growing boy in a rural community.

T: Most Canadian writers have had the same feeling. We're probably basically still a very young country with a pioneer mentality.

HODGINS: And we're suspicious of the written word, aren't we? That apprenticeship as a writer can be so painful that it seems to be if writers can do nothing else for aspiring writers, they should tell them this fact about their own lives.

T: So how is winning the Governor General's Award going to affect your writing?

HODGINS: In the long run, it's really going to help me not to care so much if a few people don't like my work. Even as an adult, I've had to fight this nagging guilty feeling about becoming a writer. With a Governor General's Award, maybe the fight will be over.

T: Would you agree the Protestant work ethic influences the reading of literature in Canada?

HODGINS: No question about it. I often get the impression reading much of the fiction written in this country that nobody in Canada ever laughs. Nobody ever makes fun of themselves, nobody ever takes life at all lightly. And yet I look at the real people around me and it seems that almost everybody I know laughs quite often every day. So if there are examples of humour in my work, it's not usually a deliberate attempt to be funny. It's simply a reflection of the way I see people, people who seem to spend a lot of their time laughing, often at themselves. Humour is a perfectly realistic part of life. But you don't get all that much comedy in serious Canadian fiction.

T: Along with that humour, I think the reader also gets a feeling from your work that the person creating everything is enjoying himself. And some of that pleasure rubs off.

HODGINS: That's good. And you're quite right, I am enjoying myself. This may be a case, ironically, of a weakness becoming a strength. I'm very, very impatient with my own work. I'm very easily bored. So I demand that almost every page entertain me. I can only hope that it will entertain the readers about one-tenth as much.

Sometimes I just fly by the seat of my pants. That is, I want to turn the page to find out what happens next. I don't always know. I'm never happy if my writing seems simply beautiful or practical. It can do everything I want a scene to do, to serve the purposes of a novel or

short story, but I still still throw it away if it doesn't somehow get me
so excited that my heart is pounding.

T: That would explain much of the audaciousness of your work.

HODGINS: Yes. But also I abandoned those safe little novels I was
writing simply because it was obvious I wasn't getting anywhere by
writing safe little novels. Some part of me said, all right, if I'm not
going to get anywhere writing safe little things I might as well go way
out and risk everything and either fall flat on my face or else maybe at
last I might get a foot in the door.

T: And so you can risk having a title like *The Invention of the World*.

HODGINS: Sure. I thought, well, I've already taken all the risks
writing this novel so why not go one step further? The interpretation
of that title I find most people getting immediately is that the author is
the inventor of a world inside a novel. But the one all important image
throughout the novel is the image of the counterfeit, so I also wanted a
title to point to the hints that are dropped about the invented as
opposed to the created world. To me, the word invention is a negative
word. I wanted it to be noticeable that I did not call it creation of the
world.

I think at one point I was aware of six or seven ways that people
could read the novel. For instance, it can also be seen as an historical
exploration of why people move to Vancouver Island. It's possible to
see the history of Vancouver Island as the history of failed colonies. So
I chose *The Invention of the World* because it implies that the different
levels of the novel are allegorical and that the primary concern is the
search for the return to the ''created'' world.

T: That was Freud's belief, that civilization is repression. Nature
makes enough borders for man already without us adding more.

HODGINS: But I'm not advocating an animal instinct. If you interpret
the novel as saying we should trust our own instincts rather than our
intellect, you could immediately jump a step further and say we should
just be running around doing what we feel like, ignoring all the
benefits of civilization and education. I'm interested in our instincts
for good, our spiritual instinct. The instinct that leads us towards
benefitting other people rather than instincts which are purely
satisfying some kind of animal desire.

T: How do you see *The Resurrection of Joseph Bourne* as being different from your previous books?

HODGINS: Well, some of the challenges I set for myself were to write a continuous narrative rather than a fragmented one. And to create a concert of voices. Using a whole small town as my protagonist, I can float from person to person for reactions to certain events. Plus, I had the advantage of using a location I hadn't used before and a number of people who were quite different from the people I had used before.

T: One thing I noticed in *Spit Delaney's Island* is how people you write about resemble the people Ken Mitchell writes about on the Prairies. Except where he examines deviancy as a survival technique, you're looking into how people use their so-called normality to protect themselves.

HODGINS: It's something I'm conscious of doing from story to story. That's a useful, profitable way of examining a person—putting him into a situation where his values are challenged and see how he reacts.

T: But you seem to be fascinated by normalcy, which in a way, is abnormal.

HODGINS: This isn't something I've thought of ahead of time but maybe there's something about this that may be important. To me, everybody is the main character in his own life story. Anyone who goes out of his way to be eccentric or to be overwhelmingly noticeable is attempting, whether he knows it or not, to be the main character in somebody else's life. And that's something I will not tolerate. I cannot stand the thought that there can be people in this world who are not even the main people in their own life story. All people are equally valid. So if that creates a tendency for liking normalcy, I suppose that is an explanation.

T: You yourself don't seem to have one trait that stands out among the rest. Sitting there on the chesterfield, you appear to be eminently normal.

HODGINS: [amused] That's a terrible thing to say!

T: Maybe that translates into real strength. [facetiously] Are you normal?

HODGINS: Well, the important thing about what you're saying is that I'm not living a role. In fact, as soon as a role is defined, I begin to resist it. I think, in my writing, the people in my stories are so important that I cannot afford to overshadow them by being a person. I can't wear kilts and get drunk in public and insult the Queen. First of all, it wouldn't be natural. But also, I couldn't risk losing my ability to meet people unhampered by an awareness that I was some eccentric person hovering over them.

T: This creates a public relations problem. Good natured, former high school teachers aren't supposed to write great works of fiction.

HODGINS: But I think the greatest novelists in the world today are people like John Fowles and John Gardner. If you learn anything about their lives at all, they are decent people. The person who cares about creating a public image is so busy thinking about "Am I living up to it?" that he's going to be less sensitive to other people.

T: Would you agree then that the most striking aspect of your work is that it appears so unegocentric?

HODGINS: Yes. I write out of curiosity, out of the mystery of these people who are around me. Inevitably I uncover more mystery than I ever solve. Whenever I try a character who is quite close to the kind of person I may be myself, I find myself losing interest in the story. I don't know what this tells you about me. [laughing] I don't even want to think about what it might tell you about me.

T: Do you think too much can be made of the fact that Jack Hodgins is writing about Vancouver Island?

HODGINS: Yeah, it's dangerous to talk that way. Of course it's important to me that I get Vancouver Island right, but if I was only interested in writing about Vancouver Island I'd write a geography book or a history book. I'm interested in writing about human beings. I just happen to be writing about people who are close to me geographically. I try not to think too much about what makes people different here. In making too much of the uniqueness of a people in a region, there's a danger that a writer could write stuff which is nothing but regional. It's important for me to find the things that people in New York or London or South Africa can also recognize. To a small degree, that's starting to happen. People will write to me from far, far away to say your characters sound like my neighbours. That's what I want to hear.

T: Do you think too many Canadian writers place an inflated value on their own individualism?

HODGINS: That's a dangerous question.

T: But it's an important question.

HODGINS: Yes, it is. I know there is a school of fiction writing which believes very strongly that the only window left open on the world now is through your self. That, I think, is perfectly legitimate for a person who sincerely believes it. But it doesn't happen to fit into the way I see the world.

T: Which is closer to Rudy Wiebe's approach to writing than say, Marian Engel's.

HODGINS: Yeah. I think if all of us lived a hundred and fifty years ago, the Rudy Wiebes and Robert Kroetschs and Jack Hodginses would be writing the epic novels and the first person novelists would be writing lyric poetry. Now we're living in a time when all the borders have been crossed. Some poets can be writing epic poems and some novelists can be writing lyric novels. It doesn't really matter. Basically I think it's a question of finding where your instincts lie. Probably you write the sort of thing that you enjoy reading yourself.

For myself, I often think of fiction as high class gossip. Really, what you're doing is saying listen, I've got a story I want to tell you about the guys who live down the road. This is what they did and isn't that something.

That's partly why I like reading Rudy Wiebe and Robert Kroetsch, and also South Americans like Vargas Llosa and Marquez, and John Nichols, the American. They have this sense of community. Everybody's in on the story. It's not exclusively the story of one person. The whole world is alive and teeming with life. There's a sense in the novel itself that the novel is a complete world. When you open the first page, you're entering a new world. When you close the last page, you're no longer in it.

Private Eye

MARIAN ENGEL

To wake her heroines and her readers from "our long colonial sleep", Marian Engel creates adventurous fictions emanating from deeply-felt personal dilemmas. Hers is a uniquely Canadian viewpoint that encourages the growth of individuality from within "a country that cannot be modern without guilt".

Bear (1976) is her best known work. Winner of a Governor General's Award, this controversial exploration of the mythic imagination charmed far more readers than it shocked. With a lyricism stemming from the subconscious, this dream-like tale of a woman's amorous relationship with a bear brought Engel the critical and popular success her earlier books had already merited.

The Glassy Sea (1978) is a feminist odyssey in which Engel's heroine joins a purely contemplative order of Anglican nuns. No Clouds of Glory (1968, republished as Sarah Bastard's Notebook), The Honeyman Festival (1970) and Monodromos (1973, republished as One Way Street) are Engel's three earlier novels. As well, she has published two books for children.

Marian Engel was born in Toronto in 1933. She was raised in Galt, Hamilton and Sarnia, educated at McMaster and McGill, and has lived in Montreal, Cyprus, the United States and London, England.

She now lives in Toronto.

photo: Paula Jardine

T: What do you mean when you say writers are chosen?

ENGEL: When I talk to Margaret Laurence or Peggy Atwood, I find we all went out and bought our little notebooks when we were eight or nine. There are a lot of writers who don't do that, but I expect the majority do. Kids know whether they have a burning ambition or not. They begin to place it. Being chosen is just a Presbyterian way of phrasing it.

T: Where does the will to stick with it come from?

ENGEL: It comes from the background. In our family we were trained as kids never to give up. It's been particularly true of the women. The girls pick out a goal and go straight to it. It can't be a gene. It must be conditioning. Before I wanted to be a writer, I had wanted to be the best whistler in the world.

T: Would you elaborate on your upbringing?

ENGEL: We moved a lot. My father was a First World War pilot who wound up teaching auto mechanics. He was a technical school teacher with a Type B certificate. During the Depression, it was the Type B teachers that they fired. They just let them go. He lost a job in Port Arthur. Then we went to Brantford and that job didn't pan out. Then we went to South Dakota because he was sick, obviously for good reason. He had ulcers. Then we wound up in Galt for five years. Then we went to Hamilton. Then we went to Sarnia when I was about twelve.

T: So you grew up under conditions where you were aware that things were not secure.

ENGEL: Yes. There was always the social insecurity of being new people. And we had relatives and neighbours to keep up with but we had very little money. Those of us who were trying to be middle class on $2,500 a year got very bitten. My God, my mother was a genius with a nickel. And am I ever mean!

When things got bad, we went up north and lived very happily in a trailer. I was over on Galiano Island visiting Jane [Rule] and Helen [Sonthoff] and we trooped over to visit a friend of mine. She lived in a trailer with a pot-bellied stove and a great garden. I sat down in that trailer and I was automatically happy. Home.

T: Did you have one of those classic childhoods where you were always lonely?

ENGEL: Yeh. My sister was six years older and I didn't have any brothers. Mother was good about that, too. She said go into the back yard, get four sticks and give them names. [laughing] Writers are chosen!

T: Do you think that early isolation is why you have an affinity for islands in your work, both literal and figurative?

ENGEL: I'm easily harassed so I'm always dreaming of permanent withdrawals. Convents, islands and great thumping houses in the country. Writing a book involves the Big Withdrawal from society, too. Mostly I do it in the winters. When it's over, what happens to me and to several other writers I know is a great plunge back into the world. If I was the only person who lived this way I'd be worried about myself. But I know many writers who do the same thing.

T: Can you write while you teach?

ENGEL: I have a horrible time. It ruins your voices. Rudy [Wiebe] seems to have no trouble. And he gives a lot to his students, too. But because I've got my kids to look after, I'm juggling all sorts of things and I know I'm not being the big humane spirit people expect a senior writer at a university to be. That small piece of me that I'm handing out every Tuesday, Wednesday and Thursday is all there is, kids.

T: How serious a jolt to your life was having kids?

ENGEL: I was terrified when I had them. I was going to have a quiet baby with spectacles who sat under the table and read. But I had twins. So I wrote my agent and asked what I should do. He wrote back and said the more responsibilities his writers took on, the better writers they became. I grit my teeth and say that. It may not be true, but it's helpful.

T: In *The Glassy Sea,* the nun says when she's being practical the dreamer in her dies. Is that work/contemplation split a problem for you, too?

ENGEL: Yes, and it was fascinating to write about. Hang it all, I haven't darkened a church door in thirty years. Except for funerals. But it will always continue as a tension for me. I will be a guilty napper, but I will still nap. In fact, I do most of my work in bed these days.

T: So that's a problem with novel writing, too—balancing the craft of writing over a long period of time with the more "creative" part of the job.

ENGEL: It's a terrible problem. I'm not the only writer to have it. You see, a writer's life is essentially contemplative. I know a lot of people who live unreflectively and are happier than I am, but I don't get any pleasure out of living that way. I probably reflect obsessively and narcissistically and excessively. Right now I'm scrambling around working to get some money, then I'm going to sit down on a stump and just think.

T: Do you have to watch your reflective nature doesn't get out of hand when you're writing?

ENGEL: I think so. You have to become another person. If there's been any change in my books it's that I've become more skillful at becoming another person. Then I have to make sure that this other person does not distort my everyday reality. My friends and relations do not, after all, act according to the scenario I have imagined for them.

T: Is that skillfulness the result of craftsmanship? Or is it because you've exorcised all your biographical material?

ENGEL: I can cheerfully say there is almost no autobiographical story left to tell that interests me. Next week, that may be another matter, of course. But now I feel I've got rid of all that material. I can really go ahead.

T: Do you worry about going through the rest of your life being pegged as the woman who wrote *Bear*?

ENGEL: Oh, God. Before it was published I remember I met a friend who's with CBC news and he said, "Are you really going to publish that book about the bear?" I said sure. He said "If you don't publish that book you'll have about eight lines in the history of Canadian literature; if you do publish it you'll have one." I knew then I had to publish that book — and then a great many more.

T: What made *Bear* convincing to me was the lyricism of the writing. Did that book seem to take you over as you wrote it?

ENGEL: It was a very strange, completely instinctual book. It was based on a lot of research that I had done on Ontario pioneers so it had a firm intellectual base. But the lyricism was just there. I won't say it wrote itself because I can remember doing draft after draft. But some of it wrote itself. I regard it as a piece of luck.

T: You mean luck in the sense that you were the perfect person to write that book? You just happened to plug into it?

ENGEL: Yes. It was a case of all the elements coming together, which they don't always do. I don't think it's the be-all and end-all of book-writing but I think it's a nifty piece of work. People can communicate with *Bear* who wouldn't like my more intellectual books because it's the acting out of a statement. That's what's good about *Bear*. It's acted out rather than preached. I tend to be preachy.

T: And as you said in *Sarah Bastard,* "All intellectual missionaries tend to lechery."

ENGEL: Did I write that? Aren't I clever! That's the happiness of writing. Occasionally you write something good but it doesn't have to be a whole book.

T: So what about your role as an intellectual missionary these days?

ENGEL: My missionary tastes are fast coming to an end!

T: Are you as happy with *The Glassy Sea* as you are with *Bear?*

ENGEL: No. It's got a problem that's inevitable. You can't possibly do as neat a job on forty years as you can on one summer. I haven't learned to deal with forty years skillfully, but it has the defects of its qualities.

T: Was the novel a conscious attempt to write a book different from *Bear?*

ENGEL: My original impulse was to see Toronto with a naive eye. I wanted to bring a stranger to Toronto and see what she would make of it. Eventually she became a nun.

T: The book struck me as an elaboration on your line, "There's a kind of virgin one only becomes with difficulty."

ENGEL: Yes, *The Glassy Sea* is perhaps an elaboration on regaining a kind of innocence. A kindness and an unworldliness.

T: But was that consciously done?

ENGEL: Writing works on many levels. You can't just do it on feelings. I think one of the things I was trying to get rid of when I wrote that book was a certain level of cynicism. Everyone I was seeing for a while, particularly aging media people, had grown so cynical. I thought everything was terribly besmirched. I was trying for myself to clean things up. I don't mean sexually. I don't even mean morally. I mean in the sense of starting to like things again.

There comes a time when you have to give up this sort of facile cynical thinking. It's college-boy smartness. You have to look for the good values in society, too. Or else there's not much reason to belong to a society.

T: Cynicism is certainly not a good quality to try and produce a good book from.

ENGEL: You're right. It belongs to young men of twenty-five, and they're notorious for writing bad books. Salinger is one of the few examples of a young person that age who has written a good book. He took a naive and innocent character who wasn't cynical.

T: You sound like you're enjoying getting older.

ENGEL: I am. I remember when I was Hugh MacLennan's graduate student at McGill, I got into a hideous argument with him because I was furious with him for being so proud of being fifty. But I realize now that I'm forty-five and not fifty, that I'm delighted to have the perspective that I have. I can see why things happened twenty years ago. That's lovely.

Length of time is a great help with writing. My young students try to write about their childhoods but they don't have enough perspective to write well. It's really unfair to be a nineteen-year-old writer because you have to continue writing but you don't have anything to write about for an awfully long time. Sure, I'd like to be young again, to look better and to have a young body. But you can't have it both ways. Would you like to be twenty again? I'd hate it. You don't know anything.

T: And yet you have that phrase, "If there's someone who is more disliked or hated than an intelligent young woman it's a mature woman who is not at the mercy of the tides of the moon."

ENGEL: Yes, I'm feeling that more and more. Men are really afraid of mature women. They're afraid of them in the same sense that they're afraid of their mothers. They're afraid of being judged. I think that's really sad.

My theory is that the young men in my generation were all

Depression kids. If their mothers had to go out and work, they were cleaning women or worked in stores. The boys I went out with, on the whole, came from small families and had the exclusive attention of their mothers when they were very young. They went on wanting the exclusive attention of their wives.

I'm not blaming it all on the men. I'm not a very good housekeeper and I was probably an irritating wife. But sometimes it makes me mad.

T: I think a lot of people your age are somewhat bitter that they were robbed of a great deal by the sexual mores of their youth.

ENGEL: The young have made us very envious. If we could have gone and followed our instincts at nineteen we feel we would have all been a lot happier.

A lot of us have been forced to realize that in this society at this time it seems to be that you can either be loved or accomplish something. That's a terrible choice to make.

T: Have you given up on the institution of marriage?

ENGEL: Not quite. [laughing] You never can tell. Being an unwilling cook and not being of an age to breed, it's unlikely I will marry again. But I still feel it's unfair that any kind of affectionate relationships should be ruled out just because I'm a writer. I've become kind of a bitchy and unreasonable person and too touchy, so I'm probably untouchable. But it makes me mad when people say you can't have affection. And there are many men I know who have the ability to write books and keep their relationships.

T: In your books there are repeated references to sexual relations being a battlefield. Has sexual warfare become any more humane in the 70's?

ENGEL: I hope so. I hope so. It's really hard to tell. I hope the younger ones are making out better than our gang. Still I always warn the younger women writers — don't use your married name and watch your relationships.

T: How do you mean, "watch your relationships"?

ENGEL: Be really aware of the fact that writing may change the balance of your life, and you may have to make a decision.

T: The reverse holds true for males, too. I can think of a lot of male writers who were miserably unhappy being married. Like Tolstoy finally running away from home in his eighties.

ENGEL: Maybe the kind of people who turn out to be writers are not the kind of people who are easy to live with or choose easy lives.

T: You don't eschew the "woman writer" label. Do you think feminist-oriented fiction has had its day?

ENGEL: I think it will have reached its zenith very soon. I think people are getting tired of it.

T: That was my reaction to the end of *The Glassy Sea.* It was like I'd heard that whole story before.

ENGEL: I wondered whether parts of that were a sell-out to the women's movement, but I don't think so. The penultimate chapters in my books are always paranoid fantasies. It's happened in every book I've written.

T: Marguerite in *The Glassy Sea* feels there must be some point to her life. Are you sure now that the point of your life is to write?

ENGEL: Yeh, I think it is. I can remember when writing was an ambition that could easily be said to be burning. It's no longer that way because I'm there. I'm very lucky. However, if writing ever deserts mc, I shall have no life at all.

T: So your motto for the "citizens of euphoria" in *Sarah Bastard's Notebook* still holds true for you today..."Only One Basket for Eggs"?

ENGEL: Yes, I'm still a one basket person. I can't help it. But I think all the eggs are different colours...

Public Eye

RUDY WIEBE

Rudy Wiebe's novels are profoundly social in scope and intent. An uncompromising moralist and pacifist, Wiebe is a Mennonite best known for his historically-based fictions which emphasize our need for communalism, self-discipline and Christian spirituality.

Peace Shall Destroy Many *(1962) examines some of the trials of being a Canadian pacifist.*

First and Vital Candle *(1966) is about one man's struggle in the Northern Ontario wilderness to believe in God while immersed in the culture of the Ojibway Indians.*

The Blue Mountains of China *(1970) dramatizes the migrations of Mennonites over the world's continents during the past century.*

The Temptations of Big Bear *(1973) is a vast historical novel which recounts how the west was lost, how the spiritual link between man and the land was broken with the coming of the white man. It earned the Governor General's Award.*

The Scorched-Wood People *(1977) is an account of Louis Riel's Metis people struggling to retain a sense of communal integrity and political autonomy in the face of encroaching nationalism.*

Rudy Wiebe has also edited six fiction anthologies, written numerous radio and television dramas and documentaries, produced an original stage play with Theatre Passe Muraille, Far As the Eye Can see *(1977), plus provided the fictional text for* Alberta/A Celebration *(1980).*

He was born in Northern Saskatchewan in 1934. He has attended universities in Alberta, West Germany, Manitoba and Iowa, edited a Mennonite newspaper and taught at a Mennonite college. He is now a professor of Canadian Literature and Creative Writing at the University of Alberta.

He lives in Edmonton with his wife and three sons.

photo: Alan Twigg

T: Your work emphasizes how closely spirituality and tough-mindedness must be linked in order for us to develop any sort of useful moral code. Most people these days don't seem willing to even consider qualities like self-denial and self-discipline, let alone try them.

WIEBE: You're right. "Indulgent" is the key word today. If we like something, we do it. That's why the whole tradition of Russian spirituality has appealed to me. If you really want to search what your soul is, you go and live on an island. You cut down the demands of the outer world to find out the demands of the inner world.

T: The Prairies is probably an ideal place for that process of self-evaluation. Would that be why the Canadian novel seems to have its roots in the Prairies?

WIEBE: Possibly. Certainly it's true the prairies have inspired a good number of our major novelists, far out of proportion to the number of people who have lived there. The first generation was [Frederick Philip] Grove and [Sinclair] Ross and W.O. Mitchell. They stuck more or less to the pioneer end of things, especially Grove. Now we're trying to go beyond that era in both directions. We're trying to look at what came before the pioneer and what has come after.

T: Would you say prairie writing, in general, is less imitative than writing in Eastern Canada?

WIEBE: Yes. Because the landscape of the prairies is much more alien to the landscape of England than the landscape of Ontario. You can see a parallel to this in Australia. They're still grappling to come to grips with an alien landscape because they had less varied immigration. But you can't build a little England in a land of marsupials. We learned that in the prairies because we had more varied immigration than Ontario.

T: Are you implying Eastern European immigrants were better settlers on the prairies than British people?

WIEBE: Sure. My parents were Russian Mennonite farmers, living in very much the same latitude as Canada. In fact, the Mennonites who came to Canada in 1870 from the steppes of the Ukraine were really the first people to settle Western Canada on the prairie. Up to that point, the Scots and the French had only settled along the river valleys, using the river lots system. They stayed close to the rivers, using them as their means of transportation. But the Mennonites in 1874 literally settled on the prairie.

They built sod houses. Now who's going to live in a sod house? A Russian peasant will, if it's necessary. Nobody thought they could make a go of it. But they brought wheat from the Ukraine. It wasn't supposed to be exported so they sewed it into the children's dolls. That's how our grain industry started.

T: So you grew up thinking of yourself as a Mennonite first and a Canadian second?

WIEBE: I had to. I lived in a Mennonite community, a settlement of two or three hundred people. Before age six I spoke no English at all. We spoke low German. My parents hadn't had a penny to get to Canada so the CPR gave them a loan and brought them all the way to Alberta. My father finally paid the CPR back fourteen years later.

All the stories my parents told us during the long winter nights were about Russia. The revolution and all that. So yes, my world was very, very Mennonite in those early years.

T: Did you ever feel a need to break away from the fundamentalism of your upbringing?

WIEBE: Well, I grew up relatively free. I was the youngest child in our family by quite a few years. And my parents were quite old people. My father was forty-five when I was born. So when we moved from northern Saskatchewan to southern Alberta when I was about twelve, I was relatively free to explore. I sensed there was something wrong with the heavy fundamentalist preaching fairly early on. When I was older I realized it was the narrow, legalistic system into which it forces you. It made of spirituality a kind of syllogism: All men have sinned...God has to reach into man's life to change life...so all you have to do to change your life is accept conversion. There's nothing spiritual about it. Christianity becomes logic. You're levered into a philosophical position by an emotional demand. These kinds of things always angered me. I knew there had to be more to the demands of a truly good life than that logical syllogism.

But I was lucky. I went to a Mennonite high school that had a lovely community spirit to it. So my Christian values were affirmed when I was young. I don't think I ever tried to smoke at all as a kid— that was a great concern of parents in those days—and we never had the hassle of adolescents growing up and pairing off and boys and girls getting into trouble. That kind of jazz was never a problem. Nobody ever thought of things like going out on a single date because there were so few kids in that school. It was a community.

T: I suppose you already recognize all the similarities between your beliefs and Tolstoy's.

WIEBE: He's becoming more and more of an influence. In fact, I usually read *War and Peace* every three or four years. Tolstoy sees where his country is coming from and knows where it's going. Also he was an outspoken moralist. But it's more than that. He was a Christian moralist who saw in the life of Christ and the doctrines of the Bible the highest ideals that man has achieved so far. Especially in the field of pacifism. Tolstoy brought pacifism to world attention at a time when it was very low on the scales during the Imperialist world of the late 19th century. To be a pacifist then was to be a ninny. But he showed the world that pacifism was not some abstract human condition. It can be rooted in action, as best exemplified by Christ.

T:' Do you think your books might be better appreciated at a future date when Christianity is not so unfashionable?

WIEBE: Actually, I've already gained a lot of ground in the seventies. People have become so tired of that emptiness which came with liberal attitudes. People are tired of that pseudo-scientific liberalism that assumes all is provable. Scientists no longer talk like that. Only outdated liberals talk like that.

So it goes in cycles. Some writers try to anticipate what's going to be popular two years from now. I just say the heck with that. To me the point is that there are eternal human values that must be spoken for. Sometimes the concept of pacifism in my books is popular; sometimes it's not. In the early sixties, at the time of the Cuban missile crisis, being a pacifist was just giving in. Then at the end of the Vietnam war, pacifism became one of the most powerful forces in North America. When that happened, *Peace Shall Destroy Many* started getting popular again.

T: In the event of a Third World War, how would our society treat pacifists?

WIEBE: I don't see the Canadian public responding to pacifists much differently than in the Second World War. A few people believe there's no such thing as a just war. But a lot of people who became pacifists during Vietnam still figure the Second World War was a pretty good war as far as wars go. We had to handle a tyrant. Besides. things were pretty tough economocally so let's go off and have an adventure. It's that kind of stupid male world that wars exemplify.

The Second World War was basically men's games. Very deadly, but for that reason, all the more enjoyable.

Maybe the women's movement can help us now. Maybe we have a lot clearer understanding because women are fitting into more things. But women are very aggressive, too. If they don't now have the killing ways that men have, maybe they just haven't learned them yet. It's like the Nellie McClung campaign for temperance. She thought temperance would immediately solve a lot of problems if women got the vote. She never imagined that women like to drink, too. Maybe that's the way it is with war.

T: Your most recent novel, *The Scorched-Wood People,* is not just the story of Louis Riel and Gabriel Dumont. It's the story of the Metis people. Do you think the novel may be getting misread as just another book about Riel?

WIEBE: Right. It's the story of a people, a people who have almost disappeared because they no longer live to express a communal will. The Metis are scattered now. For a long time they have shown very little commonality of purpose.

T: It's also happened to the Doukhobors.

WIEBE: Yes. The world has broken down their whole sense of community. History has broken them down. Riel saw this coming. In his prayers he prayed that his people would not lose sight of what they were and what they could be together. Not just as individuals.

T: In that book, Riel is a man of spirit and Dumont is a man of action. In *First and Vital Candle* there's a similar division where Josh is the man of spirit and Abe is the man of action. Is that a dichotomy you feel in yourself?

WIEBE: No, it's probably more a fiction device. It's a way of handling the complexities of human nature. It's given to me in history with Riel and Dumont and I use it for what it's worth. I tried to show that the man of action can be dominated by the man of the spirit. In his biography, *Dumont,* George Woodcock couldn't seem to grasp how such a free-spirited, guerilla leader could be dominated by Riel. Woodcock is a pacifist but — like most people — he doesn't like to believe in the power of the *Christian* spirit.

T: Some people will argue that if Riel had followed some of Dumont's instincts instead of his own, things might have been better for the Metis.

WIEBE: Things would have been momentarily different. Dumont could have covered the prairies in blood. But there was no way he could have won the war.

Big Bear understood this better than anybody, better than Riel. You can't fight the white man with his own weapons. Guns are white man's weapons. You've got to fight him with other powers.

T: *The Temptation of Big Bear* is your best known novel. Is it also your best?

WIEBE: Actually a lot of critics whose opinions I value think that *Scorched-Wood People* is a better book than *Big Bear.* I would like to think so. I would like to think that not only my skill as a novelist but also my comprehension of human beings, is increasing. Also the form of *Scorched-Wood People* was most satisfying to me in contrast to the multi-voiced *Big Bear.* It's the voice of the Metis people that writes this book. The attempt to capture that voice was very satisfying to me.

T: But Big Bear is your most powerful character. How did you discover him?

WIEBE: I discovered him while I was at university. I read William Blaisdale Cameron's *Blood Red the Sun* which discusses the Frog Lake massacre and the part that Big Bear played there. I discovered in Big Bear the ideal character for what I wanted to write. A great native man who had understood what had happened to his people, hadn't liked it, and had tried to change the course of history.

When I discovered Big Bear had actually lived where I had lived during the first part of my life, it was a perfect gift. It's like Bach saying every tune is a gift from God. His character was certainly a gift from God for me.

T: Are you coming towards the end of wanting to probe the past?

WIEBE: Oh, yeh. I've just about had it with the 1870's and the 1880's on the Canadian prairie. I think it's time I wrote something else or people will start thinking I can't do it. [Laughter] I'm working on a novel now that has nothing to do with all these things.

T: Since you're not a believer in total rationality, how much do you structure your novels beforehand?

WIEBE: I usually have a pretty clear idea where the novel's going. The first novel I ever wrote, I wrote the last chapter first. Then I started at the beginning and wrote towards it. I've never written a novel in that method again but I am quite careful.

T: In *First and Vital Candle* the Indian conjurer uses a magic ceremony to physically return a gun lost at the bottom of a river. Most novelists would have never left something like that unexplained.

WIEBE: Actually that event is based on an historically documented report from the Ojibways in Northern Ontario by a University of Pennsylvania anthropologist. When I was in Northern Ontario I met the conjurer who had been responsible. He was a very old man. He didn't talk to white men any more. This was in the early sixties. He said he couldn't do the shaking tent ceremony described in the book because people didn't believe it any more. "You cannot do the shaking tent in a circle of non-believers." I liked that. It tied in with my own feeling that we are surrounded by spirits all the time, but we just don't have the receptors to pick them up.

T: Since you're an avowed moralist, do you ever despair about the limitations of literature, about how few people you're influencing?

WIEBE: It's a limited audience, sure. I once wrote a script out of one of my weakest short stories for CBC television and between two and three million people watched it. And that's not even a big television audience. Think how many Canadians watched *Roots*! But I don't think it's necessarily the job of an artist to reach as many people as possible. The job of an artist is to make a genuine article. Like a potter who makes a pot. It exists. It carries on.

A novelist is scattering seed, I guess. In the good earth it grows. And in the long run, it will make a bit of difference.

T: Since you've led a life of relative self-denial —

WIEBE: [Interrupting laughter]

T: I mean in terms of restricting yourself to certain beliefs... Do you think your fiction writing might be an especially important outlet for you because when you indulge your imagination it can sometimes be an almost ecstatic release?

WIEBE: Oh, it is. It is.

T: The power of that release comes through in your writing. Like a way of getting high almost.

WIEBE: Yes, if the writing is going well, the writing just carries you along. I've been told I didn't write parts of *Big Bear* at all, Big Bear wrote it through me. At its best, you're quite right, that can be a kind of ecstasy. But I easily get those contact highs from other people, too. So I can go to the beer parlour, like Robert Kroetsch says, and drink nothing but Tang and come out higher than anybody there.

T: Kroetsch thinks realism may be becoming counterproductive to art. Do you think of your subjective realism as a dislocation of perception?

WIEBE: I'll leave it to the analysts to decide what kind of realism I have. But Kroetsch obviously is not a realist. *What the Crow Said,* for example, takes tall stories to an incredible end. In its own way it's more imaginative than *Beautiful Losers.* But I still have faith in the straight story. Ordinary human experiences. There's still something to be said for that kind of storytelling.

T: The awkwardness of your syntax can be quite disturbing to some readers. Do you purposely want your readers to put extra effort into your books because the more effort they put in, the more they can take away from it?

WIEBE: That's part of it. You say it well and clearly. When I read the first chapter of *Peace Shall Destroy Many* and the first chapter of *The Scorched-Wood People,* I'm very aware that neither of them is very easy reading. But in both instances, I'm trying to keep people from reading the sort of novel where you know it all the first time. I want to keep you on edge, feeling you're not getting it all. I want you to feel this so strongly that you read it again when you're finished.

T: So flawlessness can be a flaw.

WIEBE: In a way, yes.

T: Do you ever encounter resentment that a Canadian writer is experimenting with language to such a degree? As if it's okay for James Joyce but not for some guy from Alberta?

WIEBE: I get it all the time. Professors of English who are friends of mine tell me *The Blue Mountains of China* is too hard to read. I say, what? You've been reading Joyce and Faulkner all your life. Don't tell me that. We think language has to always be logical and explanatory. It isn't necessarily. Language is often parabolic. If you want to understand a Mozart concerto, you play it over again.

T: I didn't like *The Blue Mountain of China* as much either, but not because of the language. You took it for granted that your reader would be sympathetic to all your characters long before the reader got a chance to learn who each character was. Whereas your preceding novel was totally the opposite. Do you consciously try different approaches for each book?

WIEBE: Sure. You read all five and all five are different. *Peace Shall Destroy Many* is an omniscient novel. *First and Vital Candle* is a limited exploration of an individual. *The Blue Mountains of China* is almost stream of consciousness. I think once you've done a certain novel, it's such a long job that you don't want to do another book the same way. Besides, each book demands a different form. If you're going to have a novel about a people who are scattered all over the continents of the world throughout an entire century, like *Blue Mountains of China*, you can't write a third person, central-intelligence novel. I could have done that. I could have concentrated on two or three people. But I didn't think that would capture the genius and particular historical insight of the Mennonites between 1880 and 1970.

T: Could you explain the importance of naming in fiction. I know that's an idea Doris Lessing has about her work, too, but it's a difficult notion to get hold of.

WIEBE: Naming is the origin of language. Language is the way man handles his world. My child is sitting in the train with me and sees hills in the distance and he says, "What's that?" I say "hills." He says, "What are they though?" I say, "The Sweet Grass Hills." That satisfies him. You've had that experience too, I'm sure. Kids have an incredible curiosity about language. Once they catch on to what language is all about, they want to know more and more. They want names. That to me is the genius of language. It's how man dominates his environment. Man's greatest invention to me is not getting to the moon; it's the invention of language. And naming is the beginning of language.

To me, this is the genius of Jesus. He expressed his world view by telling stories. A person who wants to express a different world view than has been expressed before does not come around talking about philosophic principles. That's a back-assed way of doing it. You should begin with the stories and then deduce the principles. That's the way Aristotle arrived at his great criticism. He looked at all the extant literature of the time and he deduced certain principles from it.

That is the way all great minds work, I think. Not the other way around.

The power of Jesus over the power of St. Paul is exactly that. Jesus tells the stories and you work them out for yourself. St. Paul comes along with the principles and gets everybody mad. Even though Jesus and St. Paul were basically talking about the same things.

T: Do you see yourself doing the same thing in your work? where the truth is in the stories and not the principles?

WIEBE: Yes.

T: Your play, *Far as the Eye Can See,* is a good example of that. The rural people fight a power company and you don't propagandize.

WIEBE: And it's had some exciting effects. In Edmonton, where I saw it performed, a kind of electricity ran through the audience. People recognized their own story was being told. That's a political act. They gasped when Peter Lougheed suddenly descended from the skies. They nudged each other and said, hey, that's Lougheed! Or they laughed about the federal agriculture minister or cracks about their local paper. Laughter at ourselves is great.

We import everything in Canada. We import all our laughter, all our stories. We're the most cosmopolitan people in the world. We're expected to understand every culture but our own!

T: In your books there are strong indications that we must stay close to earth to stay close to God. Is that because rural life encourages communalism?

WIEBE: It's possible in the city, too. That's what a church can provide. The church fits into the greatest ideals we now have of community. The people I meet in church on Sunday I often visit during the week. We come together for worship service from all over the city. We talk a lot and visit a lot. As a result, my children know a lot of different-aged people. They know a lot of adults my age. They have models for adult behaviour other than myself and my wife. This is important. Often children have no models except their parents, and that can be depressing for both.

T: Do you despair about the spiritual morass North American society is in?

WIEBE: It's pretty terrible. The standard ideals are such terrible models of behaviour. We run after the Rolling Stones because they represent all the excesses that we dream about in our worst dreams. Young people often wait for the next record to come out to see what new message is going to be given. That kind of thing is very disheartening to me.

T: It seems there's a pervasive hopelessness these days that people use as an excuse to embrace selfishness.

WIEBE: I'm sure you're exactly right there. It avoids being involved with any second or third human being. But there are always young people who will reject selfish values. They realize dreams about being dropped off in front of theatres from Rolls Royces are essentially no good.

T: Margaret Laurence believes optimism is unrealistic but that a good writer has to be someone with hope. Is hope at the basis of why you write?

WIEBE: Certainly that's one thing. I think Man is good. He longs for good things. Often our basic humanity gets perverted but Man has been made by a good creator. So I'm basically hopeful in many ways.

T: Wouldn't an historian say ours is simply another society in a state of decadent decline? that the tide can never be turned?

WIEBE: Maybe. But you can always keep seeing societies in states of decline. Look at the kind of society from which my parents came in Russia in 1917. They were literally starving, socially and religiously abused and harrassed. Yet people kept on loving. People kept on having children. People kept affirming life. When I look at those times and I look at my own, I can't believe how fortunate we are. People say I wouldn't bring a child into today's world. They're crazy. They know nothing about the world. They know nothing about history.

What To Write

MARGARET ATWOOD

Margaret Atwood's unwavering resolve to hold up new mirrors to present day society, regardless of how unflattering or unsettling the resultant true images may be, makes her work to date an exemplary answer to the question of what subject matter Canadian writers should be exploring.

Her remarkable analytical perceptivity and prolific intellectual honesty have produced a diverse canon that well merits her reputation as one of Canada's most important and popular writers — and, as well, effectively prohibits any worthwhile synopsis of her basic concerns within this space. Life Before Man, *her most recent novel, which forms the basis for discussion in the following interview, examines the mating habits of contemporary Torontonians against the backdrop of the Royal Ontario Museum and simultaneously addresses the feasibility of mankind's continued tenure on the planet.*

Major collections of poetry include The Circle Game *(1966, Governor General's Award),* The Journals of Susanna Moodie *(1970),* Power Politics *(1973),* Selected Poems *(1976) and* Two-Headed Poems *(1979).*

Her extremely varied novels are The Edible Woman *(1969),* Surfacing *(1972),* Lady Oracle *(1976) and* Life Before Man *(1979).*

Dancing Girls *(1978) is a collection of short stories.* Survival: A Thematic Guide to Canadian Literature *(1972) is her major work of criticism.*

Margaret Atwood was born in Ottawa in 1939. She has lived and studied throughout Canada and Europe. Presently she lives with her daughter and novelist-husband, Graeme Gibson in Alliston, Ontario.

photo: Graeme Gibson

T: Did you come from a relatively typical liberal background?

ATWOOD: I came from a very isolated background. This is probably the key to some of my writing. I grew up isolated from society in a kind and non-violent family of scientists. When I hit society I was shocked. [laughing] I'm probably still in a state of culture shock.

T: And you always will be?

ATWOOD: Probably. Because I was only exposed to a small range of human behaviour, the good side. But the bad side is pretty bad. If you grow up being told, "On Saturdays we burn crosses on people's lawns," then you can't be so easily shocked. You become numb to it. "On Fridays we go down to the corner bar and beat each other up and then we go and kill some Jews or Catholics or blacks or whatever." You can get hardened to that kind of thing. But I've never become hardened. So whatever radicalism I possess comes out of that.

T: What's radical about *Life Before Man* is that it's the first Canadian novel I know of that seriously conveys an awareness that the human race can become extinct. Was that a conscious theme while writing the book?

ATWOOD: Yes. It's why the novel is set in the Royal Ontario Museum. And why Lesje is a paleontologist who studies dinosaurs.

T: And why the characters exhibit predatory behaviour?

ATWOOD: Absolutely. Not just the character of Elizabeth but also how our society encourages people to be that way.

T: With a book like *Life Before Man* and a movie like *Apocalypse Now!*, I wonder if we're heading into an age of examining ourselves for evil.

ATWOOD: Being aware of how awful we can be might be a self-preservation technique. Certainly when you do that it stops you from turning other people into the devil. You're unlikely to say that everything is the fault of the Germans or any other group you want to use as a scapegoat.

T: Our scapegoat in Canada has always been the United States. *Life Before Man* resembles *Surfacing* in that regard because it really helps dispel that pretension that Canadians are somehow morally superior.

ATWOOD: People can be morally superior when they are in a position of relative powerlessness. For instance, if you're a woman being victimized then you can afford moral superiority. But once you have power, you have to take responsibility. Some of your decisions may be harmful to others. I think Canada has been able to afford moral super- iority because it's been relatively powerless. I don't think, and I never have thought, that Canada's inherently better. In fact, all you have to do is look at its past record. Scratch the country and it's quite a fascist place. Look at the attitudes to the War Measures Act or the RCMP opening the mail. Canada's not a goody-goody land of idealists. If we got to a position where we needed some witches to burn, I'm sure we'd find some and burn them. That's why I find Canada potentially a somewhat scary place. Underneath, we're not much different from anywhere else.

You look at mankind and you see something like Dante's *The Divine Comedy*. You see the Inferno at one end with everybody pulling out each other's fingernails, as in the Amnesty International bulletins. Or you see the Purgatorio, shaped like a mountain, with people climbing up it or sitting still. Up at the top there's what used to be called Heaven with what used to be called God. Only now we've replaced Heaven with a kind of Utopian vision of what humanity could be if only. . .Fill in the blank. The trouble with real life is once you try to implement Utopia, you end up with the Inferno. You end up pulling out a lot of fingernails from the people who don't agree with you. That is, as we say, the Human Condition. [laughing] That was the catch-all phrase when I was in graduate school. Whenever you came to the point at which you didn't know why things were the way they were, you said that was the Human Condition.

T: Was this new novel called *Life Before Man* from the start?

ATWOOD: No, it was originally called *Notes on the Mezaoic*. Mezaoic means "middle life." The novel is the middle of the lives of several people. And they're middle class. And it's mid-history. But the title was changed because everybody said "Notes on the What?"

T: Have you sat down and figured out all the possible interpretations of *Life Before Man* as a title?

ATWOOD: I think I've got the main three anyway. For Lesje, it refers to the pre-historic era. For Elizabeth, it means that her own life is given priority over any relationship with a man. For Nate, it's connected with his political idealism. That is, humanity right now, considering all the things it does, such as shooting children, is not yet fully human.

T: That's actually a very optimistic idea.

ATWOOD: Very optimistic. Absolutely, Nate is an optimist at heart but he doesn't want to admit it.

T: But there are negative connotations to that title, too.

ATWOOD: How so?

T: Meaning that life, in a holistic scientific sense, is always going to take precedence over the insignificance of man.

ATWOOD: That's William. He's more interested in the survival of cockroaches than he is in the survival of the human race.

T: *Life Before Man* could also mean life before the eyes of man, as opposed to life lived before the eyes of God.

ATWOOD: That would fit as well.

T: I read it mostly as *Life Before Ethics.*

ATWOOD: That would be Elizabeth. She has no interest in ethics whatsoever. "Morality" is your relationship with yourself. "Ethics" is your relationship with other people. The Sixties confused people. They tried to enjoy themselves and not worry about restricting their lives in artificial puritanical ways. The problem was, once you enter into social relationships, ethics has to come in. When they stomped on morality, ethics got thrown out too. I'm not a social predictor but I do think that "morality" is going to come back in now. [laughing] Unfortunately most people still aren't too equipped to think ethically!

T: Do you think it's our swing back to conservatism that's going to solidify some standards of morality again?

ATWOOD: I don't know whether it's a question of standards. It might be more a question of fear. I think a lot of people do things because they're frightened. In times of stress, or what people think of as times of stress and hardship — because of course this country is not in stress and hardship, people are not starving in droves in the street, we're doing a lot of whining that would be pretty much sneered at in other parts of the world — people get frightened. They think they may not be able to get jobs. Or they won't be able to get the kinds of jobs that they might like to have. Whereas in the early sixties, people didn't feel like that.

So now we're retreating back into our rabbit holes. We're pulling in our tentacles so they don't get stepped on. When that happens, you want to form a monogamous relationship with somebody, hoping that it's going to keep you warm and safe.

T: This runs all through your work. The idea that fear is more primordial than love.

ATWOOD: Yeah. Because in a society like ours where people are pretty much out there on their own hook, there's no real social support system for them, no small tribe or clan or integrated structure that's going to support an individual in it; so fear is a real motivating factor. And because you don't really know where the danger is coming from, fear takes the form often of a generalized anxiety or paranoia. You don't know who the enemy is. You don't know what direction you'll be attacked from. So everybody ends up constantly swivelling around, looking for the next threat. People are afraid of whatever's out there. And rightly so.

T: And that influences who you love and how you love them.

ATWOOD: Yes. Are you loving someone out of desperation and need or are you loving someone because they're "them," as we say?

T: The marriage in *Life Before Man* paints a pretty depressing example of what happens when domesticity and sexuality can't coexist under one roof.

ATWOOD: Yes, but now marriage is retrenching itself. People are getting married a lot younger again because in times of economic hardship, people retreat to the domestic burrow. But perhaps these marriages will be formed on more equitable terms. One hopes, with marriage in the 70's, people are going into it with different expectations. In 1955, the husband was the breadwinner and the wife would have children; the husband was the boss and the wife kept her mouth shut. I'd like to think that some of that has changed. But you tell me. You're young enough.

T: I think maybe one of the problems now is that people may be getting married without enough expectations.

ATWOOD: Or without any.

T: We're groovy, we're together and if it doesn't work out we can always drift off somewhere else.

ATWOOD: None of this stuff would make much difference if it weren't influencing the lives of children. Society has always said, "You have to preserve marriage for the sake of the children." I've never really bought that one. But on the other hand, when breakups start happening on a large scale, you have to think of the consequences. We may be producing a lot of isolated, self-protective, narcissistic children.

T: At least Elizabeth does genuinely care about her kids.

ATWOOD: Yeah. Strange to say, many readers like Elizabeth. She doesn't take crap. She's not hypocritical about herself. She had a bad childhood and she got locked in to a struggle with her aunt. When she is finally able, not exactly to forgive her aunt, but at least to go through the motions of giving human support, that's positive. Even though she doesn't *feel* compassion, she acts it out anyway. After that happens, there's a chance she will be able to get outside herself. She puts politics and the women's movement down at the beginning of the book because if there's nothing in it for her, forget it. But by the end of the book there's a possibility of change. I never make Prince Charming endings because I don't believe in them. But I do believe that people can change. Maybe not completely, but some.

So Elizabeth has a lot of fans. Especially women over 35 with two kids and a shaky marriage. They think Elizabeth is all right. She's ruthless in her dealings with other people, but then people have been ruthless in their dealings with her. Violence begets violence.

T: What do you say to the argument that this book only adds to the *ennui* of the present? That bleakness begets bleakness?

ATWOOD: That's like saying everybody should write happy books. As far as I can tell, people in a crisis would much rather have that crisis admitted. When a friend of mine was dying, everybody tried to jolly him up. They said, "Oh no, you're not going to die." The fact was he knew he was dying and he wanted to talk about it. I think people in a crisis would rather have somebody say, "This is a crisis, this is real." That's much more comforting than saying here are John and Mary, they live in this bungalow, they have a washing machine and three kids, and they're really happy. What could be less cheerful if you're in a bad situation than being told normal people are happy? A lot of normal people aren't happy.

T: I agree. People always talk about censorship from the government or censorship through economics. But the main form of censorship in our society is really self-censorship.

ATWOOD: Exactly. People will say, "I don't want to hear about it" or "I don't want to read about it." But for me the novel is a social vehicle. It reflects society. Serious writers these days don't write uplifting books because what they see around them is not uplifting. It would be hypocritical to say the world is inspirational. It's not. These days the world is a pretty dismal place. You can blank that out. You can destroy your Amnesty International newsletter without reading it. But that doesn't make that stuff go away. The less you pay attention to it, the more it's going to be there for somebody else.

We think we can go on playing with our toys forever. But if you're not aware of the fact that you may die, you're much less careful about other people. One of the crucial moments in any life is when you come to that realization.

T: When did you come to that realization for yourself?

ATWOOD: Sometime in my twenties. I had had a romantic, adolescent notion of death earlier but I hadn't really felt that solid moment when you realize your life is not going to go on forever. That people you know aren't going to be here forever. That we're going to die. What was it the Greeks used to say? "Call no man happy until he is dead."

T: Do you think it was essential to you as a writer to come to terms with death?

ATWOOD: It's essential to everyone as a human being.

T: But there's always been this particularly strong awareness in your poetry that life is transient.

ATWOOD: [deadpan] Life is transient. War is hell.

T: Birds fly.

[laughter]

T: Do you get sick of hearing critics say your poetry is better than your novels?

ATWOOD: People often have difficulty handling somebody who does more than one thing. That's their problem. It's not a difficulty for me.

T: Do you think it's been an advantage for you because you can carry into prose that poet's instinct to "make it new"?

ATWOOD: I don't know whether my poetry is an advantage to me as a novelist or not. For me poetry is where the language is renewed. If poetry vanished, language would become dead. It would become enbalmed. [laughing] People say, "Well, now that you're writing successful novels I suppose you'll be giving up poetry." As if one wrote in order to be successful. The fact is, I would never give up poetry. Poetry might give me up, but that's another matter. It's true that poetry doesn't make money. But it's the heart of the language. If you think of language as a series of concentric circles, poetry is right in the centre. It's where precision takes place. It's where that use of language takes place that can extend a word yet have it be precise.

T: That's one of the best things about *Life Before Man*. It seems in this novel you've dispensed with a lot of the trappings of a conventional novel and concentrated on writing more from your poetic strength. Many Canadian reviews have criticised *Life Before Man* for what it isn't rather than trying to appreciate what it is.

ATWOOD: Yeah. I have that trouble. Some people always want to review the book that came before. When I wrote *Surfacing*, people wanted it to be *Edible Woman*. When I wrote *Lady Oracle*, people wanted it to be *Surfacing*. With this one, some reviewers wanted it to be *Lady Oracle*. They thought it was supposed to be a satire. But this new novel is more like *Surfacing* than *Lady Oracle*. Maybe this is why many people have missed its social and political content.

I cannot publish a book in Canada today without getting a third bad reviews, a third good reviews and a middle third that goes either way. I expect that. You can't be a writer of my visibility without somebody saying, "She's supposed to be such hot stuff. We think she's overexposed or overrated." That's going to happen every time.

T: *Macleans* praised the book as an excellent "women's novel." Were you aware that you lacked "the soaring perspective of the great novelists"?

ATWOOD: [laughter] That definition of a women's novel as being a book fundamentally about human relationships has to include all of Jane Austen, all of the Bronte sisters, quite a lot of Charles Dickens, *Vanity Fair* and *Middlemarch* — which to me is the best Victorian novel.

Not to mention just about all of serious modern literature with the exception of spy stories, murder mysteries and westerns. Everything else fits into that "women's novel" category. Novels have people in them. You can see their society through their interaction. Some people just can't see very well.

T: Or they don't want to see. Stories that are so modern can frighten people.

ATWOOD: Some people are frightened of my work, that's true. A real kind of heavy shock set in around *Power Politics* in 1971. But then three or four years after they appear, my books aren't shocking any more. Because that's where people have come to.

A lot of writers write about their childhood or what it was like in the small town where they grew up. Things that happened twenty years ago. On the pain level, these books are easier to read than something more immediate. When it's in the past, you know it's over. But the closer something is to you, the more shock value it can have. It could be you. That's why some people find me pretty terrifying. They confuse me with the work.

T: Also people are still very wary of any woman with power. And *Life Before Man* is quite devastating.

ATWOOD: Yes, but I think more and more, as people get used to the idea that I'm around, some of that fear goes away. I can find there's more openness now to what I'm doing than there was before.

T: My wife's comment on reading the book was that everyone can see themselves growing older in it.

ATWOOD: True.

T: And that can make people feel very uncomfortable, too.

ATWOOD: Yes, I suppose the message there is if you've got something to do, do it now. Everybody's going to croak sooner or later. Meanwhile you do have some latitude about what you're going to put into your life story. If you think about life only in terms of having a job, of future security, of doing things according to the book, you're probably just playing somebody else's script.

T: Your *Survival* hypothesis has been rather fiercely attacked as "fashionably radical, bourgeois individualism." Do you take any of that Marxist criticism seriously?

ATWOOD: No, I don't have very much time for the kind of purist leftism that defines itself as the only true religion. It's like Plymouth Brethrenism. They're so puritanical that they don't even go after new members. They're just interested in defining their own purity as opposed to the evil of everybody else. That kind of leftism is useless in this country. It has no sense of its constituency. It doesn't know how to address them. So if they want to call me names that's fine, nobody's litening.

I work on a magazine called *This Magazine*. As far as I'm concerned it's the best of the small left magazines in Canada. One of the members, Rick Salutin [playwright who wrote *Les Canadiens*], wrote a piece on *Survival* as a Marxist book. He was talking about how it had an awareness of historical development, how it took into account its place as a political instrument in that development and how it made a connection between the economy and the culture.

T: When you have a nation that is only two or three generations removed from the pioneer experience, is it really possible for us to have had anything other than a literature which is predominantly concerned with survival?

ATWOOD: That's one of the things I'm arguing. Although I don't think that's the only determining factor. In Western Canada that pioneer experience may be only two or three generations removed, but in Eastern Canada it's often eight or nine. So it's not the whole story.

T: The whole story is that our colonial status as a nation has spawned a literature of failure.

ATWOOD: No, I said a literature of survival.

T: Either way, being victimized politically has created a nation that is lacking in self-respect.

ATWOOD: Yes, Canada doesn't go for the brass ring.

T: In the seven years since you wrote *Survival* have you become any more optimistic about Canada's progression towards attaining self-respect politically?

ATWOOD: Culturally, you could say Canada's doing okay. Writers have a union now and they're standing up for their rights. We've even got a film industry of sorts. But that's a very small group of people. When you look at the economic situation you can see that things have

in fact gotten worse. More of Canada is foreign-owned than when I
published that book in 1972. So maybe our burst of culture is only a
mushroom that will disappear in three or four years. Our entertainment market may be taken over by bigger interests now that Canda is
becoming a more lucrative market. For instance, chain book stores
now control 40% of the business. If they control 60%, they will start
dictating what will be published. Publishers will send them their
manuscripts first and the chain will say what gets published. They will
have a stranglehold on writing, and the market will be even more
foreign-dominated and junk-dominated.

This is not optimism or pessimism. It's just looking at things that
are there.

How To Write

ROBERT HARLOW

Robert Harlow took the first Creative Writing course ever offered by a Canadian university, studied Creative Writing in the U.S. and later headed Canada's first accredited Creative Writing Department for ten years at the University of British Columbia, where he still teaches. Although the legitimacy of Creative Writing courses is questioned by some writers, the learn-to-write phenomenon of which Harlow has been an integral part is finding increased acceptance among Canadian universities and high schools.

Royal Murdoch (1962) and A Gift of Echoes (1965) are Harlow's first two novels, which explore and psychologically map his native northern British Columbia.

Scann (1972) is a newspaper editor's formidable, dream-like chronicle of the history and times of his northern B.C. town. Composed during a three-day retreat on an Easter weekend coinciding with the town's fiftieth anniversary, Amory Scann's medley of myths tracks a spirit of natural chaos to retrieve a lost sense of primeval order buried under civilization's social controls.

Making Arrangements (1978) is a comic tale of how three regular dead-beats from a dumpy Vancouver hotel outwit the local syndicate, evade the police, witness the world's first pay-TV sexual Olympics and then sell a smuggled Peruvian aphrodisiac to a filthy rich Arab oil sheik—all to raise a bet at the race track.

Robert Harlow was born in Prince Rupert, B.C. in 1923 and raised in Prince George, B.C. He lives in Vancouver.

photo: Dianne Demille

T: From your books, it sounds like you've had your share of rubbing shoulders with what we euphemistically call the real world.

HARLOW: Well, my father was a railroader who came out west from Maine in 1909. I grew up in Prince George when it was still a small town of 2,000 people. I did the usual things there like drive a truck, work in mills, and some timber cruising. When the war came, I was fifteen. I graduated from high school at seventeen and joined the Air Force. I was a bomber pilot for '43, '44 and '45. Then I went to UBC. I'd never even been to Vancouver, except to join up, but I had this ambition to go to university because very few people from my hometown ever did. I got my BA and then took Earle Birney's creative writing workshop in 1946.

T: That was the first creative writing workshop ever taught in Canada.

HARLOW: Yeh, that's right. All sorts of people from that class went on to do interesting things, but I think I'm the only writer.

T: What kind of influence was Earle Birney?

HARLOW: Earle was a marvellous role model, a pretty fantastic guy, because I got to see how much energy you had to expend on writing. After I studied some more at Paul Engle's workshop in Iowa and got married, I was working at the CBC as a producer. Earle phoned me up from UBC one day and asked if I'd be a sessional lecturer for eight months. I went downstairs and saw the boss, who told me I couldn't have leave. So I quit. Then they decided to let me go as sort of a sabbatical. When Earle got fed up with UBC and left, I was approached and asked if I would stay on as head of the newly established Creative Writing Department. I contemplated that decision for, oh... about twelve seconds.

T: How much had you written by then?

HARLOW: I'd written a book for my thesis at Iowa. Then I wrote parts of another two novels in the 50's. Then I published *Royal Murdoch* and *Gift of Echoes*. Later on, in 1970-71, I went on a leave of absence and wrote the bulk of *Scann* in about eight or nine actual writing months. I did it with my long-suffering family in Majorca. People think of it as a very formidable book now but I never thought of it that way as I was writing it.

T: Now with *Making Arrangements,* you've written an entirely different book.

HARLOW: I guess I believe an author should be able to write a full spectrum, not write himself over and over. Hemingway, for instance, fell into that trap a bit. He was a great writer but he did write himself over and over again. Most really good writers simply get better and better at the trade and can do a great number of things. People always say "Dickensian" as if he only wrote one kind of book. That's not true at all. His scope was fantastic. The same with Faulkner. The difference between *Sartoris* and *Light in August* is light years.

T: You once wrote, "Many authors are lost to poverty, journalism, hack writing and too much time on their hands." Why do you feel journalism is bad for writers?

HARLOW: When I said journalism, I meant the whole media thing. Journalism is just too close to real writing. It saps your energies. You have to save that energy for yourself if you're a writer. Hemingway was not a journalist when he wrote his first book. For *The Sun Also Rises* he quit work and starved and sponged off women or friends or whatever he could do. You have to be wily every day of your life. When I was doing what amounted to journalism for the CBC, I didn't really write. There were nine years when I kidded myself I was doing it. Now I save my best brains for when I write in the mornings from six until nine or ten. Then I go out to the university and use my second best brains for teaching. My third best brains are for the evening.

T: Do you ever look at a lot of excellent journalists and see frustrated writers?

HARLOW: Sure. Years ago a friend quit his job with the *Vancouver Sun* and left his family to write the Great Canadian Novel. It didn't happen. Guys dream of that all the time. I don't know how many paragraphs he had at the end of the year but it wasn't very many. Everybody says, "I'm going to go out and write," like they're going to go out and have a baby. You have to do three or four pages a day. It's a craft. It's hard work that does it. You need a lifetime of experience.

You paid me a great compliment when you said *Making Arrangements* seemed to have spontaneous humour. I don't know how many pages of stuff I tore up because I was allowing myself to get into it. That's what technique is all about in writing. To get the author the hell out of his own work so it can be its own spontaneous self.

T: Many people argue that a university can't teach the craft of writing, that all writers have to be self-educated.

HARLOW: There have always been creative schools in various forms. Like in Moscow or St. Petersburgh or Vienna at the turn of the century when people sat around and shared their ideas. That's all we do. I share my experience with young people. Now universities have finally recognized the value of that kind of learning environment and they're sponsoring it.

T: With Creative Writing, is there ever a danger that the "creative" gets stressed over the "writing"? Or do you not separate the two?

HARLOW: That's a very good question. The answer is I think there's something magic about creativity but I don't go around being "creative". That's why I refuse to discuss content in my classes. We only discuss technical arrangements that are needed to fulfill the intent of the author. For instance, last year a student had a story where a woman shoves a gun up her vagina and blows herself up. The class thought the guy who wrote the story was a male chauvinist of the worst order. So I let the discussion go along those lines and it didn't take them long to discover it was fruitless to discuss content. They had to discuss how that could work in his story. That's what happens in a workshop. It's very practical.

T: So you teach writing and not creativity.

HARLOW: Yes. When new instructors come on staff, often you'll find them holding dramatic calisthenics. But that only lasts for a few weeks. Pretty soon they realize the kids want to learn *how* to write. The only way they can do that is by teaching themselves, by writing. In a way, the person who teaches in a creative writing workshop is simply the best writer in that group. If you get one really good writer, that's a good workshop, and everyone in it is suddenly trying to write their asses off to get as good as he or she is.

T: I'd have to say that all the writers I've met of any consequence all have abnormally strong egos or drives.

HARLOW: I like to translate that word ego into drive, too. People with drive stick out. The trick is to learn how to translate that drive into the energy that goes into writing.

T: Do you ever get people who write extremely well but are too passive about their talent?

HARLOW: Sure. And they don't last long. Sometimes it's not so much passivity as lack of confidence that gets to people. Some of them can't stand any criticism at all. I had a girl turn up the other day and she'd never had her work criticized by senior students before. She came in what looked like a uniform, and with a beret on. The way she wore her clothes, they were like battle dress.

T: What happens to the ones who can't cut it?

HARLOW: The ones who get in and don't make it? I never fail them. I tell them I've made a mistake. It was my fault. I was the one who let them in. We select people by looking at their writing. We ask for a hundred pages if you're a grad student, fifty pages if you're a senior student, twenty-five pages if you come out of high school. You can pretty well tell from that. If I make a mistake, they go away and try another way of learning to write or they read for the rest of their lives. But they'll never call an artist down. They'll never say Canada Council shouldn't give a writer a buck or two to finish a book. They appreciate the work involved.

T: You wrote, "By the time the writer has shown he has talent and has begun to develop, the experience he will need as the basis of his work has mostly been gathered." I would disagree with that.

HARLOW: I think the basic experiences we have are all done by the time we're seventeen or eighteen. The way we're going to treat life and deal with experience from then on is pretty much in place.

T: You're just talking about personality.

HARLOW: The tools for handling life. Even though I know it's pop psychology to say it, you're all in place by age five. People do change when they go through puberty. The edges come off. And getting married and having children are certainly heavy experiences. But they don't usually change you fundamentally. Once the personality framework is there, you just get richer and richer as you get older. According to myth, finally you get to be wise.

T: So you believe if you're going to be a writer, it's from what happened to you in the first twenty years?

HARLOW: I think so.

T: When did you know you had to be a writer?

HARLOW: When I was nine I decided to be a travel writer. I had the gift of gab and I was always good on paper so I thought writing would be easy. But I never really started writing until quite late, when I was twenty-two or so. I'm an anomaly in that respect, but the war intervened.

T: In my teens I made a close correlation between creative energy and sexual energy. Did you think that way, too?

HARLOW: When I first was in university, the sexual tension and hysteria was incredible. We spun like dervishes for four solid years. The good girl/bad girl theory was all there. Now, with the pill, young people are more mature. The energy that might have gone into hysteria can now go into creativity. So yes, I do believe the human animal's first analogies will be sexual. However, I don't think there's any one-to-one relationship between sexuality and creativity.

T: Do you differentiate between therapy writing and someone who's writing from strength?

HARLOW: Sure. Solzenitzhen writes from controlled experience and Sylvia Plath was a therapy writer. Everybody goes through a period in their life when they're like Plath, male or female. But with therapy writing I think the author's usually in the book too much, and the result is neurotic autobiography.

T: Do you see any trend nowadays away from that subjectivism of the sixties?

HARLOW: You know what we're doing now? Fantasy. Science fiction. In the last week I've had three science fiction stories turned in. This is typical. We did it in the fifties, and it was done in the thirties when times were bad, too. In times of great change, people suddenly don't understand the world and turn to fantasy as a way of handling things. Speculative fiction has always been some kind of bottom line. Shakespeare did his *Tempest* after a long life of writing. Tolkien did his *Lord of the Rings*.

T: It's all very well to know how to write. But do you also teach your students how to read?

HARLOW: Very few people ask that question. But yes, it's absolutely essential to writing to learn to read for technique. God bless English studies. It's analysis. Writing is synthesis. The twain do not often meet. In high class criticism, which everybody hopes they write, I'm sure they do meet. Authors have to learn for themselves both synthesis and analysis. If I'm standing in line at the supermarket, I find myself picking up a nurse romance to see how and what the author is doing.

T: What should aspiring writers read?

HARLOW: Most people say to read anything that comes to hand, and I suppose that's half the answer. The other half is the hard part. All the time you're reading you should be finding out how it's done. And you don't usually start being curious about technical things until after you've begun to be serious about writing. So, one of the things I do with my students is to try to encourage them to be serious about both writing and reading all the time—see if I can't get them to teach themselves to read as authors, rather than just as readers, and that leads them immediately to seeing how things are done. Then they apply that to their own writing.

Eventually a snowball effect occurs and larger and larger questions rise up for them to answer for themselves—What *is* a novel, for instance? Or, what *can* it be? Read Dickens and you know that he invented a lot of things that it can be—those things that Sterne didn't invent in *Tristram Shandy*. Read Grass and he will show you how to turn Dickens' novel upside down and inside out and make *The Tin Drum*. Read Faulkner and you will see a half dozen other approaches. And then there are the great novella writers—Grass again, Mann, Unamuno, Moravia, Henry James, Robbe-Grillet. Mann does *The Magic Mountain* and *Death in Venice*—a ten-pound novel and a beautiful novella. James does *The Ambassadors* and *Daisy Miller* or *Turn of the Screw*. Grass does *The Tin Drum* and *Cat and Mouse*. Those aren't just long and short books. There's a technical tactic involved. Sooner or later writers reading as authors will begin to build on that tactic and will discover and use the novella for their own purposes—in the way, perhaps, Marian Engel did it when she wrote *Bear,* or Laurence when she wrote *A Jest of God,* or Solzenitzhen when he wanted to do *A Day in the Life of Ivan Denisovich*.

The novella is the basic prose form. It deals with the *energy* generated by individual moments of consciousness—or time, if you will. Once upon a time. The novel has "the times", society, added to those energised moments, and that changes it into an entirely different genre. The short story stops a moment of time so that it can happen for us lyrically, poetically. The best short stories are always poems. And, of course, there are those other parts of writing that are common to all genres that we run into all the time when we read—point of view, for instance, which is a subject vast enough to take up your time for most of your writing life. All the concerns of composition like narrative line, tone of voice, making scenes, the whole lot. There's always enough content, seldom enough technique.

T: So technique is the necessary key to content.

HARLOW: Look, let me bring in a letter here that I received this morning. I think it's germane. It's from a young woman in Paris. She's broke, getting free room and board from a rich family for doing domestic chores. This is what she says, "I started a new novel in January and I will not leave Paris until it's finished. I have never worked so well as I am here. I am ecstatic to have the chance to do this—no friends, no phone, no disturbances, no distractions. This is the only way to write a novel. The difficult thing is being totally alone with this. I have to think about technique all the time but it's such a strain. Sometimes as I reread I hear you saying, "No! No! No!" like you used to in red ink in the margins. I've written and revised 150 pages." She adds that she's reading Collette, Henry Miller and Kozinski. A nice mix, I'd say. But the point I'd make about her is that when we first met in class she hadn't read anything but a few best sellers and thought technique was for lovers. Her first try at a book was damned good, considering her technical experience. What helped most, aside from the seven months she spent in our workshop, was the reading she began to do. I think the new book will be pretty close to publishable— and for someone not yet twenty-five that's a hell of a head start, which is something she mostly got from joining a workshop, working her butt off and learning something about reading and about new authors to use as technical models.

T: That list of books you recited was pretty international, especially for a literary nationalist.

HARLOW: Right. Nowadays I'm becoming pretty chauvinist. The reason is because we have some pretty good technicians among us here in Canada. Robert Kroetsch, for instance. And have you read Betty Lambert's *Crossings*? It's a fine novel. You could write a treatise on its technical aspects. The same could be said for Reshard Gool's new book, *The Nemesis Casket*. An absolute gem.

I think the greatest thing that ever happened to literature in this country was the 1967 Centennial. The federal government had to give some money to literature because they gave it to everybody else. Now we've got a lot of excellent writers in this country. The problem now is to get the public aware of what is being produced.

T: And in a small country next to the States, that's difficult. And from your wisecrack about Toronto in *Making Arrangements,* I expect you'd also agree there are problems if you're not writing in Ontario.

Do you think "the fix is always in" in Canlit, too? just like at the racetrack?

HARLOW: No, I don't. But I've found it hard not to make paranoid cracks about Toronto. After twelve years here in the CBC and the most of the rest of my life as a resident of B.C., it's difficult to shake the feeling that you don't quite exist. When *Scann* came out in 1972, [William] French and [Robert] Fulford and [Kildare] Dobbs all refused to review it on the grounds that it was too big. Probably things have changed for the better by now so far as getting noticed is concerned, but at the moment publishing as a literary enterprise has all but collapsed and so the problem of Toronto as the centre of the universe has faded somewhat.

T: So you forgive them in the Unmysterious East.

HARLOW: No. Not at all. Now that the pressure of the collapse is on, I think they have to take the responsibility of rehabilitating the literary scene as seriously as they once took the privilege of being at the centre of things with the power to make and break literary enterprises of all kinds. If one is going to be imperial, going to live up to its demands, then one has to learn *noblesse oblige.*

When To Write

DENNIS LEE

*Dennis Lee is a poet in search of intimations of the sacred. Although he has gained considerable notoriety through sales of his highly successful children's books (*Alligator Pie *1974,* Nicholas Knock *1974,* Garbage Delight *1977,* The Ordinary Bath *1979), Lee's infrequent articulations of his desire to gain spiritual wisdom born of communion with what mankind was once free to confidently describe as the gods have also established him as one of Canada's most gifted and original poets.*

Civil Elegies and Other Poems *(1972) received the Governor General's Award.*

The Gods *(1979) is his only subsequent major collection of adult poetry.*

Savage Fields *(1977) is his major publication of literary criticism.*

Lee acknowledges that the relative breadths of historical and literary perspectives that any writer possesses to provide contemporary frameworks and ground-rules for his or her craft is a when-to-write issue easily as significant as the more obvious question regarding when a writer should ideally choose to commit thoughts to paper. How he has addressed himself to both these matters defines his unique position within Canadian letters.

Born in Toronto in 1939, Lee studied and taught chiefly at the University of Toronto prior to stints as a literary publisher, publisher's consultant and writer-in-residence. Presently he is one of Canada's most respected editors, residing with his wife and three children in Toronto.

photo: Alan Twigg

T: Most poets designate themselves as poets, then feel obliged to go about creating poems. Why are you so extremely unprolific? and why do you dislike defining yourself as a poet?

LEE: I don't know, exactly. My sense of language is different from most other poets', but I have trouble discussing it coherently. It's true, if I had to spend my life being a "Poet", I wouldn't. And in twenty years I've produced less than thirty poems that seem to me worth keeping between the covers of a book, even though I work non-stop. But this is neither poverty of the imagination, nor some special fastidious virtue. It's just the way it works. My first drafts are so godawful, I need an incredibly strong pull from whatever is trying to get written before I can write anything at all.

T: What about your objectives? Do you always know what you're trying to do when you write a poem?

LEE: I write to find out what the poem wants to do.

T: How do you connect that approach to your feeling that you're writing outside the mainstream of Canadian poetry?

LEE: Well, back east there's a tradition of the well-made poem, of people trying all their lives to add three more poems to the mythical anthology of great verse in the English language. And in the west there's a sense of people trying to work from the quick of words, from the process of moment-to-moment being.

This is going to sound quixotic or just like some nifty thing to say, but I mean it literally. When I get together with an empty piece of paper, the main message I get as far as poetry by Dennis Lee is concerned is: Don't Bother. I have lots of private experiences and opinions, of course, but why clutter up the airwaves with more of that stuff? If that's all there is, better the paper stays empty. So I start from square one, which is silence. Often enough I just stay there.

This is very different from a poet who walks down the street, sees a child hit by a car driven by a drunken driver, and feels compelled to go home and write about it. Or who falls in love and needs to tell what it's like. That's great, of course. That's being a Poet. But I'm the kind of writer who is always mooching around in an empty space that words may or may not decide to enter, waiting on them tongue-tied.

T: So you're not trying to be socially useful? Or to have some cathartic, therapeutic experience by writing?

LEE: That's right, I'm not. At least not while I'm writing, which is what counts. When people ask, "Do you write for yourself or your readers?", both alternatives are wrong. The only target, the magnet, the one thing that exists for you is the thing that is trying to get itself into words, and isn't there yet.

What happens when "it" is finally born there on the page is a different matter. Then the writer can be concerned for the reader, or self-centred, or whatever. But that's after the event.

T: "The event" being that something which gets a hold of you and says, "Write me."

LEE: Right. I hate to sound so mystical about it. It must sound like a pile of crap. But how I've managed to make even 25 or 30 poem-like objects in the last decade is almost beyond me. I often wait so long for something to vouchsafe itself that I can't help asking what am I doing it for, mooching around like that? And then when it does come, you go from famine to feast. There are so many dimensions and overlaps and tonalities to even the simplest thing. You get overwhelmed by the multiplicity of what-is. That's when craft is necessary, just to keep up with it through the scores of drafts.

T: Writing your kind of poem could be likened to editing what-is. Maybe the qualities that make you a good editor have made you a poet?

LEE: That's a good connection to make. And as an editor, I also start by being purely reactive.

T: What's the tie-in between this purely responsive stance and your contention in *The Gods* that artists have been doing "unclean work" and "murdering the real"?

LEE: That's a complicated question. First of all, the notion of artists being murderers of the real has to be seen in a particular historical context. We have to look at the writing of the last 200 years.

Before that, dimensions of meaning were experienced as residing in the day-to-day world. "What-is" was sacramental, it mediated meaning. But with the advent of the "objective world" of Descartes, of a universe composed of value-free facts, the "feelings" and "meanings" and "values" were severed from the objective world and exiled to the domain of the private subject. The cosmos was no longer taken to be intrinsically meaningful.

By 1800, say, the crisis of living in a de-valued real world had come to be felt *as* a crisis. All the great Romantics had to wrestle with it. Since then, the artists' progressive attempts to resolve it have led mainly through symbolism, and then through various metamorphoses of symbolism: mundane reality must be a symbol of a higher level of meaning.

Symbolism was undercut by post-symbolism where all you can do is celebrate the activity of tracing meanings—or making them up. You no longer believe there is a higher level at which you'll find meaning; that's the old, prescientific idealism. But you go on celebrating the absurd courageous existential activity of *creating* meaning in art, not believing in the meanings themselves. Like Mallarme and later Yeats and Rilke and Joyce.

T: If I understand you correctly, you're saying artists celebrated the idea of creating meanings or values as a compensation for having lost touch with them.

LEE: Exactly. As a compensation for having lost belief in a meaningful cosmos *and* in a higher realm of value. For instance, Joyce set up the sequence of the chapters in *Ulysses* to mime the sequence of books in *The Odyssey*; not because he believed the latter really embodied a literal scheme of meaning, but because all he could affirm was the hope that the patterns of art will somehow make sense of life. He gives us a value-free aesthetic pattern. Well, whoopee! It's an aesthete's solution, a formalist solution, which glorifies the value-imputing imagination of the artist, but at the expense of confirming the devaluation of the real world even further. And in fact it ends up devaluing the "value-imputing imagination" too; there's no longer any credible content to the values it's supposed to be creating. Pound gets all kinds of brownie points for re-activating old myths in *The Cantos*. But nobody takes them seriously, except as demonstrations of what a formalist virtuoso he was. We don't *believe* in them as "values".

T: So you're saying each time this process is repeated, the substance of "value" keeps retreating from us further.

LEE: Yes. Each time the great heroic artists extend what their predecessors did to try and resolve the crisis, they have to re-locate the "value" in still more involuted, rarified, improbable quarters. In the process they de-value the day-to-day reality further and further. They "murder the real" instead of resuscitating it.

T: How do you see today's artists continuing along this route?

LEE: By now, all a lot of the best artists can do is simply rev up our nerve-ends, substitute sensation for meaning altogether. Moment-to-moment art gives you the kind of kicks that eating stimulants or jacking off or killing people can. Nothing *means*: but at least there's always one more *frisson* of raw sensation that can be cranked out. This is decadence, it seems to me: primitive brutalism accompanying high sophistication.

T: Can you give me an example?

LEE: Well, James Dickey's stuff is a good example. Technically his poetry is strong, it's beautifully written. But humanly it's horrendous. The cutting edge of his modernity is this impulse to jolt your nerve-ends one crunch further, one more time, with each new line. And he's good, he's one of the best; he can actually do it. Same with Ted Hughes. Look at the combination of magnificent word-sense and super-gothic blitzkrieg of the nerve-ends in *Crow* or *Gaudete*. This is not some two-bit kid of twenty having wet dreams and power trips on the page; this is one of the best poets of the last few decades, following the deep instincts of his maturity. What a terrible era. These are our authentic necessities now, and they stink.

T: How do you justify your own work as being any different?

LEE: Well, the only step ahead I could find in *The Gods* was to try and identify our condition, to enact it consciously and then name it.

T: But you also write very directly about physical sensation in the love poems. I could say, aren't you asking your "carnal OM on a rumpled bed" to carry a great burden of meaning?

LEE: That's true, but it kind of misses the point. The love poems in the first part of the book actively *enact* the process of becoming idolatrous. They start with the innocent high spirits of falling-in-love, and end up with the man confessing that he's turned the woman's body into one more idol, because there's so little else that feels real. The poems explore that process, with their eyes open, and they discover this limitation on how far we can make one intense experience the locus of all meaning and value. So I don't think you can tax the poems with just being unwitting symptoms of the problem.

T: Does this mean you think revealing these problems in *The Gods* transcends them?

Lee: I wish it did, but I don't think it's that simple. But at least the book blows the whistle on that kind of idolatry as an unconscious pattern of behaviour. Implicitly and explicitly it questions the whole project of modernity. And it questions being a poet within the stream of modernity, which is what I balk at in particular.

Do we really want to continue this psychic slaughter of what-is from generation to generation? Shouldn't we ask ourselves if it's not self-perpetuating? if it isn't self-defeating? And if the line of heroic advance that always seems to beckon us out of the morass isn't it in fact the straight line further into it?

T: So you're anti-romantic.

Lee: Oh, totally. And part of being a romantic is that you always have to find some new taboo to rebel against; the *frisson* makes you feel real for one more go-round. But my love-making poems are not "shocking" or "fearlessly outspoken". In those terms they have nothing to offer, they're dull. I'm not trying to go any further down that road. I'm not cruising for new taboos to infringe. I'm looking to stop the whole knee-jerk performance. Romantic revolt is a great yawn by now. Taboo is dead, we killed it.

T: If romanticism didn't exist, or modernity generally, could you have written this book?

Lee: No, I'm a creature of my era like anyone else; I write from inside time, my own time. However my temporal arena is not just the 1960's and 70's. My work has a long-haul vista, for better or worse. Some of it must seem dull or bizarre to a person who reacts as though the world began in 1960 because I'm taking my particular moment as the last few centuries.

T: Do you foresee a day when you might believe in "the gods" in more than a strictly metaphorical sense?

Lee: That is *the* question. I can only answer it by saying I believe, with some sobriety, that the best human beings of the past, for whom a sense of the sacred often interpenetrated their lives, were not just crazy or naive or seeking solutions to their three-year-old toilet training problems. I respect their knowledge of the gods, whatever it consisted of. I can't participate in it on their terms, of course. But the possibility of enduring that knowledge afresh, as who *we* are, without just lobotomizing ourselves, matters to me very much. Unfortunately a lot of the terrible perversions of the twentieth century may have also come out of that hunger.

T: Explain that.

LEE: Well, I don't know an awful lot about the history of Nazism. But during the early thirties, before becoming a Nazi was a matter of sheer survival, there were people of stature who poured themselves into the Nazi cult because it seemed to take seriously their hunger for a lost sense of the sacred. Not that this is any justification for men like Heidegger or Gottfried Benn. Quite the contrary. It shows that this hunger is not something to play dilettantish games with, because it can lead you desperately astray.

T: Would this reaction make particular sense in an ultra-materialist society?

LEE: Probably. I don't know enough about Germany's history to say. Certainly in North America right now we're being swamped with sleazy, 15th-rate appeals to such a hunger. The whole conservative swing right now has this dimension to it, it seems to me. It's partially a stifled expression of a spiritual hunger for a sense of *tremendum*. People are reaching out for some deeper bedrock sanity that goes beyond liberal convenience, and trendy disposable gratifications. Weird though many of the expressions of that longing are.

T: Are you still influenced by whatever religious instruction you received as a child?

LEE: I'm sure I am. In fact, I would like to know more about the particular tradition I was born into. There are things I rejected that I respect a lot more now.

T: What tradition was that?

LEE: The suburban United Church.

[Laughter]

T: I was hoping for something a little more exotic.

LEE: No, no, that's the whole point about it. In terms of blah, there can't be many blah-er religious traditions than that. Only Unitarianism gone to seed might be more blah. That polite, philistine, spineless, *nice* suburban Protestant Christianity was what I grew up in. I was shaped by the experience of lacking a concrete sense of the sacramental.

T: That could be the whole function of watered-down Christianity. Perhaps it's not supposed to give you what you need at all; it's an icon, it's function is to perfectly reflect your state of hunger.

LEE: That's the best justification for the suburban United Church I've ever heard. But actually, it's the older Methodist/Presbyterian tradition I've started to respect now. I mean the rectitude, the honesty and the sense that you live an unadorned life. The sense that you work hard at something solid and don't try to impress people with insubstantial glitter. Those are fairly limited virtues, I know. But if you live in a city like Toronto, now, where you're so inundated by trash-with-flash that you practically need hip-waders, that old Wasp integrity, stultifying though it was, starts to look pretty valuable.

T: Then what made you rebel against it?

LEE: In my middle and later teens I wanted something much purer and more intense, and as it happened I soaked myself in the Christian mystics; I read them haphazardly, and daydreamed about being one myself. But then some time by the age of twenty-five I recognized, not very willingly, that my ordinary growing up was being delayed by trying to live in that fantasy, *my* fantasy. So I relinquished it and rebelled against the Wasp tradition in more conventional ways.

T: What do you think you've rebelled towards?

LEE: I guess I've felt the greatest affinity since then with the Society of Friends. But I've backed away from churches completely. I have no affiliation still.

T: What kind of religious instruction or sense of the world do you try to imbue your children with?

LEE: I don't know how to handle that. My youngest child is eight and his iconography is very much shaped by American mass culture, superheroes and so on. He picks it up by osmosis, like all his friends. What do you do to counteract that flood of rancid pablum, in ways that won't just make it seem forbidden and glamorous?

T: Have you examined your motives for writing *Alligator Pie* and *Garbage Delight*? Maybe that's where some answers lie.

LEE: Well, one point of germination for my kids' writing was the impulse to play...I should stop and say I mean play as a direct, shapely release of energy for its own sake...Growing up in a post-puritan society, I'd learned to repress certain kinds of feeling pretty effectively: joy, anger, reverence, delight. So you could say my kids' poetry goes back and frees up the play of a lot of those feelings.

T: That would explain why your kids' poetry is so successful. It works for you while it works for the kids.

LEE: That's right. And people of my generation probably need to free up. The trouble is now there's so much emphasis on the Fun culture, on getting your kicks, that I start to worry whether my kind of playing in words couldn't easily get co-opted. Even the possibility makes me squirm. Does my stuff get read as if it were Saturday morning TV cartoons? Real play is different from just getting kicks; it's grave or tender just as often as it's rambunctious.

I've got one or two more kids' poetry manuscripts that I'm finishing up, then I think that will exhaust what I can do, in poetry at least. I'd be turning myself into a Dennis Lee factory. If I do any more children's writing I think it'll have more to do with sorting out how to be human when you're three years old or six years old.

T: Does this mean you'd become a moralizing writer? as opposed to working from the "play" angle?

LEE: I hope I'll never become a moralizing writer. Perhaps I'll write something for children that doesn't make a person think of "play" and "moral" as being mutually exclusive categories.

T: Some people say *Sesame Street* is very good and some say *Sesame Street* is very bad. If you had to lock a kid in a room for a month and choose one of two programmes for him to watch, *Sesame Street* or *Mr. Dressup,* which would you choose?

LEE: There'd be no choice, really, over that length of time. If a kid saw nothing but *Sesame Street* he'd have a good time, but he'd go manic; if a kid saw nothing but *Mr. Dressup* he'd have a good time, and he wouldn't get depressive.

T: Because *Sesame Street* is all ingest, ingest, ingest. There's no time allowed for digestion.

LEE: That's right. Morris Wolfe once wrote a piece in *Saturday Night* in which the basic structure of time on TV was analyzed as JPM's, which are jolts-per-minute. *Sesame Street* is brilliant but it works on the high JPM system. A show like *Mr. Dressup* respects the longer, gentler, more meandery rhythm of a child's attention span.

T: Have you ever worried about television role models usurping your own model as a parent?

LEE: I've already got a fine supply of inadequacy as a *person*. If I had to spend a lot of time contemplating my performance as a "role model", in competition with TV, I'd probably crack up.

From that point of view, the way I lead my life day-to-day doesn't make a whole lot of sense. When I'm not traipsing around the country making a spectacle of myself, I spend most of my time upstairs on the third storey wrestling with rhythms on a page. When I come down — and I mean from upstairs — that's assuming I've managed to be in the same city as my children in the first place — I'm a weird mixture of high and low from all that. I make too-large demands on the people around me as a result. So actually I'm pretty dissatisfied with my way of being a parent. There may be less inept ways to manage than the ones I've found, but when you scribble and you have a scribbler's temperament, there don't seem to be many alternatives.

What about you? Are you satisfied with raising your kid so far?

T: I often feel the same sense of inadequacy. I feel an obligation to counteract all that outside stimuli but it takes so much energy!

Also I think because our ground-rules for raising kids are no longer so obviously defined by society, it becomes more and more difficult to supply your kid with the necessary boundaries and limitations. I think what's happening as a result of that is that parenting is becoming very personal and open-ended almost as a compensation.

I have absolutely no idea whether this is good or bad. But I know that when I'm pleading with my four-year-old not to argue with me, I'm right there inside the sandbox and that must be historically rather bizarre. Today you have all these parents, including the fathers, trying to relate to their kids as equals. Let's hope it's wonderfully positive in the long run. But I sense that children do not want or even require this camaraderie. They want distancing. They want to feel you're separate and that you've got things under control.

LEE: I feel the same. Often my relationship with children has been a reaching out for that fraternal thing; sometimes in a nice way, sometimes neurotically. Both at once, maybe. I mistrust it increasingly, too. As I get older, I'll probably be a more brusque, meat'n'potatoes, cut-and-dried kind of parent. At least that would be the negative definition of it.

I've got this in-between feeling generally. There's a free-floating part of me that would like to pedal back in time or psychic space, and disconnect from all that shallow, secular, trendy downtown Toronto civilisation. I'd like to stand back from my ways of making a living, making a life, and take a deep breath. If I miss the brass ring or whatever, well, tough luck on me. I'd be in that waiting space I spoke of in terms of when I write. A person could reach out for things which ring a lot truer.

T: It sounds like you never stop re-evaluating yourself.

LEE: Well right now I'm teetering on the edge, I've just turned forty. I feel this glorious male menopause coming on. [Laughter] First I finish writing a couple of things, see, wind up my obsessions of the last decade; then I have a male menopause. I expect it's already marked down on some invisible calendar. It's likely set for a Thursday afternoon... I just hope they serve coffee.

Why To Write

Hubert Evans is Canada's senior active writer, a man Margaret Laurence has called "The elder of our tribe."

Born in Vankleek Hill, Ontario in 1892 and raised in Galt, Ontario, Evans worked as a reporter before enlisting in 1915. He was wounded at Ypres in 1916, then received an honourable discharge with the rank of Lieutenant in 1918. He married in 1920 and settled at Roberts Creek, B.C. He and his wife later lived in northern B.C. Indian villages before returning to their coastal home in 1953. His wife died in 1960.

The New Front Line (1927) was written in the aftermath of Evans' experiences as a soldier in the First World War; a novel since out of print.

Mist on the River (1954) is based upon Evans' observations of the hardships encountered by Indians populating B.C.'s Skeena River area; a novel now regarded as a Canadian classic.

O Time in Your Flight (1979) recounts a year in the life of an Ontario boy in 1899; a critically acclaimed novel rich in historical detail and clear narrative style.

As well, Hubert Evans has published one biography, two volumes of poetry, three juvenile novels, 12 plays, 60 serials, and 200 short stories. He has worked as a professional writer in Canada since building his present seaside home at Roberts Creek in 1926.

photo: Brian Sugiyama

T: Tell me about how you came to write O *Time in Your Flight.*

EVANS: The second time I went to the hospital to get my heart pacer batteries renewed, they opened me up and found something else was wrong. I was in bed for weeks. I thought by golly, time's a-wastin', I better get some of the family history down. So my son-in-law brought me one of those dictaphones from his office. I was awake a lot at nights so I just started in stream-of-consciousness. I could taste the food and smell the smells. Some nights I'd talk two chapters.

Those days I could still see to do a little hunt n'peck typing so in the daytime I typed it out pretty well just as I said everything. It ran to 65,000 words. I had a copy made for the children and then I sent a copy to the Ontario Public Archives. But in the back of my old freelancer's mind, I must have figured I might be able to use this. I told them I wanted it kept under wraps until 1980.

Then four or five years ago I couldn't go out and saw wood or go fishing any more on account of my heart. I was sort of at loose ends so I did 90 pages of the book. But the viewpoint I had wasn't any good. It was too subjective and modern.

You see I'm an oldtimer. After sixty years I still see a story as a play. The characters are on an imaginary stage and I'm a member of the audience. I just try to get them to show themselves. This can be very limiting. On the other hand, I think it narrows down the focus.

T: So you needed a more objective approach to get you going.

EVANS: Right. So I decided to see the whole world through the eyes of a nine-year-old that was me. Anything the boy couldn't comprehend at the time, I just left out. I tried to do as little interpreting as possible. It was like the title. I don't explain where that phrase O *Time in Your Flight* comes from because I never knew it was from a poem when I was a boy. It was just something my mother said.

This has been one of the main tenets of my writing all along: It's far better to have a reader miss a point than hit him over the head with it. If you get the reader concluding, ''I know what that character is up to,'' then you've got participation. The reader becomes part of the story when he's seeing around corners.

T: I imagine writing novels for young people would have helped you learn that approach pretty quickly.

EVANS: Yes, it's been very helpful. I've often thought that.

T: And it would also force you to simplify your language.

EVANS: Exactly. Now if I was running one of those creative writing courses in a university, I would have an exercise where people tell stories in Basic English. English has taken on far too many words. There are too many tools.

I know an old chap who retired near here who used to be a big time businessman. One day he decided he was going to take up carpentry. So he goes out and buys several hundred dollars worth of electric tools. But this is a guy who can't even sharpen a hand saw or a chisel! Both my grandfather and father were excellent carpenters even though they had very few tools. They knew how to sharpen them! By golly, they knew how to use them and when not to use them.

It's the same with language. We've got all these words, all these tools. Think of one of the Lake poets writing on the death of a child, then think of Issa, the Japanese poet in the 1500's. Issa on the death of his child uses only twelve words. Whenever I recite it, it still moves me:

> Dew evaporates
> All our world is dew
> So dear, so fleeting.

T: Reviews as far back as the 1920's mention your spare, "lean and vigorous style". Did you have to learn to write that way?

EVANS: I'm a two-time high school dropout. The second time I left school I went to work for a newspaper called the *Galt Reporter*. My boss there had been the editor of a prestigious paper called the *Chicago Inter-Ocean*. When I arrived he said two things to me. Learn to use a typewriter within two weeks or you're out. And as far as possible, use words that the boy who sells your paper can understand. Then you'll be writing good English. That's always stuck.

T: Would you say your approach to writing is very much like your approach to life?

EVANS: Yes, I suppose that's true. I knew my wife ever since we were thirteen and we both always had the same idea. To travel light. To not have any encumbrances. To own only what you can carry on your back. For instance, we said we would never own land. Then her home broke up back east and we got sent this piano. Then we had kids. We had to have a roof over our heads so I built this house.

T: How did you become a Quaker?

EVANS: It's a long, long story. My wife was a graduate of the University of Toronto. One of the books she got me reading was Carlyle's *Sartor Resartus*. That book really became my Bible. "Always the black spot in our sunshine. This is the shadow of ourselves."

You see I went through two years and three months in the trenches in World War One. I tell you, I got pretty damned cynical. I had got to a stage where I would say how the hell does anybody know what beauty is? I remember saying this to myself. I remember thinking a tree may be as ugly as the hair on my arm.

In Carlyle's *Sartor Resartus* his protagonist reaches this point and says he's not going to put up with it. He decides the world is not a "charnel house filled with spectres." From that day on, his attitude changed. Well, in those days there was a thing in Philadelphia called the Wider Quaker Fellowship. My wife and I asked to join because we were universalists.

The Quakers have no creed. They have no minister. It's an attitude. If you believe in life and growth, you can be a Quaker.

T: Did you always want to be a writer?

EVANS: I always thought about it. After I came out of the army I went up north for a year and started writing. In those days, if you could put a short story together, you could sell it. But you couldn't make a living just by writing for Canada. So I wrote pulp stories. The most popular kind back then were war stories by American guys who'd never even been there. I couldn't write about violence so I wrote outdoor stories. Animal stories.

T: What made you start writing for kids?

EVANS: My wife said she'd rather have me digging ditches than writing pulp. Mind you I've never written anything that I'm ashamed of, but I've written a lot of things that really didn't need to be written. She suggested I write for teenagers because you can still change a person's viewpoint up to the time they're twenty.

T: How old were you then?

EVANS: I was thirty or so. The first thing I did was a syndicated column about factual things I'd seen with animals. The Judson Press in Philadelphia wrote me and asked me to do a book about it. I wrote about sixty-five of these columns in six weeks. The book sold quite well.

T: Was making a living as a writer in the 1920's easier than today?

EVANS: Much easier. If you could tell a story, the market was there. Today I don't know how people can make a living with fiction. TV has changed everything so much.

T: Did you get much notoriety in those days?

EVANS: Well, listen. When I was doing those outdoor nature stories, I was living in a very fine house in North Vancouver. This was the late 20's. A piece ran in every daily paper across Canada saying Hubert Evans lives in a one room shack far away from civilization! [laughter] The truth was I'd never had it so good. I was really in the money.

T: But you've lived through long periods of being virtually unknown.

EVANS: Yes, yes, yes. [laughter] Of course these days if a writer wants to make headlines he practically has to perform some unnatural act with a farm animal.

T: Perhaps if you hadn't separated yourself geographically. . .

EVANS: No, I'd had it up to here with cities. This is what I wanted. I wrote to various postmasters along the coast looking for a sheltered cove, a sandy beach, good anchorage and a creek. I came to Roberts Creek and bought this half-acre of waterfrontage for $1,000 cash.

T: If you hadn't always written for money, do you think you would have produced more than three adult novels?

EVANS: Maybe I would have. But I haven't got that intense perception and psychological imagination that say a Margaret Laurence or a Graham Greene has.

T: What made you write your novel about the Indians of northern B.C.? [*Mist on the River*]

EVANS: Well, I had quite a number of chums in the army who were Indians. But it was really my wife's Quaker concern over Indians that took us north in the first place. She had this book by an American called *Indians Are People Too*. This is what I wanted to do with *Mist on the River*. Just show them as people. Basically I was just being a reporter.

  I could have written about the injustices Indians faced. You know, like *The Ecstasy of Rita Joe*. I've seen all that. I know all that. But I had commercial fished and trapped and built dugout canoes with these people. I could roll a cigarette and sit on my heels and talk with them. I was one of them. I wanted to show how they were really just like us.

T: Donald Cameron has described that book as "a good man's compassionate regard for another's pain."

EVANS: Bertrand Russell said, "If we want a better world, the remedy is so simple that I hesitate to state it for fear of the derisive smiles of the wise cynics. The remedy is Christian love or compassion." D.H. Lawrence kept on this, too. What the world needs is compassion.

One of my problems as a writer is that I've never been able to write about middle-class, Kerrisdale-West Vancouver people. My head tells me they've got their tragedies and disappointments and dramas like everyone else, but this is one of my blind spots. I'm sorry to say I can't get inside their heads the way I do with older people or down-and-out people or children.

T: Maybe it's because those people will never allow you any communal feelings with them.

EVANS: It's true, I think we do all need to feel ourselves part of a larger family. Living with the Indians for eight years in the Skeena country taught that to my wife and me. The Indians have still got this. But most of us have really lost it.

Of course there are lots of Indians I don't take to, just like there are lots of white people I don't take to. But there's a quotation by Albert — how do you pronounce it? Is it Camus? Is that the right way? He said there is no question here of sentimentality. He said, "It is true that I am different by tradition from an African or a Mohammedan. But it is also true that if I degrade them or despise them, I demean myself."

T: That harkens back to that Camus quote above your writing desk.

EVANS: I can repeat that one by heart. "An artist may make a success or failure of his work. He may make a success or failure of his life. But if he can tell himself that finally, as a result of his long effort, he has eased or decreased the various forms of bondage weighing upon Man, then in a sense, he is justified and can forgive himself."

Canadian Literature

MARGARET LAURENCE

Margaret Laurence's deep compassion and technical expertise have made her Canada's most revered novelist.

Born in Neepawa, Manitoba in 1926 of Irish and Scottish ancestry, Laurence was educated in Winnipeg where she later worked as a labour reporter. Married in 1947, she lived in Vancouver and the emerging African colonies of the Somaliland Protectorate and Gold Coast before a formal separation from her husband in 1962. She then took her two children to London, England to pursue a full-time career as a writer.

Twice recipient of the Governor General's Award, she is the author of fourteen books, the best known of which are her "Manawaka" fictions:

The Stone Angel (1964) introduced her imaginary town of Manawaka as well as one of the most memorable characters in Canadian literature, a prideful ninety-year-old heroine named Hagar Shipley.

A Jest of God (1966) depicts the dilemmas of Rachel Cameron, a middle-aged schoolteacher who struggles for the capacity to love.

The Fire-Dwellers (1969) centres upon Stacey MacAindra, a Vancouver housewife who feels bewildered by an uncommunicative husband and a society which encourages anxieties to be smothered.

A Bird in the House (1970) allowed Laurence to come to terms with the dark childhood shadows of death and a domineering grandfather in a collection of autobiographical short stories.

The Diviners (1974) is an ambitious culmination of her Manawaka series which explores and celebrates the significance of ancestral pasts.

Margaret Laurence lives in Lakefield, Ontario.

photo: Alan Twigg

T: What's really struck me in the course of interviewing the authors for this book is the extent to which the state of mind of an artist is usually inextricably tied to the state of his or her society. You must recognize this in your own work.

LAURENCE: Oh, certainly. The thing is, whether I recognize it or not, it's bound to be there. For instance, I don't write a novel with the idea of commenting on society. Or I never set out and say, "Well, now it's Canadian-novel-writing time." I think of all my characters in my Canadian books a great deal more as human individuals than I do as Canadians. I simply have a character in mind, or a group of characters, and I want to deal with their dilemmas. I want to communicate with them.

What happens is the dilemma of one particular woman often turns out to be the dilemma of a lot of women. When *The Fire-Dwellers* was published, a lot of women wrote to me and said how did you know this was how I felt? I didn't know. I wrote that book by trying to connect with one human individual.

T: And that can have far-reaching effects. Yet there are some people who would argue that such fiction is apolitical.

LAURENCE: Yes, I think very many people would define political writing as something which is strictly in the political realm of governments and social issues. But I think what is political in most serious novels is something quite different. For instance, in *The Stone Angel* old age is itself a political dilemma. Death. We're not supposed to think about it. But it's there. It's going to happen to all of us.

If you are writing out of what you know, inevitably what you know is your society around you. So if a writer is aware of social injustice, which I think I very deeply am, then that will be there, too. For instance, people sometimes ask me whether I'm consciously writing feminist novels. No, I am not. Even though I myself feel I am a feminist, I won't write in any didactic or polemical way about it. My protagonists are women and I simply try to portray their dilemmas as truthfully as I can. I'm not doing it for any other reason than because I am interested in a character as a human individual.

T: And that's how literature can be useful.

LAURENCE: Yes. I remember very clearly thinking before I started *The Stone Angel,* "Who will be interested in the life of an old woman of ninety?" Then I thought *I* am interested. Of course it turned out I wasn't alone. The fact that Hagar struggles so hard to maintain some human dignity throughout the period of her dying has meant a great deal to a lot of people. In fact, to my great surprise, I discovered that novel is actually being used in a number of geriatrics courses and nursing courses for the aged. That pleases me enormously.

T: So increasing awareness is itself a political act.

LAURENCE: Yes, I think so. Otherwise I would not be writing novels.

T: Do you think writers actually create change or is their role simply to reflect it?

LAURENCE: This is the question of the chicken and the egg. I don't know. The writer's consciousness is formed by the society, then the writing in turn helps to do something to affect the society. It's a two-way street. For instance, the feeling we got in the 60's that we were a culture that mattered to ourselves and the world has helped our writers, but our writers also helped in forming those feelings.

T: You once wrote, "What I care about is trying to express something that, in fact, everybody knows but doesn't say." Do you think Canadians might be especially dishonest with themselves?

LAURENCE: No. When I said that, I didn't mean people who were being hypocritical. I was referring to people who experience lots of feelings in their lives but they are in some way inchoate. They aren't verbal people. This is part of what writers do. They speak for people who cannot speak for themselves.

T: I asked that question because the pioneer experience and the influence of Victorianism have tended to make Canadians keep their emotions under wraps. That sort of repression could encourage double standards.

LAURENCE: I agree. But, as I hope it comes out in my books, I don't think this country's puritan background has been all bad for us. With Hagar [*The Stone Angel*] and the generation of my maternal grand-father, who I've written about in *A Bird in the House,* they created a very repressive atmosphere. Hagar really damaged her children. Yet at the same time that generation imbued us with an ability to survive. Besides, I don't think the puritan work ethic is all that wrong! [laughter]

T: But there's a National Film Board profile of you which indicates your childhood was pretty bleak.

LAURENCE: Well, even though my grandfather was a very authoritarian man, I myself had the great advantage of growing up in a house where my step-mother, who was my aunt, and my other aunts, were extremely strong and liberated women. I never had the feeling that as a woman I couldn't choose the profession that I wanted to choose. Two of my aunts were nurses, my stepmother had been a high school teacher of English and my mother had been a pianist.

Also, my stepmother was an extremely enlightened woman for her day. For example, when I was young, she never tried to censor my reading. I can remember when *Gone With the Wind* came out, there were many mothers of daughters who would not permit their little prairie flowers to read this wicked book. But I could always read anything. Mind you, I admit there was not that much hard core porn in the Neepawa Public Library!

T: Do you think the pendulum has swung too far the other way these days?

LAURENCE: Well, a lot of the porn magazines I find *vile*. I detest them. But it's not because they deal with sex. It's because they deal with sex in an exploitive and very largely cruel way.

In terms of novels, I don't believe in writing sex scenes for the sake of bringing in a lot of sex. But if you are to wipe out sex entirely, that's wiping out one whole area of life. I think if you're writing truthfully about a character, you've got to deal to some extent with that side of their lives. As much as the novel demands and no more.

T: You've said that many people misread literature. Can you explain what you mean?

LAURENCE: Misreading comes in when people are unable to see what's going on in a novel because they focus on the wrong things. I'm thinking of people who want to have my books banned, particularly *The Diviners*. A lot of those people not only admit to the fact that they have not read the book, they are proud they have never read it. Their eyes are blind to everything except the few sexual passages and some of the so-called swear words. That's a sad and tragic way of reading a book. That kind of reader doesn't want to read. To put it in its broadest sense, the motives are not of love but of hate.

T: Or of fear.

LAURENCE: That's right. One thing the book banners commented on with *The Diviners* was that I dealt with the quote "seamier side of life". Well, the seamier side of life exists. Also they complained that I showed the native people in the worst possible light. I was simply incensed and enraged by that reaction! I was trying to show the Tonnerre family as real complex human individuals who had suffered at the hands of society. We are culpable. To say that I was showing them in an unfavourable light, as though I was a racist, is ridiculous. Perhaps the book banners wanted *Hiawatha*. But that's not how real life is.

People say to me, well, if it's banned by the school boards then all the kids are going to read it. But I'd just as soon they didn't read it under that particular aegis.

T: When *Settlers of the Marsh* [by Frederick Philip Grove] was banned from public libraries the year you were born, Prime Minister Arthur Meighen wrote Grove's publisher and congratulated him on publishing the book. In our apparently liberal age, why have so few politicians come to the defense of *The Diviners*?

LAURENCE: I really don't know. But because we've seen a few of the more unenlightened politicians actually wanting to control the Canada Council in the last few years so grants wouldn't be given to writers they disapproved of, I think it would have been nice if more politicians would have spoken up.

T: Trudeau could have said the government has no business in the libraries of the nation.

LAURENCE: [laughter] Well, there have been a great many people across Canada who have spoken up in defense of *The Diviners*. In fact, during the controversy in Peterborough County, quite a few Anglican and United Church ministers and their wives wrote to me and the local newspapers expressing their support. Some of the other books which small pressure groups wish to see banned from the schools, if you can believe it, are Ernest Buckler's *The Mountain and the Valley* and W.O. Mitchell's *Who Has Seen the Wind?*, which to my mind is a profoundly religious book.

T: We heard a lot of predictions about the possible demise of the novel as well as the possible demise of the church during the 60's when man was busy landing on the moon. Do you think there's a connection?

LAURENCE: I don't really know. People have been saying the novel is dead for a long, long time. As far as I'm concerned, it's still extremely alive. It simply finds new forms. And God, though very often proclaimed dead, is also very much alive in my opinion.

T: I think if there is a connection between religion and art, it's that they both emphasize man is not wholly a rational being, that the truth about ourselves must also be "divined".

LAURENCE: I accept that connection. Certainly a very great deal of all serious art is in some way religious, even if the writers and painters don't admit it. This is so with literature because, like faith, it frequently points to the mystery at the heart of things, the mystery and wonder at the core of every human individual. That sense of mystery and wonder comes out of a great deal of writing, as it does with religious faith. Many writers, including myself, who even though they were not thinking in any specific religious terms, have experienced something while writing which I think of as a kind of grace. This came very naturally to ancient and tribal peoples. They described it as possession by the gods. Nowadays when people say they have written something that surprises them, in my terms there's a sense of grace happening there.

T: In a good book maybe some of that grace gets passed along to the reader.

LAURENCE: One hopes so. I certainly feel very fortunate to have worked as a writer most of my life because I do feel I have been given a certain amount of grace. Whether deservedly or not, we don't know. But I feel extremely fortunate to have spoken to three generations; the generation before me, my own generation and the next one. People say to me sometimes do you expect your books will be around for a hundred and fifty years? I don't know and I don't care. I feel I've been lucky in being able to speak to a number of people in those three generations.

T: Do you get many letters from readers?

LAURENCE: I've been very fortunate. People write to me quite often. By far the larger proportion of these letters has been extremely warm and positive. I get a few poison-pen ones, but not that many, thank goodness. And of course I get letters from people who say that I'm sure that you will be tired of hearing this but your book *The Diviners* meant a great deal to me for such-and-such a reason. Well, I would rather hear that than a good review. It means people who are not involved in the world of books professionally are taking the trouble to say your work has spoken to them. That means a great, great deal to me. That's what literature is all about.

T: Robertson Davies claims Canada still expects nothing from its writers.

LAURENCE: Well, I can only speak personally on that. One difficulty I've had in the last few years is that Canadians almost expect too much. Writers are extremely vulnerable people. It really frightens me when people say to me what are you working on now? when's your next novel coming out? They mean it in the best possible way. But I sometimes think, gosh, can I really do anything more? I'm grappling with trying to write something right now. But it really scares me.

T: Do you sometimes wish you could turn off all the tape recorders like this one and retreat from having a public role?

LAURENCE: I do feel that sometimes. There are moments when I would like to rent a nice cabin in the arctic somewhere. On the other hand, I do feel very responsible for doing what I can to help writers who are younger than myself in whatever ways I can.

T: Was there someone in particular who helped you out when you were young?

LAURENCE: Yes. The writer who really went out of her way to help me was Ethel Wilson. I got to know her during the five years we lived in Vancouver, before my first novel was published. She had read a couple of my short stories in *Prism* so she wrote to the magazine expressing her enjoyment of the stories. Then she wrote to me personally. During the years in Vancouver I was absolutely starved for the company of other writers. Ethel Wilson provided that. The sense that somebody did understand. There's no question that I would have gone on writing, but she provided me with an enormous amount of encouragement. I owe her a great, great deal. There's no way that I can ever repay her personally. The only thing I can do is pass it on.

T: You've lived in Vancouver, England, Africa and now Ontario. Yet the heart of your work still appears to be the Prairies. Do you still consider yourself a Prairie writer?

LAURENCE: Yes, I still consider myself a Prairie writer. That's where I spent the first twenty-two years of my life and I still have a strong sense of place about the Prairies. Literature has to be set somewhere. This is one of the great strengths of our writing. Whether it's Jack

Hodgins on Vancouver Island or Harold Horwood in Newfoundland, our writers have a strong sense of place. Even if you're writing out of an urban situation, like Morley Callaghan, you can still write with a tremendous sense of the earth, of the place. We're fortunate that the whole nature of Canada is that we're a conglomerate of regions because this has given an added dimension to our writing.

T: When do you feel Canadian literature began to come of age?

LAURENCE: It began to come of age around the Second World War. The generation of writers before me—like Hugh MacLennan, Ernest Buckler, Sinclair Ross and Morley Callaghan—were the first people not to base their stories on British or American models. They wrote out of the sight of their own eyes.

T: So you see yourself as part of a second generation.

LAURENCE: Yes, I do. A second generation of non-colonial Canadian writers. Now there's a whole new generation of Canadian writers who can almost take this "valueing" of ourselves for granted. I like to keep reminding them that we owe a lot to that generation of writers before me. They worked in terrific isolation. A book wasn't considered any good if it didn't get a seal of approval in London or New York.

All this has changed a great deal during the 60's and 70's. A lot more people are interested in the literature of this country. But in those days we never valued what we had as a nation. For instance, when I was in high school we never read one Canadian book. Then at university I studied the contemporary novel but all the writers were American. This was when Hugh MacLennan and Gabrielle Roy were writing some of their finest work.

I don't suggest that we should wipe Shakespeare and Thomas Hardy out of our schools. Anybody who is writing in the English language, after all, is in some way an heir to Wordsworth and Milton and Shakespeare anyway. But Canadian writers are taking the language and making it our own. This connects with young people. They want to see what they are and where they came from. Their geographical place. Their people. I have gone to literally dozens of high schools in Canada. The kids are incredibly keen to find out more about Canadian literature. It's because they recognize it as theirs. With a book like *The Stone Angel* they say, well, that's just like my grandmother. It's truly their culture.

T: Could there be a link between the extent of a country's nationalism and the quality of its literature?

LAURENCE: Not necessarily. I think a writer can be a good writer and have no conscious feelings about nationalism at all. But here we should stop and define what we mean by nationalism. It can take different forms. Nationalism can be that imperialist feeling Britain had at one time or it can be the nationalism of Nazism, of wanting to conquer the world. A jackboot forever stamping in the face. The way I feel about Canadian nationalism is quite different. We don't have any territorial ambitions. We simply want to possess and own our own country.

T: A few writers, such as Mordecai Richler, have been reluctant to accept that label "Canadian" writer. Do you think one writer can be more Canadian than another?

LAURENCE: Of course Mordecai Richler is a Canadian writer. It isn't anything that you choose. I don't have to proclaim I'm a Canadian writer any more than I have to proclaim that my eyes are brown. It's just part of me.

T: Is being a "Canadian" writer still restrictive financially?

LAURENCE: Kid, being a writer of any kind is restrictive financially! [laughter]

T: Is that the main reason the Writers' Union of Canada was formed?

LAURENCE: It was formed in order to try and get some better conditions. For example, to help our members get better contracts with their publishers. To try to get some sort of miniscule compensation for library use of our books. To lobby the government for better laws regarding the importation of foreign editions. We like to think of ourselves as a practical working union. We are, however, extremely different from a trade union in that the Writers' Union doesn't have the power to strike.

But there's another reason that isn't economic. When the Writers' Union was first formed in 1973, I was the first interim chairman. In the only address that I made, I said that I thought of the writers of this country as being members of a kind of tribe. Even though the Writers' Union has got much larger and we sometimes argue heatedly at our general meetings, there is still that tremendous sense of belonging to a community. And we all need that sense of community.

T: Have you ever asked yourself why someone might prefer to read your books in particular?

LAURENCE: They find something in them that relates to their own lives or has relevance to their own place of belonging. It's the same reason they might read anyone's books, I guess.

T: Except few books express such an encouraging belief in the power of the human will, of changing oneself.

LAURENCE: Yes, there is that. There is this feeling in all my books not of optimism — because you'd have to be a fool to be optimistic in this world — but of hope.

T: And I think people also appreciate being able to get so close to your characters. When that happens, literature can offer people a safe form of intimacy. Perhaps it almost teaches us how to love.

LAURENCE: Well, I hope that a sense of love does come across. If it does, it's because what I feel most of all when I'm writing my books is that each individual human being has great value. Each person is unique and irreplaceable. They matter. Of course, that is a very Western world outlook. But it's profoundly my own.

Alan Twigg (b. 1952) is a fifth generation Vancouverite, contributing editor of *Quill & Quire,* theatre critic of the *Vancouver Free Press* and a literary critic for Vancouver *Province.*

This is his first book.